DATE DUE

ND 7 '01		
NO 26 02		
FE 4 03		
MK 13 '04		
AG 12 '09		

DEMCO 38-296

CHINESE CIVILIZATION IN THE MAKING, 1766–221 BC

Chinese Civilization in the Making, 1766–221 BC

Li Jun
Faculty of Oriental Studies
University of Cambridge

A catalogue record for this book is available
from the British Library.

ISBN 0–333–61890–4

 First published in the United States of America 1996 by
ST. MARTIN'S PRESS, INC.,
Scholarly and Reference Division,
175 Fifth Avenue,
New York, N.Y. 10010

ISBN 0–312–16563–3

Library of Congress Cataloging-in-Publication Data
Li, Jun, 1961–
Chinese civilization in the making, 1766–221 BC / Li Jun.
p.   cm.
Includes bibliographical references and index.
ISBN 0–312–16563–3 (cloth)
1. China—Civilization—To 221 B. C.
DS741.65.L514   1996
931—dc20   96–34821
                                                CIP

10   9   8   7   6   5   4   3   2   1
05   04   03   02   01   00   99   98   97   96

Printed and bound in Great Britain by
Antony Rowe Ltd, Chippenham, Wiltshire

To Mariella

Contents

Preface

Many attempts have been made by scholars from different schools of thought to explain the characteristics of ancient Chinese civilization. This book reexamines the available original evidence and seeks to provide a new perspective on the structural changes of ancient China. Specifically, it applies the concept of the Asiatic Mode of Production (AMP) to an analysis of the Shang and Zhou Dynasties (1766–221 BC).

First, I apply the methodology of analytical Marxism to discuss the AMP as referring to a stratified society in which land is owned formally by the state, but in practice by small communities.

Secondly, I argue that this redefined understanding of the AMP is compatible with the Marxist theory of history, and in particular that the AMP exhibits its own economic dynamics.

Thirdly, I establish the empirical validity of the AMP through a detailed analysis of three aspects of ancient Chinese society: (1) productive forces, especially the degree and nature of technological development; (2) the relations of production, especially changing forms of land ownership; and (3) the nature of the main labour force.

On the basis of this analysis, I argue, first, that it is premature to define the Shang Dynasty (1766–1122 BC) as either feudalism or slavery. Owing to the lack of detailed knowledge, we are not in a position to provide a definite answer on the nature of the Shang society. Second, I contend that productive forces in both the Western Zhou (1122–771 BC) and the Chun Qiu period (722–481 BC) were just one step beyond those of primitive society. For the most part, production was carried out collectively, on the basis of kinship groups and the main labour force were neither slaves nor serfs, but rather ordinary members of sublineages. Finally, I argue that, as a result of great increases in productivity made possible by dramatic technological developments, private ownership of land emerged towards the end of the Zhan Guo period (476–221 BC). Subsequently, the coexistence of different modes of production replaced the dominance of the AMP.

Part of Chapter 2 has been published as 'The Asiatic Mode of Production: Stagnation Without Salvation?', *International Journal of Moral and Social Studies,* Vol. 8, No. 3: Autumn, 1993. I am most grateful to the journal for allowing me to reproduce it in this book.

Acknowledgements

This book is the revised version of my D. Phil. thesis submitted to Oxford University in 1992. In preparing the book I have accumulated a huge debt of gratitude to many scholars throughout the world. I would like to express my deepest debt of gratitude to Professor G. A. Cohen whose combination of an unfailing sense of humour with severe criticism makes me feel privileged to be under his supervision. His excellent guidance has been a constant source of inspiration. I am also extremely grateful to my second supervisor, Dr C. Zhiren Lin, whose insightful suggestions and constructive criticism have been a major stimulus to my research. I am most grateful to my examiners, Dr S. Allan and Dr D. Faure, for their penetrating criticism and generous advice, which have greatly increased my understanding of analytical methodology.

I greatly benefited from Dr P. Nolan and Dr M. Loewe of Cambridge University, Professor Melotti of Rome University, Italy, Professor Yu Yongding of the Chinese Academy of Social Science, Beijing, D. Hopkins, Dr Zhang Yongjin of University of Auckland, New Zealand, Dr Jia Bingbing and Dr M. Pobjoy of Oxford University for their helpful comments on drafts of chapters at various stages. I am very grateful to Professor Tokei of the Hungarian Social Academy who kindly sent me two of his books. I would like to thank the staff in the Oriental Library and the Oriental Reading Room of the Bodleian Library, Oxford University, especially David Helliwell and Shu-ching Naughton, for their tolerance of my constant disturbance. I also have to extend my thanks to the staff in the Oriental Faculty Library and the University Library of Cambridge University. They enabled me to find the necessary materials to revise my arguments in this book during my two-year experience there. I am most grateful to my friend Hou Junshu in Beijing for his painstaking search for rare Chinese materials on my behalf. My sincere thanks also go to John M. Smith at Macmillan for his excellent editorial work. He makes me realize that truth is always in details.

I am deeply grateful to the Sino-British Friendship Scholarship which has kept the wolf from the door and enabled me to pursue my academic interests with ease.

This book could not have been written without the ever-present support of my parents who have cultivated my curiosity for knowledge.

My heartfelt thanks go to my wife Mariella Giura Longo for all manner of her support. Her love, criticism and companionship have greatly encouraged me to finish the book. It is devoted to her to express my admiration for her tolerance of my impatience.

Introduction

The concept of the Asiatic Mode of Production (AMP) is one of the most controversial issues in Marxology. It has been described as 'the Loch Ness Monster of historical materialism, rarely sighted and much disbelieved' (O'Leary, 1989: 331). Not surprisingly, the literature on this topic, as one of the highly-praised experts puts it, 'has grown from a rock to a cape to a peninsula' (Krader, 1975: xi). Much has been written not only by historians and economists, but also by political scientists and specialists in many other academic fields.

Why does the concept attract the attention of so many scholars from such a wide range of disciplines? A brief answer is offered by E. Gellner, 'the AMP is the projection to the Marxist scheme of thought and terminology of one or two of the deepest fears and preoccupations of political thought' (Gellner, 1989: vii). One of the most recent detailed studies of the concept is provided by O'Leary, who contends: 'The concept of an Asiatic Mode of Production is the bastard child of historical materialism' (ibid.: 1). In an attempt to dismiss the explanatory value of this concept, he seeks to demonstrate that 'historical materialism is damned with the AMP' (ibid.: 3). He reaches this conclusion because he takes for granted the thesis that societies dominated by the AMP are permanently stagnant.[1] This interpretation is apparently against the central premise of the Marxist theory of history which says that there is an overall tendency, throughout history, for productive forces to grow. Forms of society 'rise and fall when and because they enable and promote, or frustrate and impede, that growth' (Cohen, 1988: 155).

Furthermore, China has often been cited as one of the best examples to illustrate the so-called permanent stagnation of societies dominated by the AMP (Tokei, 1979, 1989; Wittfogel, 1981; Cohen, 1982: 267). Has China ever been a country dominated by the AMP? If the answer is positive, when did China experience it? Finally, does the AMP imply a permanent stagnation?

Opinions are widely divided on the above questions. For scholars who deny the validity of the concept of the AMP, Marx's remarks on China furnish 'a final illustration of the limits of his comprehension of Asian history' (Anderson, 1974b: 492). This view is derived largely from the fact that some of Marx's comments on China and other non-European societies were contradictory. For example, in *Capital*, Vol. 1, Marx wrote: 'In the ancient Asiatic, Classical-antique, and other such modes of

1

production, the transformation of the products into a commodity, and therefore men's existence as producers of commodities, plays a subordinate role, which however increases in importance as these communities approach nearer and nearer to the stage of their dissolution' (Marx, 1976: 172). This indicates that Marx regarded the AMP as one of the ancient modes of production.

But in *Capital*, Vol. 3, Marx said: 'In contrast to English trade, Russian trade leaves the economic basis of Asiatic production [in China] quite untouched' (Marx, 1981: 452). Here Marx referred to China as being dominated by the AMP until the early nineteenth century.[2] This conclusion is apparently inconsistent with the previously quoted assertion which implies that the AMP belonged to the remote past. These conflicting comments by Marx offered excuses for scholars to reject completely the validity of the AMP and its application to China.

On the other hand, orthodox Marxists maintain that the theory of the AMP is 'politically harmful and methodologically incorrect', since it 'is associated with the view that oriental society was stagnant and therefore that European capitalism played a messianic role' (Godes, 1981: 104). According to them, '[e]very attempt to give an affirmative answer to this question must lead to only one answer, to a recognition that the AMP is nothing other than feudalism. The orient, in a very unique fashion, went through the same steps of social development as Europe' (ibid.: 103).

Contrary to the above claims, there have been scholars outside China seeking to confirm the existence of the AMP in Chinese history. For example, in the 1920s some Russian scholars such as Mad'iar (1928) sought to analyze the Chinese rural economy in the light of the AMP. They considered the concept as specifically relevant to Chinese agrarian history.

However, for scholars in favour of the application of the AMP to the study of Chinese history, there are diverse interpretations as to when China was dominated by the AMP. In their book *'Tszin-Tian'*[3] (1930), Kokin and Papaian classified the Western Zhou (1122–771 BC) as a society characterized by the AMP while others tended to consider the whole of Chinese history as being dominated by the AMP before the first British invasion of China in 1840 (Mandel, 1971; Krader, 1975; Melotti, 1977; Sawer, 1977; Tokei, 1979, 1989; Wittfogel, 1981). As Tokei contended: 'The ownership form of the "Asiatic" mode of production remained essentially unchanged until the 19th century, that is, until the onslaught of Western imperialism and capitalism' (Tokei, 1979: 83).

In China, scholars have never failed to take a great interest in the concept of the AMP. Much has been written as to whether this concept is compatible with the Marxist theory of history and which period of Chinese history can be characterized by the AMP. Conflicting hypotheses are advanced, but all are said to have been supported by varying interpretations of the same sources.[4]

This book is a preliminary attempt to clarify the above confusion. It seeks to defend, both from a theoretical and an empirical point of view, the validity of the concept of the AMP.

Chapter 1 is a redefinition of the concept of the AMP within the general framework of analytical Marxism.[5] I shall contend that, although they do not form a systematic theory about the AMP, Marx's scattered remarks, if well reconstructed, can provide a sound basis for a clear definition of the concept. In order to fully appreciate the significance of the AMP in the comparative studies of economic formations, I shall argue that it is essential to grasp Marx's methodology first. Marx compared modern capitalism with all pre-capitalist societies to confirm the specificity of the former. Then he compared pre-capitalist societies to see the origins of capitalism. The concept of the AMP was used by Marx to characterize some non-European societies which did not develop further than they did before industrial capitalism emerged in the West. However, nowhere did Marx confine the existence of the AMP to modern times. Hence the significance of the AMP is to show that some actions at a given level of productive forces are at best unlikely or at worst impossible.

Based on the recent reformulation of the Marxist theory of history by G. A. Cohen,[6] I shall argue in Chapter 2 that the so-called permanent stagnation of the AMP is conceptually flawed, because the AMP has its own dynamics. Therefore, the concept of the AMP does not contradict historical materialism. Moreover, I shall contend that the geographical prefix of the AMP does not prevent it from being a scientific concept in the analyses of diverse societies. Marx's attitude towards colonialism is not determined by so-called Eurocentrism, but by his dialectical consideration of the world; that is, that the impending urge of capital to expand throughout the world is inherited in its own contradiction, which will dig its own grave.

In order to test the empirical validity of the AMP, I shall apply the concept to the analysis of ancient China[7] in the subsequent four chapters. In Chapter 3, I shall examine the available contemporary records to see whether the first dynasty in Chinese history – the Shang – warrants some classifications offered by scholars in both China and the West. I shall argue that first-hand evidence does not support either feudal or slavery explanations of that period, since authentic information is not sufficient to allow us to provide a definite answer on the nature of the Shang at the present stage.

Chapter 4 will be a study of the first part of the second dynasty – the Zhou (1122–221 BC), known as the Western Zhou (1122–771 BC), and its relationship to the AMP. I shall first examine the state of productive forces to see whether individual farming was possible by that time. Second, I shall explore the precise meaning of the *fengjian* system and seek to argue that it is a misconception to equate it with feudalism. Finally, I shall contend that the main labour forces in the Western Zhou cannot be defined as either slaves or serfs. Evidence will be provided to illustrate that the AMP was the predominant mode of production in the Western Zhou.

Chapters 5 and 6 will be concentrated on the technological, economic and social changes in the Eastern Zhou period (771–221 BC). I shall argue that this period was a watershed in Chinese history. The invention of cast iron gradually reduced the cost of farming and other implements. Along with the increase in productivity, private landownership was eventually established by the end of the Zhou dynasty. All the changes demonstrate that the Zhan Guo (the Warring States) period (476–221 BC) represented a transition from a society dominated by the AMP to a society in which different forms of landownership coexisted.

Chapter 7 will sum up the discussion. First, as one of the distinctive modes of production, the concept of the AMP constitutes an inextricable part of the Marxist theory of history. Marx's comparative study of the AMP and other modes of production such as slavery and feudalism does not carry any pejorative connotation. It aims at seeking inner mechanisms of diverse economic formations.

Second, the concept of the AMP can be applied to only a certain period of Chinese history, namely, the period from the Western Zhou to the Chun Qiu (the Spring and Autumn) times (722–481 BC). Therefore, Marx was apparently wrong when he implicitly classified the whole of Chinese history before the first half of the nineteenth century as dominated by the AMP. Nevertheless, I shall contend that the importance of Marx's comments does not depend on his being right in each case. Even when some of his specific observations become questionable, 'the initial lead provided by his perceptions loses none of its value for understanding history' (Mukhia, 1985a: 175). In other words, the AMP provides a useful key in explaining ancient Chinese history during the above-mentioned period.

It is, however, important to note that no attempt will be made to offer a detailed account either of every aspect of such a long period of ancient Chinese history or the relevant contemporary literature on the AMP. I shall limit myself to delineating those major aspects directly related to the concept of mode of production. For example, the state and development of technology will be stressed, because '[t]echnology reveals the active relation of man to nature, the direct process of the production of the social relations of his life' (Marx, 1976: 493).[8] Nonetheless, it would be wrong to identify the development of the productive forces merely with the development of technology. There are many other aspects which are equally important in evaluating the level of the productive forces such as the increase of agricultural output on the basis of the extension of cultivation, the exploitation of new resources and the growth of population (cf. Cohen, 1988: 104–5). But I shall touch only on some of these crucial features, since the long-range perspective of this book does not permit me to exhaust every relevant point of the developments of the productive forces.

Finally, I shall, whenever possible, substantiate my arguments with available primary sources such as oracle-bone inscriptions, bronze inscriptions, contemporary literature and other archaeological finds. However, since some original materials are ambiguous, essential secondary sources will be consulted. Being vast in quantity, they must necessarily be used selectively and special attention is paid to the results of recent scholarship.

1 The Concept of the Asiatic Mode of Production

In the Preface to *A Contribution to the Critique of Political Economy* Marx wrote: 'In broad lines Asiatic, ancient, feudal, and modern bourgeois modes of production can be designated as progressive epochs in the economic formation of society' (Marx, 1970: 21). This crucial sentence formally introduced the concept of the Asiatic Mode of Production. This is the only place where Marx succinctly listed it as one of the modes of production. Both before and after he penned this passage, Marx wrote many comments about different forms of religion, history, economy and so on in non-European societies, without clearly defining which of these countries were dominated by the AMP. Therefore, two related questions arise: first, how significant was this mode of production in Marx's conceptualization of the world? Second, to what extent can such a conceptualization explain different developments of world history? These two questions have been discussed in great detail by O'Leary in his recent book, *The Asiatic Mode of Production* (1989). He has argued rigorously that neither Marx nor Engels ever abandoned the substantive conceptual commitment suggested by the AMP (O'Leary, 1989: 146).[1] However, O'Leary sought to use his knowledge of Indian history to dismiss the explanatory value of the concept. Without rehearsing detailed arguments suggested by O'Leary, we can conclude that Marx never denied his famous account in the Preface in any of his writings. Even during the last years of his life, Marx still kept a special interest in the concept, and sought to give a satisfactory answer to the problems the concept had created.[2]

Unfortunately, his death prevented him from finishing the work. Marx left us only scattered comments on the concept, and most of his references to it were indirect and very often incidental. This ambiguity has given rise to many, and often contradictory, understandings among scholars with diverse perspectives, for almost a century. Scholars in favour of the concept can be divided into two groups. In the first group are those who tend to argue fiercely about the characteristics of this mode of production, about its fundamental differences from other modes of production, about the nature of the tensions and conditions that operate in its depths, etc. (Hobsbawm, 1964; Lichtheim, 1967; Draper, 1977; Melotti, 1977; Sawer, 1977; Godelier, 1978; Plekhanov, 1981), while scholars in the second group remain satisfied with what is simply a surface identification of the

6

AMP and regard it as absolutely stagnant (Mandel, 1971; Tokei, 1979, 1989; Jaksic, 1990).

On the other hand, scholars against the concept are delighted to stress, firstly, the logical inconsistency between Marxist philosophy of history and the AMP. Secondly, they emphasize the so-called 'numerous conceptual deficiencies, and its explanatory imperfections' (O'Leary, 1989: 6). It is not surprising that arduous effort has been made to give it 'a decent burial' (Anderson, 1974b: 487; Lubasz, 1984; O'Leary, 1989: 335). Yet, despite the repeated attacks on the concept,[3] the AMP continues its existence as one of the academic sphinxes in social science.

The purpose of this chapter is thus an attempt to give a clear definition of the concept of AMP in order to test its explanatory validity. The first section will define the concept of mode of production, while the second section will be focused on Marx's repeated attempts to define the AMP in his lifetime. I shall contend that his relevant comments on the AMP, albeit in scattered form, offer important insights for a rigorous conceptualization. In the third section I shall seek to reconstruct Marx's methodological approach to the AMP and argue that Marx employed the concept of the AMP to explain the origins of capitalism. Marx believed that capitalism cannot be understood completely unless it is compared with pre-capitalist societies. Hence, for Marx, capitalism was the methodological indicator to study all pre-capitalist societies. In the fourth section some similarities and differences among pre-capitalist societies will be distinguished in order to see their inner mechanisms. For the purpose of the present study, I shall confine myself to comparing the AMP with slave and feudal modes of production. I shall seek to demonstrate that, as a distinctive mode of production, the AMP constitutes one of the most important elements in Marxist theory of history.

1 DEFINITION OF MODE OF PRODUCTION

Mode of production is one of the most fundamental concepts in Marxism. Marx discovered this concept chiefly in the process of formulating his theory of materialistic history.[4] Though he never made a strict definition of the concept, three different definitions can be found in Marx's relevant writings. Following G. A. Cohen, who has made the most famous recent defence of the Marxist theory of history, they are (1) the material mode; (2) the social mode; (3) the mixed mode (Cohen, 1978: 79).

The material mode of production denotes the manner, or the mode in which 'men work with productive forces' (ibid.: 84). The productive forces refer to 'those facilities and devices which are used to produce effect in the forces of production; means of production on the one hand, and labour power on the other' (Cohen, 1988: 4). Means of production include instruments of production of all kinds, raw materials, and so on, while labour power is the combination of the physical and mental capacity of men involving such things as skills and technical knowledge.

The social mode of production denotes 'social properties of the production process' (Cohen, 1978: 80). It has three dimensions; (1) the aim of the production; (2) the form of the producers' surplus labour; (3) the mode of exploitation.[5] Furthermore, these dimensions are closely related and can be demonstrated in a specific relation of production. Relations of production are relations of economic power people enjoy or lack over labour power and means of production (Cohen, 1988: 5), namely, over productive forces.

Sometimes Marx also used the mode of production in a comprehensive fashion to convey a combination of the material and social mode of production. Though he never made clear which of the three modes he referred to when he wrote certain passages, Marx seemed more often than not to employ the concept in a way which includes both material and social dimensions. Therefore, 'a mode of production' is used in this book as a combination of material and social modes of production.[6]

2   MARX ON THE ASIATIC MODE OF PRODUCTION

In this section I shall, first, seek to provide some background knowledge of the AMP. I contend that, although he was deeply influenced by German classical philosophy, especially Hegelianism, Marx's main reason for employing the concept of the AMP lay in his attempt to give world history a theoretical explanation; and the purpose of that explanation was to provide a logic which would satisfy an overthrow of capitalism. Secondly, I shall give a brief review of Marx's repeated attempts to provide a definite conceptualization of the AMP in his lifetime. I shall argue that Marx did not have a static and simplified version of the AMP. Though he was not fully satisfied with what he had achieved on the concept by the end of his life, Marx's scattered remarks nevertheless offer important insights for a clear definition of the AMP.

It goes without saying that the whole European intellectual tradition had an undeniable impact on Marx. As scholars have argued,[7] ever since ancient Greece there has existed in the West a conceptualization of oriental despotism. It refers to a social and economic structure specific to Asia. This perception has been explained by European thought in different terms such as geographical, racial and historical factors. By the nineteenth century, when Marx started his conceptualization of world history, the idea that Eastern countries lacked within themselves the conditions for further organic development had been deeply embedded in the minds of European intellectuals. Marx was no exception. He absorbed the relevant existing literature, especially the Hegelian philosophy of history, which claimed that universal history was the progressive objectification of the self-conscious spirit, i.e. freedom, in the state. However, in the oriental despotism of Eastern societies only one was free, that is, the emperor, while in ancient Greece some were free, namely, the citizens, and it was in the Germanic state that freedom was enjoyed by all (Hegel, 1905: 18–19). By comparison, oriental history is conceived by Hegel as static (Croce, 1957:57).

However, Marx's immediate reason for formulating the concept of the AMP was related to the imminent rationalism of his theory of world history. Since the chief purpose of that theory was to prove an eventual collapse of capitalism, Marx, wherever possible, sought to discover the inner mechanisms of different societies in world history.

During the 1840s Marx was preoccupied with the establishment of the main structure of his new conception of world history. In the *Economic and Philosophical Manuscripts of 1844* Marx regarded the history of human beings between primitive community and ultimate communism chiefly as a history of self-alienation, and private property as the objectification of alienated labour (Marx, 1961: 120).

In *The German Ideology* Marx and Engels (1968) further considered history as consisting of four forms of property ownership. The first form was tribute ownership which belonged to primitive production. The second form was the ancient communal and state ownership. It was not yet private property, but marked the first step in the alienation of property away from its producers. The division of labour was quite advanced, as evidenced by the differentiation between town and countryside. The third form was feudal ownership, characterised by small-scale cultivation of land using serf labour and by small capital handicraft industry, using the labour of apprentices and journeymen. The final form of ownership was characterised by the domination of capital over wage labour. It was manifested in the subordination of the countryside to the town and the world-wide progress of commerce. It is evident that, first, this sketch of world history was implicitly based on the experience of European history (Marx and Engels, 1968: 77). Secondly, Marx and Engels regarded state property, not private property, as the basis of the earliest class societies. Finally, since this was their first attempt to formulate systematically their new discoveries, it is not surprising that some of their expositions were relatively vague, and that the Hegelian influence can be easily detected. For example, the Hegelian amalgam of state with community can be found in Marx's interchangeable usage of the two concepts: communal and state property (ibid.: 33–7).

In the *Manifesto of the Communist Party* Marx and Engels (1959) defined the history of all pre–communist societies as the history of class struggle, which was the social manifestation of the contradiction inherent in a particular mode of production. This contradiction in production was resolved through class struggle, and society advanced to its next historical stage. In the ancient world it was the struggle between slaves and slave-owners; in the feudal era it was mainly between the feudal lord and the peasant serf; in the capitalist society it is between the bourgeois and the proletariat.

At this time Marx and Engels had no special interest in the nature of non-Western societies. Most of their writings on the subject were more theoretical rather than empirical. For example, in the *Manifesto of the Communist Party* China was mentioned only in a negative sense while capitalism was praised as being superior and apt to conquer and unify the entire world. Capitalism 'batters down all Chinese walls' and 'compels all nations, on pain of extinction, to adopt the bourgeois mode of production … In a word, it creates a world after its own image' (Marx, 1968: 32–3).

It was after the failure of the revolution of 1848 that Marx started his systematic conceptualization of the capitalist society. In the process he read the works of the British political economists, such as Adam Smith, Richard Jones and J. S. Mill, and travelling accounts about Indian and other non-European societies.[8] Those writings contained descriptions and analyses of the so–called stationary and unprogressive non–European societies. The influence of these readings can be easily detected in Marx's writings of the early 1850s.

From 1853, to earn his living, Marx began to write articles for the *New York Daily Tribune*. It was in those articles that the social and economic nature of non-European societies was analyzed by Marx for the first time. His articles on India, such as 'The British Rule in India' and his letters to Engels outlined what can be regarded as Marx's first definition of the AMP.

First, Marx regarded the absence of private property as the key to understanding oriental societies, and the geographical factors were generally emphasised. For example, he wrote, 'Bernier correctly discovers – the basic form of all phenomena in the East… to be the *absence of private property* in land. This is the real key, even to the Oriental heaven…' (Marx, 1968: 427). Who owned the land? In a letter to Engels, Marx said, 'the *king is the one and only proprietor of all the land* in the kingdom' (ibid.: 426).[9]

Secondly, Marx considered the need for large-scale public projects organized by the government as one of its most important components, and this in turn necessitated governmental intervention in other aspects of people's social life. Although this geographical-materialist explanation was first suggested by Engels in a letter to Marx (ibid.: 424), Marx adopted the suggestion enthusiastically in his article 'The British Rule in India':

> Climate and territorial conditions, especially the vast tracts of desert, extending from Sahara, through Arabia, Persia, India and Tartary, to the most elevated Asiatic highlands, constituted artificial irrigation by canals and waterworks the basis of Oriental agriculture (ibid.: 85).

Thirdly, Marx did not believe that the above geographical factor could by itself account for the lack of social and economic development in the East. Therefore, he brought social structure, for example the village system, into his analysis. According to Marx, Eastern societies were mainly composed of isolated villages. Since they were self-sufficient, there was a lack of communication and mobilization. As Marx succinctly stated, each of these villages 'possessed a completely separated organization and formed a little world in itself' (ibid.: 431).

Finally, Marx thought that the combination of agriculture and handicraft manufacturing was the fundamental obstacle for the progress of India and other non-European societies. 'Those family-communities were based on domestic industry, in that particular combination of hand-weaving, hand-spinning and hand-tilling agriculture which gave them self-supporting power' (ibid.: 88). And it is this power that underpinned the atomization of the village communities (ibid.: 128). Obviously Marx considered the destruction of the self-sustaining villages as a precondition of progress. Thereby, England was credited as the unconscious tool of history in bringing about a social revolution in India (ibid.: 89; 125–8; 430).

Between 1857 and 1858, in preparation for the writing of *Capital*, Marx wrote many notes which were published posthumously with the title of the *Grundrisse*, in which he analyzed the so-called pre-capitalist economic formations. In particular he stressed the primacy of production, because he held that production in all pre-capitalist forms was different from that of capitalism.

Furthermore, Marx sought to explain the origins and specificity of capitalism. He maintained that capitalism was distinguished from all previous modes of production by the complete separation of the direct producers from their means of production, and the monopoly of the means of production by one class, that is, the capitalist. Since he regarded the separation of the worker from the soil as one of the preconditions for the emergence of capitalism, Marx regarded all previous modes of production as antonyms of capitalism, because in them there was no separation of the direct producer from the means of production.

By now Marx continued to regard the self-sustaining villages as the basic foundation of the AMP. However, there were some shifts of emphasis when he tried to clarify his previous ambiguities about the concept.

First, he believed that land in societies dominated by the AMP was actually owned by the community despite its appearance that the state was the owner:

> Oriental despotism therefore appears to lead to a legal absence of property. In fact, however, its foundation is tribal or communal property, in most cases created through a combination of manufacture and agriculture within the small community which thus becomes entirely self-sustaining and contains within itself all the conditions of production and surplus production' (Marx, 1964: 70).

Marx here saw the complex nature of landownership in the East. At the same time he attempted to articulate the mode by juxtaposing state (higher) and village (smaller) community. Since the common property also formally belonged to the state personified as the ruler, 'surplus labour is rendered both as a tribute and as common labour for the glory of the unity, in part that of the despot, in part that of the imagined tribal entity of the god' (ibid.). Therefore, as scholars have convincingly argued, Marx analysed different developments of societies mainly from the economic point of view in the *Grundrisse*. The political sphere now became a subordinate problem (Krader, 1975: 115–17, 313; 140–64; O'Leary, 1989: 235–61, 270–5).[10] The theoretical and practical significance of the concept of the AMP lay in the dualistic nature of landownership, that is, that land belonged to both state and community.

Secondly, Marx discussed two different forms of property relations. The first one included Asiatic and other communally based types of property relations, while the second encompassed both slave and serf based on private forms of landownership. As some supporters of the AMP have contended, this characterization of forms of property constitutes the basis for a multilineal scheme of history, namely, there are many different paths of development from primitive society throughout the world (Hobsbawm, 1964; Marx, 1973: 495; Melotti, 1977; Sawer, 1977). Nevertheless, there still remain unsolved problems such as how these forms are differentiated from one another and in what sense they pose real alternatives, and how the multilineal explanation of the world is compatible with Marx's theory of history.

It was in the Preface to *A Contribution to the Critique of Political Economy* that Marx put forward the concept of AMP unambiguously for the first and the last time in his life: 'In broad lines Asiatic, ancient, feudal and modern bourgeois society can be designated as progressive epochs in the economic formation of society' (Marx, 1970: 21). Since Marx did not give further qualification to this sentence, it can be explained in two ways. The first interpretation is that Marx listed these modes of production according to chronological order, that is, that world history is a temporal sequence of these modes of production. This means that historical development is unilineal.[11]

On the other hand, scholars holding the second view seek to contend that Marx here only gave an analytical description of epoch-marking progress[12] in the economic development of history (Melotti, 1977: 26; Sawer, 1977: 207). Although some of Marx's writings can be understood in terms of the first explanation, a closer study of all his comments on the issue reveals that Marx penned these modes of production as analytical rather than as descriptive concepts. He aimed at distinguishing different social and economic structures. For instance, in the *Grundrisse* Marx definitely suggested that feudalism was not based on the contradiction in slavery, and that it developed on the edge of the Roman Empire among the German tribes ('military' feudalism) (Marx, 1964: 68–99). Furthermore, nowhere did Marx explicitly indicate that the AMP was a precursor of the slave mode of production. These examples imply that we cannot universalize any mode of production as we please. It is vulgar Marxism which describes history as simplified universal development, namely, that every society, regardless of its specific peculiarities, has to experience those modes of production listed by Marx in the above quoted passage (cf. Hobsbawm, 1964: 36; Melotti, 1977). Any attempt to give the 1859 Preface a unilineal explanation is thus a gross distortion of Marx's theory (Marx, 1973: 495–513).

Finally, it is worth emphasizing that in the last years of his life Marx read the latest works of anthropology and sociology. He made many comments for further analysis of pre-capitalist social formations. Both the depth and extent of his research exceeded those of his earlier explorations. All his notes suggest that Marx had modified his theory about pre-capitalist societies. In many places he sought to redefine the concept of the AMP (cf. Krader, 1975: 343–412; O'Leary, 1989: 147–50). In particular he changed his mind over the nature of the village communities he had once described as 'the key to the secret of the unchangeableness of the Asiatic societies, an unchangeableness in such striking contrast with the constant dissolution and refounding of Asiatic states, and the never-ceasing changes of dynasty' (Marx, 1967a: 358). For instance, as a result of discussion with Russian populists, Marx considered the Russian villages as the potential basis for future socialism in Russia without going through capitalism.[13] All these notes demonstrate Marx's continuous effort to resolve problems raised by his previous discussions on the concept on the AMP. He was willing to absorb new knowledge and correct himself in the process of formulating his theory of history.

On the other hand, since he did not have time to reconsider systematically the nature of non-European societies in the light of the latest knowledge about those societies, Marx was not able to establish a rigorous definition of the AMP. Many problems remain unsolved. For example, there is no consensus as to which passage among Marx's writings refers to a descriptive account of pre-capitalist social forms, which one denotes Marx's attempt to locate conceptually the AMP in his whole project of the theory of world history, and what the relationship is between the two.

Based on these ambiguities, Currie seeks to argue the so-called invalidity of the AMP (Currie, 1984: 251–64; 1985),[14] while Wittfogel claims that Marx 'committed a sin against science' by suppressing his Asiatic discovery in his later years (Wittfogel, 1981: 370–7, 380–9).[15]

Of course, there are objective reasons for such misunderstandings or distortions, because Marx's massive writings on different occasions can be interpreted to support different versions of the AMP.[16] The ambiguous nature of the concept thereby has left a great deal of room for diverse explanations of Marxism.

However, we cannot discount the subjective reasons for creating so much confusion about the AMP. It is impossible to be value-free when writing on any such social and political issue. Thus, it is not surprising that scholars with different political orientations argue for different expositions. The latest argument against both the AMP and Marxist theory of history has been offered by O'Leary, who has sought to demonstrate that 'historical materialism is damned with the AMP' (O'Leary, 1989: 3).[17]

Contrary to the above argument, I shall contend in the next section that scholars like O'Leary, despite their systematic treatment of Marx's original texts, have failed to understand Marx's methodological approach to world history.

3   A METHODOLOGICAL APPROACH TO HISTORY

As indicated above, Marx's main concern in his life was to explain the structural mechanism of capitalism as a system of production predicated on the relationship between capital and wage-labour. For Marx, all pre-capitalist societies are essentially local systems and economically limited. It is capitalism that will prevail in the world. Hence the historical perspective inaugurated by modern capitalism provides the starting point for the understanding of Marxism (Marx, 1973: 409–10).

At the same time, Marx was also very much concerned with the process of capitalist growth, especially the strong barriers of pre-capitalist societies to capitalist expansion (Marx, 1967c: 333; Wolpe, 1980: 3–5). Therefore, Marx first intended to reveal the struggle between the expansive urge of capitalist society and the conserving forces of the pre-capitalist economic structures, between these 'diametrically opposed economic systems' (Marx, 1967a: 765). Second, Marx maintained that, despite capitalism's expansive tendency, the outcome of this struggle was dependent, in the final instance, upon 'the character of the old mode of production itself' (Marx, 1967c: 332).

Nevertheless, Marx never overlooked the revolutionary effect of English capitalist expansion on non-European societies. For instance, in *Capital*, Vol. 3, Marx compared two different impacts of Russian and English commerce with China, and concluded: 'In contrast to English trade, Russian trade leaves the economic basis of Asiatic production quite untouched' (Marx, 1981: 452). Why? Because Russian commerce did not represent a superior mode of production. Thus the important factor in analysis of the nature of different countries is the structural character of the societies concerned (Marx, 1967a: 82). From this standpoint, the crucial task is to grasp the structural mechanism of each specific society before assessing the impact of world capitalism on it.

Unfortunately, scholars, more often than not, tend to either ignore or neglect Marx's methodology, and merely seek to apply the economic rationality of capitalism to the study of pre-capitalist societies. In particular, they maintain that all modes of production imply the same economic mechanism of surplus extraction. A typical example of such an approach can be found in the writings of Hindess and Hirst. They claimed to be concerned with providing formalistic definitions that have theoretical validity (Hindess and Hirst, 1975). Influenced by Althusserian Marxism (Althusser, 1969), they rejected the theoretical validity of Marx's formulation of the AMP simply because in it the state is supposed to be both landlord and sovereign, and hence taxes and rents coincide. This means that there is only one general mode of surplus appropriation through the state. They held that it is impossible to derive a mode of production from the tax/rent couple as a mechanism of surplus appropriation. For them all the appropriation of surplus must be economic, as is the case in capitalism.[18]

Therefore, they failed to understand that it is capitalism that for the first time has accomplished the separation of the economic mechanism of surplus extraction from other means of coercion (Banerjee, 1985: 15).

However, even those like Hindess and Hirst, who rejected the conflation of the political instance in determining the mechanism of the appropriation of surplus in the AMP, had to explain the characters of other pre-capitalist economic formations, such as the ancient mode of production in ancient Greece and Rome, in terms of its mode of surplus extraction by the legal right of citizenship (Hindess and Hirst, 1975: 79). Law and politics entered directly into the very constitution of the infrastructure in their analysis. It is not surprising that they abandoned their criticism within a short time (Hindess and Hirst, 1977; Banerjee, 1985: 16).

Hence Marx's methodology is neither a pure abstractionism for the sake of theory nor an evolutionism which starts from the dawn of history and then arrives through a chronological scheme to the present reality of his time (Banerjee, 1976: 237). In fact, it is the capitalist production of his time that constitutes the starting point of Marx's enquiry. For example, when speaking about the paradigm of labour, a simple abstract category valid for all epochs, Marx dealt with the most complex social organization to date, that is, capitalism, because he believed that the abstract category of labour attains its richest possible concreteness when labour in general becomes the actuality, with its utter indifference to any specific kind and form of labour (Marx, 1973: 102–5).

Nevertheless, this does not mean that Marx kept himself confined to the essential forms of capitalism. For Marx one cannot understand the specificity of these forms of capitalism completely unless one compares them with other social and economic structures (Marx, 1973: 84–108; 1976: 125–77).[19]

Why did Marx use this method? The answer is not difficult to find: the concealment of the actual nature of things in the commodity culture of the capitalist mode of production is so widespread and deep-rooted that bourgeois forms of life assume almost natural, if not immutable, appearance. But 'the whole mystery of commodities, all the magic and necromancy that surround the products of labour as long as they take the form of commodities, vanishes... as soon as they come to other forms of production' (Marx, 1967a: 76). Therefore, only this methodology can combine its critical existential grasp of capitalism with its historical grasp, so that the distinctive mechanism of capitalism will be reviewed in all its specific nuances by its contrast with pre-capitalist economic formations. This is essential to understand differences between capitalism and pre-capitalist economic formations. In other words, only after the present, that is, the latest and most concrete reality is known, can we proceed to grasp the nature of history's previous reality and major discontinuities in the process of history. For example, in *Capital*, Vol. 1, Marx first tried to show that categories such as commodity and money are the expressions of conditions and organization of bourgeois society. Then he claimed that these forms of capitalism bear 'the stamp of history' (Marx, 1967a: 169). They are capable of providing insights to those of the earlier modes of production, even if as glimpses of a forgotten past. It was after all on their ruins and remains that capitalism came into the world, still dragging many unconquered remnants. 'The bourgeois economy thus supplies the key to the ancient, etc.' (Marx, 1973: 105).

On the other hand, Marx reminded us that the above methodological approach, that is, to look at the remnants of pre-capitalist societies merely as they exist within capitalism, is not sufficient to reveal the essential differences between various pre-capitalist societies, because those unconquered remnants of pre-capitalist elements in bourgeois society do not reveal the specific complexities and distinctive mechanisms of all pre-capitalist modes of production. These elements of the past may exist now in a stunted form, or they may even be crippled. According to Marx, if continuities in history point to the general, it is discontinuities which specify the particular. This dialectic of continuity and discontinuity in the historical process holds a crucial position in Marx's conceptualization of the nature of pre-capitalist societies (Banerjee, 1985: 20).

For example, the historical category of commodities is, according to Marx, the historical premise of capitalism. Although production and circulation of commodities exist in all pre-capitalist societies, they have never dominated social production. They only constitute one of the historical premises of the capitalist mode of production. As Marx unambiguously stated: 'In themselves, money and commodities are no more capital than the means of production and subsistence are' (Marx, 1976: 874). It is within the capitalist mode of production that commodity production and circulation become dominant. If we apply this principle to the analysis of pre-capitalist societies, without considering other factors in those societies, it is impossible to detect the inner dynamics of those societies and their differences with capitalism. 'We see here how even economic categories appropriate to earlier modes of production acquire a new and specific historical character under the impact of capitalist production' (ibid.: 950).[20] This functional distinction of categories is essential if we want to grasp the inner mechanisms of the changing modes of production.

In short, to understand the nature of pre-capitalist societies one must first understand the mechanism of capitalism. As Marx clearly indicated, only once the self-criticism of bourgeois society had begun could political economy arrive at 'an understanding of feudal, ancient, oriental economics' (Marx, 1973: 105). The reason is simple: that will enable us to understand the structural discontinuities which differentiate societies. A critical theory of capitalism is hence the first precondition for grasping the nature of previous modes of production in history (Banerjee, 1985: 23).

Moreover, Marx emphasized that, to conceptualize correctly all pre-capitalist societies, we should not confine our analysis to the categories of capitalism. It is also necessary to extend our conceptualization to capitalism's forms of growth, and that will lead us to past forms of history. For instance, the accumulation of wealth is a presupposition of capitalism. It played a great role in dissolutions of old relations of production before the final establishment of capitalism. But, in pre-capitalist societies, however much wealth one may have, it is not capital. It is to be transformed through a historical process of social change into capital. 'Only when the capitalist mode of production has become predominant, when it does not merely exist sporadically, but has subordinated to itself the mode of production of society; when in fact the capitalist directly appropriates the whole surplus labour and surplus products in the first place... – only then does profit become the principal source of capital, of accumulation, of wealth' (Marx, 1972: 420–1). 'And it is through this process that the capitalist inserts himself as (historic) middle-man between landed property, or property generally, and labour' (Marx, 1973: 505). This process was ignored by classical political economists, because they sought to justify capitalism as a natural form of production while condemning all early economies as artificial (ibid.: 105).

Thus, the analysis of the presupposed forms of capital's growth can clarify the position of the bourgeois society. The fact that it represents nothing but a specific mode of production in history points backwards to those pre-capitalist societies. We cannot thereby understand those specific forms unless we comprehend the historical background of the capital's forms of growth with our knowledge of the mechanism of capitalism, in which the individual is separated from the objective conditions of his work, wage labour from capital (ibid.: 488). It is at this point that the historical approach enters into the enquiry, because this historical dimension can reveal the dynamics and logic of those pre-capitalist societies (cf. Banerjee, 1985: 25). As Marx stressed, what is more important than anything else is the method of investigation. It should indicate 'the point where historical investigation must enter in, or where bourgeois economy as a mere historical form of the production process points beyond itself to earlier historical modes of production' (Marx, 1973: 460). It then becomes evident that to grasp the inner logic of history, we have to compare the capitalist mode of production with pre-capitalist modes of production in all possible spheres. Indeed, for Marx the same process of analysis represents two aspects of one construct: 'The presentation of the specific, distinguishing characteristics is here both the *logical* development and the key to the understanding of the *historical* development' (ibid.: 672).

In this way Marx brought together two perspectives. In the first place, he used the concept of capitalism as a methodological indicator to study pre-capitalist societies. Naturally, Marx stressed the differences between capitalism and pre-capitalist societies. As capitalism is the point of departure, the application of this concept to reveal the specificities of pre-capitalist societies has a special significance. In other words, from this standpoint, all pre-capitalist societies can be classified in a single genre and belong to 'the *first* social forms'. They witness the development of man and his productive power 'only to a slight extent and at isolated points' (ibid.: 158). Cultivators were bound to the soil and labour was not free from constraints of extra-economic fetters. Consequently, there were not enough incentives and financial support for the productive power systematically to develop specialization and technological innovations.[21] In contrast, capitalism, based on 'the personal independence founded on *objective* dependence is the second great form, in which a system of general social metabolism, of universal relations, of all–round needs and universal capacities is formed for the first time'. In 'the second great form', the workers are separated from their means of production and labour becomes legally free, meaning that it is free to be exploited by capital. Contrary to those first social forms where the forms of unfreedom correspond to the context of everyday life, capitalism bears the contradiction: the form of free labour relations is opposed to its content of unfreedom.

However, despite all its defects, Marx repeatedly emphasized that only this 'second great form' can create the presuppositions of the third form, socialism (ibid.: 158).[22] This is one of Marx's most important arguments. It closely relates to the fate of all pre-capitalist societies. If Marx's book is correct in asserting that capitalism will destroy all earlier modes of production,[23] it is then premature for a non-capitalist society to implement socialist ideas before catching up with capitalism by adopting its mode of production first. Socialism's experience in so-called underdeveloped societies in the twentieth century seems to have confirmed Marx's argument.

Therefore, this comparative study between capitalism and its pre-social formations first clarifies the actual forms of capitalism and its precursors. Second, it explains many social phenomena in pre-capitalist societies.

However, it is essential to grasp capitalism first. Otherwise, all the earlier modes of production would either look like the formal structures of the present capitalism or assume completely irrelevant shapes.

Since the mystery of capitalist production has been revealed by Marx in his major works, we are now in a better position to understand the distinction between capitalism and pre-capitalist economic formations.

Nevertheless, this is only the first step to see the significance of the AMP as one of Marx's contributions to social science. To rightly locate the concept in Marx's theory, we must take the second step, namely, to distinguish the similarities and differences between pre-capitalist societies. It is this second perspective of enquiry which will enable us to know the logic of each of those pre-capitalist societies.

Of course, we first need sufficient information on those societies. But pure empiricism will not help us penetrate into the inner mechanism and dynamics of those modes of production, because it maintains that an application of any theory involves a fundamental denial of historical truth (Banerjee, 1985: 28; Chaudhuri, 1992: 48). Marx, though he did not provide a systematic treatment of the problem, offered valuable guidance in his writings. To be sure, this does not mean that we must treat all of Marx's writings on the subject as correct or equally important. As is well known, most of his knowledge in this field was built on the limited economic, social and anthropological studies made during his time. Therefore, it is understandable that Marx emphasized different aspects of Indian and other non-Western societies at different times. It would be unreasonable to expect Marx to be correct in every relevant comment. From this perspective, specific analysis of each pre-capitalist society still requires serious attention. No doubt this is both a complex and demanding task. However, for the purpose of the present study which intends to establish the AMP as a distinctive mode of production, I shall confine myself to comparing the AMP only with slave and feudal modes of production.

4   SLAVERY, FEUDALISM AND THE ASIATIC MODE OF PRODUCTION

Marx's discussion of slavery and feudalism, like his writings on the AMP, is not systematic. He frequently used these concepts, but he never defined them adequately. This has created conceptual confusions. Despite the efforts of scholars to give them precise definitions,[24] there has been no consensus as to their locations in the whole project of the Marxist theory of history.[25] Having no intention to enter the relevant controversies,

I shall, firstly, follow the generally agreed definitions. Secondly, against those who try to globalize slavery and feudalism,[26] I shall argue that regardless of the need for further empirical information, the available sources have already demonstrated a possible application of the AMP into the analysis of some non-Western societies.

According to Marx, the slave mode of production refers to a society in which slaves were privately-owned commodities. They did not own any means of production. Nor did they have control over their labour. Marx believed that Roman history represented the purest form of slavery in which the city was the centre for the residents of the countryside (Marx, 1964: 97). As Marx wrote: 'The private landed proprietor is therefore simultaneously an urban citizen. Economically citizenship may be expressed more simply as a form in which the agriculturalist lives in a city' (ibid.: 79–80). The test of the dominance of a slave mode of production lay not in the numbers of the slaves but in their social location, namely, in the extent to which the elites depended on them for their wealth.

The feudal mode of production denotes a society in which the basic relations of production were those which regulated the appropriation of land and its products. They bound and opposed the lord to the peasant, the owner of the land, and, in part, of the peasant's person to the immediate producer. The peasants were compelled to provide compulsory labour and to pay rent in kind or money. Extra-economic coercion was used by the landlords to guarantee a constant flow of income. 'The essence of the feudal mode of production in the Marxist sense is the exploitation relationship between landowners and subordinated peasants, in which the surplus beyond subsistence of the latter, whether in direct labour or in rent, in kind or in money, is transferred under coercive sanction of the former' (Hilton, 1976: 30; cf. Anderson, 1974a: 147–53; 1974b: 407).

In view of my discussion in the second section of this chapter, the AMP is understood to refer to a society within which land was formally owned by the state, but in practice belonged to the small communities. Taxes were paid directly to the state through the tax collectors in the name of tribute. The majority were subject to a small number of individuals who represented a higher community. This power first took root in functions of common interest such as the religious, the economic and the military, and eventually transformed itself into an exploitative one.

Definitions of different modes of production indicate that there are some common features in these pre-capitalist societies: first, the majority of the people in these modes of production lived at a subsistence level; second, the existence of men as producers of commodities played a subordinate role in production. Production was chiefly for consumption; third, extra-economic coercion existed to a lesser or greater extent.

However, even if we come to know 90 per cent of similarities between two societies, it does not help us understand why societies have evolved differently. It is the other 10 per cent of differences which counts. That is why Marx insisted on distinguishing different socio-economic structures. In particular Marx took care to differentiate the AMP from other modes of production. In the *Grundrisse* Marx stated that from primitive tribal society, different communes evolved in the course of time. Marx divided them roughly into four categories: classical, Asiatic, Germanic and Slavonic. Moreover, two main forms of property relations developed out of these communes: that is, communal and private. According to Marx, Eastern societies represented the former while ancient Greek and Roman slavery represented the latter (Marx, 1973: 495–6).

In *Capital*, Vol. 3, Marx also stressed: 'Under slavery, feudalism and vassalage... it is the slave-owner, the feudal lord, the tribute-collecting state, who are the owners, hence sellers, of product' (Marx, 1967c: 326). 'Under those earlier modes of production the principal owners of the surplus-product with whom the merchants dealt were namely, the slave-owner, the feudal lord, and the state' (ibid.: 331). There are many other passages conveying a similar idea (Marx, 1967a: 217; 1967b, 36; 1967c: 326, 331, 791), but all seem to indicate that the essential differences which divide pre-capitalist societies into different categories lay in the nature of the exploitation of the labourers and their state of dependence in each case:

> In all forms in which the direct labourer remains the 'possessor' of the means of production and labour conditions necessary for the production of his own means of subsistence, the property relationship must simultaneously appear as a direct relation of lordship and servitude, so that the direct producer is not free, a lack of freedom which may be reduced from serfdom with enforced labour to a mere tributary relationship.... This differs from slave or plantation economy in that the slave works under alien conditions of production and not independently. Thus, conditions of personal dependence are requisite, a lack of personal freedom, no matter to what extent, and being tied to the soil as its accessory, bondage in the true sense of the word. Should the direct producers not be confronted by a private landowner, but rather, as in Asia, under direct subordination to a state which stands over them as their landlord and simultaneously as sovereign, then rent and taxes coincide, or rather, there exists no tax which differs from this form of ground-rent. Under

such circumstances, there need exist no stronger political and economic pressure than that common to all subjection to that state. The state is then the supreme lord. Sovereignty here consists in the ownership of land concentrated on the national scale (Marx, 1967c: 790–1).

This is probably one of Marx's most revealing passages on the relationship between the AMP and other economic formations. Together with his other discussions on the subject and evidence suggested by recent scholarship, we are now in a position to reinstate some of the most important features which Marx thought the AMP had.

Firstly, Marx made it clear that there were at least three different forms of surplus extraction in pre-capitalist societies: the 'Asiatic', the feudal and the slave. In the AMP, the peasants had to face the state which represented and, by taxation, economically realized, communal ownership. As a result, there was no need for any special method of enforcement in the collection of ground rent apart from those binding each individual to the community and the state.

By contrast, in slavery it was the slave owners who extorted the surplus from the slaves by virtue of their ownership of both land and people, and in feudalism society was based on property rights and the right of the lord over the serf's labour.[27] 'Feudal landed property gives its name to its lords, as does a kingdom give its name to its king. His family history, the history of his house, etc. all this makes the landed property individual to him, makes it formally belong to a house, to a person' (Marx, 1961: 60). This property right gave the landlord a legal basis to alienate peasants from their means of production. The nature of feudal rent, for instance labour services, payment in kind, or money varied, but the surplus produced for the peasants' superior is obvious and undeniable (Kosminsky, 1956: vi–vii; Dobb, 1963: 19–35, 37; Anderson, 1973b: 17, 402; Shaw, 1978: 133–8; Roemer, 1988: 135–9).

Secondly, in slavery, the slave was at the mercy of his owner and he had no freedom. Similarly, the feudal mode of production also created personal dependence, albeit to a lesser extent in comparison with the former. As Marx emphasized, in feudalism 'instead of the independent man, we find everyone dependent; serfs and lords, vassals, land suzerains, laymen and clergy. Personal dependence here characterizes the social relations of production just as much as it does other spheres of life organized on the basis of that production' (Marx, 1961: 61).

By contrast, in the AMP land was owned in practice by the community, although it officially belonged to the state. Since the level of the productive forces was relatively low, production was conducted chiefly through communal farming. Under such conditions, producers did not have to depend on a specific landlord, and this lack of independent lords released them from the social and economic bondage to which a serf in feudal Europe was subjected.

However, does this imply that they were in a better situation than those producers in slavery and feudalism? The answer is negative, because they were limited by their communal existence, which was under the direct control of the state.[28] Marx once depicted this situation as 'the general slavery' of the state (Marx, 1973: 495).[29] Such a description has created different interpretations. For instance, in China scholars often quote the above comment of Marx to argue that China has experienced slavery (Guo Moruo, 1976). But read in its context, it is very clear that Marx first used this concept to demonstrate exactly the differences between societies dominated by the AMP and Roman slavery where the producers were considered as among the 'natural conditions of production for a third individual or community' (Marx, 1973: 495). Second, Marx merely introduced the concept metaphorically, just as he freely used wage-slavery for an entirely different system, namely, modern capitalism. Therefore, the phrase 'general slavery' only refers to a condition in which the existence of the individual was nothing more than an accident. To be more precise, the individual was one of the purely natural elements in preserving the survival of the community. As a result, he remained unconscious of himself as an individual with juridical and political rights. He was not a slave from the point of view of Roman slavery, because he did not live actually in a specific slave relationship either to the community or to another individual as a slavemaster. However, the slave-like relationship did exist, albeit in a generalized or universalized form. It was applied to the community itself, which was exploited as an organism by the state above it.

Thirdly, in slavery slave-owners had absolute power over slaves, and in feudalism the landowner confronted the producers also as an alien power. Apart from their differences, there existed antagonism in social relations in the two systems. Furthermore, private landownership constituted the foundation of all slave and feudal forms of surplus extraction. In writing about the Greek *polis* and Roman history, Marx stressed that private ownership of land had been the solid bases of these societies. 'The history of the Roman Republic, ... is the history of landed property' (Marx, 1976: 176; cf. Marx, 1964: 73–83, 102, 109). 'Communal property – as state property, *ager publicus* – [is] separated from private property. The property of the individual is here not, ... itself directly communal property. ... The commune – as state – is, on one side, the relation of these free and equal private proprietors to one another, their bond against the outside, and is at the same time their safeguard' (Marx, 1973: 474–5). Property was therefore integrally bound up with citizenship. It was only as a *civis* that an individual could be a proprietor in Ancient Rome.

In feudalism, Marx wrote: 'The domination of the land as an alien power over men is already inherent in feudal landed property. The serf is the adjunct of the land' (Marx, 1961: 61). Thus the landlord had his privileges (although not as much as a slave-owner had), his jurisdiction, and his political position, and so on. He could behave as the king of his estate, while the serf did not own the means of production or labour conditions of his own means of subsistence, such as land. Since the serf was tied to the lord, he had to provide to the individual landlord a certain amount of unpaid surplus labour in the form of demesne and farming, etc. The communal organization of these producers hence appeared less as a kinship community than as the functional component of the exploitation of individuals. For Marx, it is always the direct relationship of the owners of the conditions of production to the direct producers which reveals the innermost secret, the hidden basis of the entire social structure (Marx, 1967c: 791).

By contrast, in the AMP land was cultivated collectively, but the ultimate ownership remained in the hand of the state insomuch as it personified all the communities:

> Since the *unity* is the ... precondition of common ownership, it is perfectly possible for it to appear as something separate and superior to the numerous real particular communities. The individual is then in fact propertyless, or property – i.e. the relationship of the individual to the *natural* conditions of labour and reproduction, the inorganic nature which he finds and makes his own, the objective body of this subjectivity – appears to be mediated by means of a grant from the total unity of the individual through the intermediary of the particular community. The despot here appears as the father of all the numerous lesser communities, thus realising the common unity of all (Marx, 1964: 69).

This passage clearly indicates, first, that, since the same piece of land belonged to both the community and the state whose rights were realized through taxation, this implies that the communal landownership was not formally differentiated from state land-ownership; landlord and land-owner were one. Hence the surplus of the peasants was extracted in the form of tax not by any private slave-owner or landlord, but by the state. Second, the cultivator was bound to the land not by private right to the state, but by customary right, and thus custom and public law were not differentiated in the AMP.

Moreover, the concept of citizenship which gave a person independent political and economic rights was unknown for the people in the AMP as well. This can happen only in a society where awareness of individual rights is less developed away from primitive community. This characteristic of the society, along with its communality, indicates that the individual's organic, umbilical ties to his community and to nature have not been severed. Finally, since the method of the extraction of the surplus was collective, social conflicts in the AMP were less direct and visible.

On the contrary, in societies in which social changes increase 'a conscious attitude to the conditions of production as to *one's own* – an attitude established by the community for the individual, proclaimed and guaranteed as law; in so far as the existence of the producer therefore appears as an existence within the objective conditions *belonging to him*' (ibid.: 92), developments of the originally communal ownership inevitably modify all previous forms until the final establishment of private property. We can find the typical example of this form of property in ancient Greek and Roman slavery where members of the community had already acquired separate existence as private proprietor from their collective existence as an urban community. Moreover, individuals were allowed to lose their property there (ibid.: 72, 93–4).

Nevertheless, in the AMP, this *loss*[30] was hardly possible, except as a result of entirely external influences such as conquest, because 'the individual member of the community never establishes so independent a relation to it as to enable him to lose his (objective, economic) tie with it. He is firmly rooted' (ibid.: 94). Therefore, ownership means that 'certain persons enjoy the monopoly of disposing of particular portions of the globe as exclusive spheres of their private will to the exclusion of all others' (Marx, 1981: 752). The above definition of ownership is certainly far from precise. Ownership should be defined in terms of a set of rights. First, it includes the right to possess a physical object such as a dwelling, a piece of land, etc. Second, the possessor has the right of control of the benefits of his or her property. He or she should not be prevented from taking actions with his or her property such as selling it. Third, the property must be protected by an authority system. Finally, the concept reflects a social relation that defines the property-owner with all others. Hence, strictly speaking, empirical possession cannot establish ownership. Rights are not only the relationship between a person and an object, but also the relationship between a person and others with respect to the object. In other words, rights can only exist when there is a social mechanism that gives duties and binds individuals or communities to those duties. From this standpoint, there is no concept of ownership in a society in which there is plenty of land and people can occupy it without limitation. But when a society has created all the conditions mentioned above, it is inevitable that people will formulate the concept of ownership. The absolute right to appropriation derives from the need for all to secure their sustenance and from the right of all to the fruits of their own labour.

However, owing to different circumstances, both geographical and cultural, various forms of ownership evolved in history. Between them there are substantial differences in nature, size and internal structure across a broad spectrum. But they share a common feature: that is, all the institutional arrangements are created to permit different forms of ownership to survive. They are the manifestations of the essence of societies with definite memberships and clear boundaries.

Fourthly, in the AMP, division of labour was developed in a way different from that of slavery and feudalism. In *Capital*, Vol. 1, Marx produced a vivid description of how the simplicity of the organization of production in the AMP remained more or less the same for centuries and concluded: 'The law that regulates the division of labour in the community acts with the irresistible authority of a law of Nature, ... The simplicity of the organization for production in these self-sufficing communities that constantly reproduce themselves in the same form, and when accidentally destroyed, spring up again on the spot and with the same name...' (Marx, 1967a: 357–8). Obviously, since division of labour in the AMP happened in a spontaneous or natural way and was historically closer to man's origins, there was greater domination of the natural, communal and extra-economic conditions. As a result, 'each individual has no more torn himself off from the navel-string of his tribe or community, than each bee has freed himself from connexion with his hive' (Marx, 1967a: 334). The AMP thereby represented an unclarified unity of man and nature, of the individual and community, and of politics and society.

On the other hand, the whole social structure in the AMP can be described as a patriarchal extension, because it preserved the functioning of the primitive village community in the midst of the more elaborate superstructure (Hobsbawm, 1964: 37–8). Hence it was not easy to change its social and economic relations. 'The more traditional the mode of the production itself, i.e. the more the *real process* of appropriation remains the same, the more unchanging will the ancient forms of property be and therefore also the community as a whole' (Marx, 1964: 93; cf. Marx, 1973: 495). To be sure, there always exists a tendency of change to a lesser or greater extent everywhere. However, the lack of clear-cut class distinction which Marx regarded as one of the important sources of social progress prevented a quick growth of independent and competing economic and social groups in the AMP.

By contrast, conflicting social relations complicated division of labour in both slavery and feudalism. Apart from slave-owners and slaves, there were free and semi-free peasants and artisans in ancient Greece and Rome. In feudal Europe there were not only lords and serfs, but also vassals, suzerains, laymen, clergy, and so on. 'Feudalism itself had entirely empirical relations as its basis.... Feudalism is the political form of the medieval relations of production and commerce' (Marx and Engels, 1968: 190, 364). Under such conditions, there emerged the guild industry which provided potentiality for further development of productive forces. The division of labour among guilds, although not within them, encouraged the growth of handicrafts in quality and efficiency. Along with the increase of labour skills, tools became more sophisticated and precise. Then came the separation of production and commerce which soon called forth a new division of production between individual towns, 'each of which is soon exploiting a predominant branch of industry' (Marx, 1964: 131).

Eventually, however, the local restrictions of earlier times gradually began to be broken down, and the relations of production, which protected and supported previous production, became unsuitable for the further development of the productive forces (Marx, 1964: 112–31). It was capitalists who, preoccupied with profit, promoted further division of labour and established a new dominant mode of production, that is, modern capitalism. For Marx, this is a necessary condition 'to create the material basis of the new world' – 'on the one hand the universal intercourse founded upon the mutual dependency of mankind, and the means of that intercourse; on the other hand the development of the productive powers of man and the transformation of material production into a scientific domination of natural agencies' (Marx, 1968: 131).[31]

Fifthly, there was a significant difference in relations between city and countryside in these three modes of production. Both ancient slavery and feudal Europe had a growing antagonism between cities and countryside. As Marx explicitly stated: 'The history of classical antiquity is the history of cities, but of cities founded on landed property and on agriculture; ... the Middle Ages (Germanic period) begins with the land as the seat of history, whose further development then moves forward in the contradiction between town and countryside; the modern [age] is the urbanization of the countryside' (Marx, 1973: 479). The merchants in feudalism, taking advantage of the conflicts between the crown and the feudal lords, eventually became a countering force in opposition to the state.

In time, the communes of the burghers became both economically powerful and politically independent within the feudal society. The feudal lords could not ignore their demands. Indeed the establishment of the communes of the burghers was one of the inevitable steps in the process of the emergence of the bourgeoisie. As a result of long struggle between different classes, political power was gradually decentralized. The bourgeoisie finally won the battle by establishing modern capitalism (Bloch, 1962a: 56, 227; 1962b: 383, 446–7; Hibbert, 1953: 15–27; Pirenne, 1971: 20; 1925; 1937). The significance of this system was summarized by Marx in his early work *On the Jewish Question*:

> The [bourgeois] political revolution ... raised state affairs to become affairs of the people, which constituted the political state as a matter of *general* concern, that is, as a real state, necessarily smashed all estates, corporations, guilds, and privileges since they were all manifestations of the separation of the individual from the community. ... It broke up civil society into its simple component parts: on the one hand, the *individuals*; and on the other hand, the *material* and *spiritual* elements constituting the content of the life and social position of these individuals. It set free the political spirit, which had been, as it were, split up, partitioned, dispersed in the various blind alleys of feudal society. It gathered the dispersed parts of the political spirit, freed it from its intermixture with civil life, and established it as the sphere of the community, the general concern of the nation, ideally independent of those *particular* elements of civil life. ... Public affairs as such, ... became the general affair of each individual, and the political function became the individual's general function (Marx, 1975: 165–6).[32]

However, in the AMP, cities were chiefly centres of administration. Most of the industries were monopolized by the state, and their main purpose was to satisfy the needs of the courts and nobilities. Therefore, even if there were increasing differences between towns and villages in terms of population and purpose of production, and so on, relations had never been the same as in European history in which the state and the villages were brought into increasing contact. In its final analysis, the urban development and accumulation of surplus in the AMP was not an expression of internal commodity production but of the transformation of this surplus into commodities. In the absence of the antagonism, the cities in the AMP hence did not enjoy the same range of economic relations as Western cities did (Marx, 1964: 77–8; cf. Marx, 1968: 426; 1973: 467, 479) .

To be more specific: first, the merchants and artisans in the AMP could not be in a position like their counterparts in feudalism playing the feudal lords against the king in their attempt at consolidating power. Thus cities in the AMP could not become the centres of bourgeois power to struggle against the state power, because the system ruled out any possibility of developing a potential bourgeois class. The merchants and artisans always remained subordinate to the political power. Consequently, they were not able to demand political autonomy or political privileges as the European bourgeoisie was.

Secondly, the bureaucrats in the AMP lived in the cities. They could be very powerful within their areas of control, but they were no more than public functionaries. They had no privileges apart from those received from the king. Although there developed certain legal systems such as criminal law,[33] there had never been civil law such as Roman law to guarantee the rights of the people.

Finally, the absence of a conflict of interests between the peasants and landlords over the question of disposal of the land failed to lead to the labourers' separation from the land – another prerequisite of the emergence of capitalism (Marx, 1964: 67). The peasants in feudal Europe could flee into cities to earn their livings, while peasants in the AMP had no such an alternative.

Finally, there was a strong sense of a contractual feature in the vassal's obligation of fidelity to his lord on a basis of militarism in Western feudalism (Hall, 1962: 7). By contrast, kinship relationship between the king and his appointees occupied a position of supreme importance in the AMP. Therefore, familism was the essence of the entire social organization in the latter.

All these factors blocked an endogenous development of capitalism in societies dominated by the AMP. Moreover, they help to show why Marx regarded the AMP as one of the progressive stages in human history in his famous Preface to *A Contribution to the Critique of Political Economy* in 1859.

Human civilization first started from the ancient East because of many inventions in the Bronze Age. Compared with primitive society, this was certainly a great step forward. Marx called the AMP a 'progress', because the development of cooperation within it already multiplied the effectiveness of human labour power which 'gave rise to the palaces and temples, and the armies of gigantic statues of which the remains astonish and perplex us' (Marx, 1976: 452).

Nevertheless, for reasons discussed above, governments in societies dominated by the AMP were not interested in the process of improving conditions of production at all as long as it could guarantee surplus extraction to support the maintenance of the court and army. From the point of view of farmers, it was for the sake of survival that they repeated their work year after year. Since it is not easy for the existing productive forces to become powerful enough to break the encasement of their relations of production, the traditional villages could not provide the basis for the emergence of a civil society. On the contrary, only its dissolution was the matrix out of which civil society was formed. By now we readily find the substantial differences between the AMP and slavery, the AMP and feudalism.

A yet more complex question arises: does the AMP imply a total stagnation in societies dominated by it?

2 The Asiatic Mode of Production and the Marxist Theory of History

Is the AMP compatible with the Marxist theory of history? Many scholars believe that the concept contradicts the claim of an overall social progress in historical materialism (O'Leary, 1989: 152–202). However, in this chapter I shall examine two claims which are said to have prevented the AMP from being a scientific concept. The first claim asserts that societies dominated by the AMP are permanently stagnant, while the second maintains that the concept of the AMP has a derogative connotation. Moreover, this so-called derogative connotation is said to be a reflection of Marx's Eurocentrism. In the first section I shall seek to demonstrate that both social and economic relations in the AMP are in constant movement. The so-called stagnant character of the AMP should be understood in the context of a comparative study between different economic structures in history. Therefore, it is arbitrary to presume that an endogenous development of capitalism is *a priori* impossible from societies once dominated by the AMP. In the second section I shall contend that the charge of Eurocentrism against Marx is at best misleading. It derives from scholars' failure to understand Marx's methodological approach towards historical research between different societies. A brief review of Marx's sophisticated attitude towards colonialism is an attempt to indicate that Marx's remarks on non-European societies are nothing but a logical extension of his critique of capitalism. The point of Marx's analysis of colonialism is not to highlight what is good about European capitalism, but to stress what is wrong with it.

1 THE ASIATIC MODE OF PRODUCTION AND STAGNATION

It cannot be denied that Marx time and again talked about the stagnant nature of non–European societies. In particular he seemed to have been carried away by his own descriptions of Asiatic societies in those articles written for the *New York Daily Tribune*.[1] From then on, the idea that stagnation is an inextricable part of the AMP has been accepted by both Marxists and their critics.

Here are some examples:

[T]here was a complete lack of *dynamism* within the Oriental system (Sawer, 1977: 46).

The Asiatic mode is not so much a case of the successful hampering of the productive forces by their relations as it is a paralysis of both aspects of production: its specific character stunts all material and social progress. Asia remains frozen on the threshold of civilization, outside the mainstream of history (Shaw, 1978: 129).[2]

[T]his mode of production [AMP], arrested in a transitory place, has indeed no dynamics, no real history at all (Tokei, 1979: 83).

Critics of Marxism claim that a stagnant AMP contradicts the essential premise of the Marxist theory of history, which is supposed to have a universal application. For instance, Gellner declares:

The notion of the Asiatic Mode of Production thus destroys the crucial Marxist diagnosis of the general ills of mankind (the identification of *the* original sin) by allowing the existence of another and independent sin (namely functional or self-serving political domination), and thereby also undermines the hope of a guaranteed salvation tied to the eradication of that one and only original sin (Gellner, 1988: 51).

Read in isolation, some of Marx's writings seem to suggest this interpretation. However, in this section I shall argue that the idea that societies dominated by the AMP are stationary needs qualification. Firstly, I shall contend that the stagnant character of the AMP makes sense only if we look at the concept from the standpoint of comparative studies between different economic structures in history. It does not necessarily imply a permanent stagnation, because both economic and social relations in the AMP are in constant movement. Therefore, it is arbitrary to assume that an endogenous development of capitalism is *a priori* impossible from societies once dominated by the AMP. Specific studies of the differences between societies can lead us to no more than this conclusion: the AMP did not develop further than it did. Secondly, I shall discuss why economic dynamisms have different manifestations in world history.

As indicated in the second section of the first chapter, Marx's conceptualization of the AMP is not precise. He became aware of this when he wrote the *Grundrisse*, in which he sought to make the concept compatible with the major premises of his theory of history. For example, talking about the production and reproduction of humanity in all pre-capitalist societies, Marx mentioned 'the advance of population' as one of the factors which might destroy the foundation of the AMP. And the communal system, Marx wrote, would decline and fall, 'together with the property relations on which it was based' (Marx, 1973: 486). It unambiguously implies that the AMP could be propelled into the next stage by its own internal mechanism.[3]

It is true that Marx did not spell out how population growth specifically affects the internal changes in societies dominated by the AMP. However, based on the results of recent historical research, we now can construct an AMP which will avoid a theoretical contradiction with the logic of Marx's theory.

As is well known, the starting point of Marx's analysis of the world is production and reproduction of human beings and their environments. 'Whatever the social form of the production process, it has to be continuous' (Marx, 1976: 711). Furthermore, 'production is itself determined by other moments. For example, if the market, that is, the sphere of exchange, expands, then production grows in quantity and the divisions between its different branches become deeper. A change in distribution changes production, such as concentration of capital, different distribution of the population between town and country, and so on. Finally, the needs of consumption determine production. Mutual interaction takes place between the different moments. *This* [*is*] *the case with every organic whole*' (Marx, 1973: 99–100).[4] Similar comments can be found throughout Marx's writings. Hence Marxism is predicated upon the dialectical nature of the process of production, which is always changing. Sooner or later, it will subvert its own conditions of existence and lead towards the next forms of social and economic organization. From this perspective, no mode of production can be absolutely static, because, without continuous exchange between man and nature, human beings cannot survive. During this process man changes his environment and vice versa.

Consequently, any social structure which represents broad specific human situations can never remain permanently the same. They are determined by time and space, by history and society (Krader, 1975; Banerjee, 1976). Therefore, every society is subjected to a process of internal integral change. In the process of reproduction these changes produce something different from what has existed before. Along with it, there is a constant change of social relations which would affect the dissolution of the village community. These relations are moments and their development over time would open new possibilities. The AMP cannot be an exception, for it has its own dynamism. Although it is much less visible than those in Western societies, no serious scholars would deny its existence. However, its 'natural' evolution was preempted by other societies which had already entered capitalism.[5] It is unfortunate that a historical laboratory cannot be set up to isolate non-capitalist societies from the ever-expanding capitalist economy. We shall thus never be able to demonstrate whether they, or some of them, had the potential to propel themselves to a higher stage of production, that is, capitalism.[6] But there is no convincing reason to exclude the possibility of the growth of capitalism from societies once dominated by the AMP.[7]

Now it becomes clear that the AMP must be understood, firstly, in the context of comparison between capitalist and pre-capitalist societies to explain the conditions of the emergence of the former. Secondly, the AMP indicates a specific social and economic formation whose elements such as monarchy, centralization and labour are organized so differently from those of feudalism that it will be much too dogmatic to classify both into one category. Finally, Marx designated the AMP in an attempt to compare European feudalism from which modern capitalism first came to the world with some non-European societies to see the historical results of their different developments. Therefore, comparative studies of different economic formations may lose much of their value, if they fail to discover the inner dynamisms of those formations. Such a danger always exists, if we do not have a thorough knowledge about a country we are studying. Any simplification will not do full justice to the differences among divergent societies. Thus the purpose of comparative study is not to suggest superiority of one nation and inferiority of another, but to deepen our understanding of both and a form of self-discovery (Keightley, 1989).

Marx did not clarify these points himself, but his methodology of investigation undoubtedly points in this direction. For instance, even in the later years of his life Marx showed his strong disagreement with the Russian sociologist Kovalevsky who had described India as 'feudal'. Since he did not make a systematic study of the differences between feudalism and Indian reality, Marx's comments are fragmentary as well as suggestive. They succinctly indicate that he always kept this comparative methodology in mind, whenever he sought to analyse the inner structures of various societies. As it is crucial to my argument, I would like to reproduce some of Marx's major points here.

Marx repeatedly refuted Kovalevsky for several reasons. First, Marx pointed out that in feudal Europe land was regarded as 'the *poetry of the soil*'. The common people were deprived of the right to own the land they cultivated. In contrast, '[t]he *soil* is nowhere *noble* in India' (Krader, 1975: 383).

Secondly, Marx noticed that serfdom, as an essential component in feudalism, did not exist in India. The imposition of Islam by the Muslim rulers in India made Indian property 'as little feudal as the impot foncier [land tax] makes the French landed property feudal' (ibid.: 373). 'At the close of the Mongolian Empire the so-called *feudalisation* was found only in certain districts, in most of the others *common* and *private property* remained with the indigenous possessors and the administration of the functions of the state remained in the hands of *officials named by the central government'* (ibid.: 384).

Thirdly, the existence of the *ikta* (benefice system or grants for military service) in India by no means proved that medieval Indian society was feudal, since we can also find such things in ancient Rome, and Roman society was definitely not feudal.

Fourthly, the picture of administration of justice, especially in civil law, in Mughal India was totally different from that of the feudal system in Europe, where the superior lord could not enter the jurisdictional domain of his vassal. The role of European feudal nobility as protectors of free and unfree peasants was almost insignificant in India and one of the most important sources of European feudalism was therefore obstructed (Banerjee, 1985: 36).

Fifthly, the nature of the state was different from that of the feudal principalities of Europe. For instance, '[b]y Indian law political power was not subject to division between sons' (Anderson, 1974b: 407). Hence, another essential factor of European feudalism was absent in India (Krader, 1975: 203).

Marx made similar remarks in his notes on John Budd Phear who sometimes also described the village community in Bengal as feudal. For instance, Marx wrote, 'Mr La Touche's *Settlement Report of Ajmere and Mhairwarra* ... falsified the facts by the phraseology borrowed from feudal Europe. ... In Europe, in contradistinction to the East, *in place of* [type of] *tribute* was substituted a *dominion over the soil* – the cultivators being turned out of their land and reduced to the condition of serfs or labourers. In the East, under the village system, *the people practically* governed themselves' (Krader, 1972: 256–83).

Marx based his knowledge mainly on the writings of his contemporaries, some of whose descriptions of non–European societies have been proved either biased or inaccurate. In respect of Indian history, many historians and sociologists have provided evidence to show that many Westerners' accounts of the traditional India before the last century were grossly exaggerated. Inevitably Marx made mistakes in judging the specific characters of non-European societies. One of the most famous examples is his claim that 'India has no history at all, at least no known history. What we call its history, is but the history of the successive intruders who founded their empires on the passive basis of that unresisting and unchanging society' (Marx, 1968: 125). Following this logic, Marx did believe that capitalism could not emerge internally and independently within a non-feudal society.[8]

Furthermore, he simplified the relation between the state and direct producers in traditional India. On the one hand, he over-emphasized the role of the state in providing conditions of production such as irrigation, especially in his writings of the early 1850s. On the other hand, it has been proved that the so-called complete isolation of villages did not exist in India (Raychaudhuri and Habib, 1982; Habib, 1985; Chaudhuri, 1985; Sharma, 1986).[9]

The same is true of Chinese history. Recent historical scholarship in both China and the West unambiguously indicates that the later imperial Chinese economy was much more dynamic than was commonly described (Rawski, 1991: 84–8). Not surprisingly, Weber's claim that the pre–European rise of industrial capitalism was impossible in China (Weber, 1951) has been seriously challenged by scholars. Detailed studies show that many features which were previously believed to have existed only in the Western pre-industrial societies are identified in detail in traditional Chinese society (cf. Gardella, 1992: 317–39). Elvin even concludes that '[r]eading in the literature of China two or three centuries before the modern age, there are moments when it is hard to believe that an industrial revolution had not begun' (Elvin, 1973: 285; cf., Needham, 1970). Hence there is no convincing reason to believe that capitalism would never have appeared in China endogenously and that the Confucian ethic is not compatible with fast economic development (Chao, 1986: 5; Feuerwerker, 1990; Rozman, 1991).

Despite all the defects in his writings, social scientists continue to find supporting evidence for Marx's general approach to non-European societies, and some crucial features attributed by him to them, for example the combination of agriculture and handicraft as the broad basis of the whole economic structure. The contradictory comments and the lack of precision in Marx's analysis do not affect the essential distinction he drew between societies dominated by the AMP where the control over the surplus was ultimately monopolized by the state and Western societies where such control was exercised by social classes consisting of the private owners of the means of production.

Why do economic dynamisms have different manifestations in the world? Again Marx and Engels offered us valuable guidance. Talking about how human beings evolved from primitive communism to the first stratified societies, Engels started with the improvement of technology, division of labour and the existence of a surplus which provided the possibility for the emergence of a minority of individuals to appropriate a share of this surplus. Since they were the heads of the tribes, they had

> a certain measure of authority and are the beginnings of state power. The productive forces gradually increase; the increasing density of the population creates at one point, interests, at another conflicting interests, between the separate communities, whose grouping into larger units brings about in turn a new division of labour, the setting up of organs to safeguard common interests and combat conflicting interests. These organs which, if only because they represent the common interests of the whole group, hold a special position in relation to each individual community – in certain circumstances even one opposition – soon make themselves still more independent, partly through heredity of functions, which comes about almost as a matter of course in a world where everything occurs spontaneously, and partly because they become increasingly indispensable owing to the growing number of conflicts with other groups. It is not necessary for us to examine here how this independence of social functions in relation to society increased with time until it developed into domination over society... and how finally the individual rulers united into a ruling class. Here we are only concerned with establishing the fact that the exercise of a social function was everywhere the basis of political supremacy; and further that political supremacy has existed for any length of time only when it discharged its social functions' (Engels, 1987: 166–7).

Here it is important to note that Engels used the phrase 'beginnings of state power'. It unambiguously implies that there were different beginnings in the formations of state power.

In three different passages of the *Grundrisse*, Marx discussed factors of geography, climate, physical conditions, social, and tribe characters, effect of historical moments such as migrations and relations to other tribes to explain different developments of diverse societies (Marx, 1964: 68–72, 83). Moreover, in *Capital,* Vol. 3, Marx talked about the same economic basis – the same in its major conditions – displaying endless variations and gradations in its appearance, as the result of natural conditions, racial relations, historical influences acting from outside, etc., and 'these can only be understood by analysing those empirically given conditions' (Marx, 1981: 927–8). In another place, he stressed the important role of traditions[10] in all pre-capitalist societies:

> It is evident that tradition must play a dominant role in the primitive and underdeveloped circumstances on which these social production

relations and the corresponding mode of production are based. It is furthermore clear that here as always it is in the interest of the ruling section of society to sanction the existing order as law and to legally establish its limits given through usage and tradition. Apart from all else, this, by the way, comes about of itself as soon as the constant reproduction of the basis of the existing order and its fundamental relations assumes a regulated and orderly form in the course of time. And such regulation and order are themselves indispensable elements of any mode of production, if it is to assume social stability and independence from mere chance and arbitrariness. These are precisely the form of its social stability and therefore its relative freedom from mere arbitrariness and mere chance. Under backward conditions of the production process as well as the corresponding social relations, it achieves this form by mere repetition of their very reproduction. If this has continued on for some time, it entrenches itself as custom and tradition and is finally sanctioned as an explicit law (Marx, 1967c: 793).

Although he considered tradition as one of the common features in pre-capitalist societies, Marx, together with Engels, revealed the outline of the process in the formation of the AMP. Since it was the old public authority which acquired a new function, class differentiation took place in hidden forms in the AMP. It was chiefly manifested in unequal access to both the means of production and surplus of labour. For instance, because the heads of communities received the surplus formally in the interests of their communities, it is difficult, if not impossible, to determine the point at which the communities were exploited by those providing services.

Nevertheless, what is certain is that, depending on different environments and other factors, human beings form diverse traditions affecting relations of production, especially forms of property relation, and of exploitation throughout the world. Indisputably societies evolve in different directions. As indicated above, Marx's exposition remains unfinished. We cannot expect Marx to tell us what kind of specific form every tradition takes and to what extent each has shaped different routes of development. Moreover, even Marx could not avoid making mistakes.[11] It is up to scholars in divergent disciplines to have thorough investigations and much more work needs to be done. To be sure, 'success will never come with the master-key of a general historico-philosophical theory, whose supreme virtue consists in being supra-historical' (Marx, 1983: 136).

Therefore, the AMP can be considered as one of the distinctive socio-economic organizations in some non-European societies developing out of primitive communism. In comparison with Western European history, the

AMP was one of the most natural developments of world history, because in such an economic system, land was practically possessed by the community, and the tax system directly evolved from the tribute previously paid to the ancient community for the benefits of all, such as religious rituals and the survival of the community.[12] Indeed, in the name of paying homage to the position of the representative, the form of the surplus extraction in the AMP was carried on in such a 'natural' way that it would appear unreasonable not to do so.[13] By the time the majority realized that the very institution which they supported had turned against them, it was too late to change the situation, since it had been 'sanctioned as an explicit law' (ibid.).

Consequently, on the one hand, the low level of the productive power kept the social and economic relations at a low stage; on the other hand, tradition continued to play a crucial role in value-orientation or even philosophy of life.

2   THE ASIATIC MODE OF PRODUCTION AND EUROCENTRISM

The concept of the AMP is said to have reflected Marx's Eurocentrism by both Marxists and their critics (Carrère d'Encausse and Schram, 1969: 8; Wittfogel, 1981).[14] One of the most crucial reasons to support such a claim is that it is the only mode of production with a geographical prefix among those modes of production listed by Marx in the famous 1859 Preface. For Marxists, this seems to suggest, explicitly or implicitly, inferiority of non-Europeans. Therefore the concept of the AMP should be eliminated from Marxism, because it is not compatible with the Marxist theory of history which believes in equality of all human beings.

By contrast, critics of Marxism claim that Eurocentrism is the supreme virtue of the concept of the AMP (Lichtheim, 1967; Avineri, 1968: 28).[15]

In this section, however, I shall argue that the charge of Eurocentrism against Marx is at best misleading. It derives from the failure to comprehend Marx's sophisticated approach to colonialism. If we conceptualise the AMP with Marx's methodology outlined in the preceding chapter, it is not difficult to see that Marx's study of non-European societies is nothing but a logical extension of his critique of capitalism. For Marx, colonialism represented a perfect example to confirm his theory of history, namely, that the expansion of capital throughout the world is the realization of its inherited contradictions, which will dig its own grave. Hence there is no difference of races, since it is Marx's firm belief that all nations are capable of pursuing the same things as soon as they get rid of those restricting conditions.

As noted in the second section of the foregoing chapter, in the formation of his own theory, Marx was undoubtedly influenced by European intellectual traditions, especially the British classical economy and Hegelian philosophy. Nevertheless, there is a fundamental difference between Marx and his predecessors. For Hegel, history is an expansion of consciousness (the world spirit), 'giving itself form in cultures, which subvert themselves through their success in advancing consciousness' (Cohen, 1978: 26). It is the Prussian monarch who was the ultimate expression of this general consciousness.[16] Moreover, the classical economists sought to justify capitalism as the only 'natural' society, while condemning all previous societies as artificial (Marx, 1973: 83–8).

But, for Marx, '[h]istory is the history of human industry, which undergoes growth in productive power, the stimulus and vehicle of which is an economic structure, which perishes when it has stimulated more growth than it can contain' (Cohen, 1978: 26). Marx devoted his life to discovering the historical conditions of different economic structures. And the final outcome of the changes of those economic structures, Marx maintained, is the realization of communism. Since he sometimes called it the end of prehistory of all humanity,[17] communism, hence, cannot be realized sporadically at will. In fact, when they postulated systematically their new discovery for the first time in *The German Ideology*, Marx and Engels made it absolutely clear that communism must be realized universally:

> Empirically, communism is only possible as the act of the dominant people 'all at once' and simultaneously, which presupposes the universal development of productive forces and the world intercourse bound up with communism.... The proletariat can thus only exist world-historically, just as communism: its activity can only have a 'world historical' existence. [This is] world-historical existence of individuals, i.e. existence of individuals which is directly linked up with world history (Marx and Engels, 1965: 46–7).

On the other hand, Marx held that only capitalism has the universal urge to create a world market which can provide the material basis of communism. Inevitably, all pre-capitalist societies will be dragged into the process of capital accumulation. It is from this standpoint that Marx began his analysis of European colonialism in non-European societies. Therefore, to have a proper understanding of Marxism, we must first bear in mind its international nature. Nowhere do we find that Marx confined his research to a single society in terms of narrow-minded nationalistic interests. Read in context, instead of a simplified Eurocentrism, Marx had in mind several interrelated perspectives in his attitude towards capitalist expansion in all pre-capitalist societies.

First, Marx denied positive significance to the existence of economic structures in all pre-capitalist societies in comparison with capitalism. He contended that the former represented a lower stage of productive forces, and hence a lower stage of economic formations. In order to emphasize the necessity of replacing them with the capitalist mode of production, Marx produced vivid descriptions of the backwardness of those societies. One of the most famous passages can be found in 'The British Rule in India' in which Marx wrote:

> Now, sickening as it must be to human feeling to witness these myriads of industrious patriarchal and inoffensive social organizations disorganized and dissolved into their units, thrown into a sea of woes, and their individual members losing at the same time their ancient form of civilization and their hereditary means of subsistence, we must not forget that these idyllic village communities... restrained the human mind within the smallest possible compass, making it the unresisting tool of superstition, enslaving it beneath traditional laws, depriving it of all grandeur and historical energies. We must not forget the barbarian egotism which, concentrating on some miserable patch of land, had quietly witnessed the ruin of empires, the penetration of unspeakable cruelties, the massacre of the population of large towns with no other consideration bestowed upon them than on natural events, itself the helpless prey of any aggressor who deigned to notice it at all. We must not forget that this undignified, stagnatory, and vegetative life, that this passive sort of existence, evoked on the other part, in contradistinction, wild, aimless, unbounded forces of destruction, and rendered murder itself a religious rite in Hindostan. We must not forget that these little communities were contaminated by distinctions of caste and by slavery, that they subjugated man to external circumstances instead of elevating man to be the sovereign of circumstances, that they transformed a self-developing social state into never changing natural destiny, and thus brought about a brutalizing worship of nature, exhibiting its degradation in the fact that man, the sovereign of nature, fell down on his knees in adoration of Hanuman, the monkey, and Sabbala, the cow (Marx, 1968: 88–9).[18]

As noted in the preceding chapter, we shall certainly miss the point if we are led by those comments to pass judgement on the adequacy of Marx's book that there were no real social and economic changes in Asia. The point is to be faithful to Marx's methodology, which regards humanity as a totality.[19]

Secondly, Marx's explanation of the function of colonialism is inextricably related to his critique of capitalism. There were few in the last century who were so outspoken as Marx in his criticism of capitalism. For example, Marx strongly condemned the process of primitive accumulation of capital in English history as 'ruthless terrorism' (Marx, 1976: 895). He showed his great sympathy to the 'degraded and almost servile condition of the mass of the people, their transformation into mercenaries' (ibid.: 881).[20] For Marx, capital comes into the world 'dripping from head to toe, from every pore, with blood and dirt' (ibid.: 926).

Thirdly, Marx condemned the inhumanity of capitalist expansion in the non-European world no less than his contempt of capitalist exploitation of the working class in its own country. In many articles, Marx demonstrated his indignation at the sheer brutality of the British opium trade with China and the cruelties inflicted by the British on India, especially in the wake of the Mutiny (Marx, 1968: 181–250). He had no hesitation to call colonialism Western barbarism.

The profound hypocrisy and inherent barbarism of bourgeois civilization lies unveiled before our eyes, turning from its home, where it assumes respectable forms, to the colonies, where it goes naked (ibid.: 130).[21]

Fourthly, despite his condemnation of colonialism, Marx distinguished subjective motivation from objective historical results, namely, that he dissociated moral indignation from historical judgement. Since he postulated the ultimate victory of socialism over the prior universalization of capitalism, Marx thereby endorsed the capitalist expansion as a brutal but necessary step to accelerate the progress of humanity. Just as the horrors of industrialization were dialectically necessary for the triumph of communism, so the horrors of colonialism are necessary for an early coming of a world revolution of the proletarians (Avineri, 1968: 12). It is from this standpoint that the British penetration could break down the old social structures in all pre-capitalist societies.

England has to fulfil a double mission in India: one destructive, the other regenerating – the annihilation of old Asiatic society, and the laying of the material foundations of Western society in Asia (ibid.: 125).

Is it possible to achieve the social progress 'without dragging individuals and peoples through blood and dirt, through misery and degradation?' (ibid.: 189) The answer is negative.

England, it is true, in causing a social revolution in Hindostan, was actuated only by the vilest interests, and was stupid in her manner of enforcing them. But that is not the question. The question is, can mankind fulfil its destiny without a fundamental revolution in the social state of Asia? If not, whatever may be the crimes of England she was the unconscious tool of history in bringing about the revolution.

Then whatever the bitterness the spectacle of the crumbling of an ancient world may have for our personal feelings, we have the right, in point of history, to exclaim with Goethe:

> 'Sollte diese Qual uns qualen,
> Da sie unsre Lust vermehrt,
> Hat nicht Myriaden Seelen
> Timurs Herrschaft aufgezehrt?' (ibid.: 89)[22]

This famous passage has been interpreted as a mere imitation of Hegel's doctrine of the 'cunning of Reason' (List der Vernunft) by most scholars writing on the AMP. This is definitely an overstatement. To refute it, the best way is to quote Marx.

It is true that Marx, on the one hand, openly claimed to be 'the pupil of that mighty thinker [Hegel]' (Marx, 1976: 103). But, on the other hand, Marx stressed that his dialectical method was, 'in its foundations, not only different from the Hegelian, but exactly opposite to it. For Hegel, the process of thinking, which he even transforms into an independent subject, under the name of "the Idea", is the creator of the real world, and the real world is only the external appearance of the idea. With me the reverse is true: the ideal is nothing but the material world reflected in the mind of man, and translated into forms of thought' (ibid.: 102). Thus, with Hegel, the dialectic 'is standing on its head. It must be inverted, in order to discover the rational kernel within the mystical shell' (ibid.: 103).

Furthermore, the passages cited indicate that it was not out of benign altruism that capitalists brought a new mode of production to the non-European societies. Although the process of transformation from all pre-capitalist societies to socialism was accelerated by European bourgeoisie, the capitalists were totally unaware of the ultimate consequences of their own acts. That is why Marx described European colonialism as perpetrating a despotism equal to, if not greater than, that of the native rulers (Marx, 1968: 84).

Fifthly, Marx time and again discussed in some detail the impact of capitalist expansion in non-European societies. For example, in India, Marx contended, the British sword had created a political unity which had never existed before in its history. For Marx, that unity would be strengthened and perpetuated by modern means of communication. Moreover, '[t]he native army, organized and trained by the British drill sergeant, was the *sine qua non* of Indian self-emancipation, and of India ceasing to be the prey of the first foreign intruder. The free press, introduced for the first time into Asiatic society, and managed principally by the common off-spring of Hindoo and Europeans, is a new and powerful agent of recon-struction. The Zemindars and Ryotwar themselves, abominable as they are, involved two forms of private property in land – the great desideratum of Asiatic society' (ibid.: 126).

Consequently, although colonialism was developed in different societies around the world, it would produce a similar effect. Therefore, just as Marx never reduced the process of industrialisation to mere moralistic condemnation of the greed of capitalists, so the motivation behind colonial expansion should not be mistaken for its historical significance (Avineri, 1968: 13).

Sixthly, Marx held that the real beneficiary of colonialism, e.g. the British rule in India, was not the British economy as a whole, but the ruling classes. To support this idea, Marx differentiated the benefits derived from India by the British economy and society as a whole, and the specific benefits derived from India by individuals and groups in England. He contended that as far as the British public was concerned, the cost of administering India exceeded the income derived from it. Over the decades the constantly growing debt of the East India Company had been paid out of the pocket of the British taxpayer, and these expenses were in excess of all benefits the economy derived from India (Marx, 1968: 222–5, 254, 440).

Moreover, Marx pointed out that it was those several thousand bond-holders of the East India Company and employees in the various branches of British administration who benefited from India. Marx discussed in detail the net patronage connected with the East India Company and those Cabinet officers engaged in Indian affairs. The result was that India was a goldmine only for them. In each of the different branches of the Indian administration – clerical, medical, military and naval – salaries in India were disproportionately higher than those paid for comparable positions at home. But since the gross income of all those individuals derived from India was much below the costs of Indian administration, and since the burden of the Indian administration was ultimately borne by the taxpayer in England, British rule in India was in fact an indirect way of taxing the British people for the benefit of their upper classes. Members of those families and their relatives were shipped off to India to make their fortunes in the Indian service (ibid.: 222–5).

Through this class analysis, Marx arrived at a more profound indict-ment of British imperialism than is usually attributed to him (cf. Avineri,

1968: 16–17). It was the British people, and not only Indians, who were being exploited for the benefit of the British ruling classes to keep their colonial power. The British economy as a whole could do better without colonialism. Indeed, Marx's firm grasp of the critical and revolutionary nature of the dialectic enabled him to have a deeper understanding of colonialism (Marx, 1968: 345–52).

Seventhly, Marx argued that colonialism had another two dialectical effects: not only were non-European societies becoming more dependent on Europe, but the latter was becoming more dependent on the former in its later development (Avineri, 1968: 15). As Marx wrote:

> The ruling classes of Great Britain have had, till now, but an accidental, transitory and exceptional interest in the progress of India. The aristocracy wanted to conquer it, the moneyocracy to plunder it, and the millocracy to undersell it. But now the tables are turned. The millocracy have discovered that the transformation of India into a reproductive country has become of vital importance to them, and that, to that end, it is necessary, above all, to gift her with means of irrigation and of internal communication. They now intend to draw a net of railroads over India. And they will do it. The results must be inappreciable (Marx, 1968: 126–7).

The ultimate dependence of Europe on Asia is also implied by Marx when examining the economic balance of payments regulating the flow of funds from the metropolis to the colonies, especially to India. For example, in his discussion of the consequences of the Indian Mutiny, Marx argued, '[t]hese financial fruits of the "glorious" reconquest of India have not a charming appearance; ... John Bull pays exceedingly high protective duties for securing the monopoly of the Indian market to the Manchester free-traders' (ibid.: 352; cf. ibid.: 440–1).

Last but not least, Marx demonstrated how the bourgeoisie creates the premises of its own destruction. Marx had no doubt that colonialism would be overthrown by the peoples of the colonies, together with the working class in Europe. Nevertheless, Marx contended,

> The Indians will not reap the fruits of the new elements of society scattered among them by the British bourgeoisie, till in Great Britain itself the now ruling classes shall have been supplanted by the industrial proletariat, or till Hindoos themselves shall have grown strong enough to throw off the English yoke altogether. At all events, we may safely expect to see, at a more remote period, the regeneration of that great and interesting country, whose gentle natives are, to use the expression of

Prince Saltykov, even in the most inferior classes, 'plus fins et plus adroits que les Italiens,'[23] whose submission even is counterbalanced by a certain calm nobility, who, notwithstanding their natural languor, have astonished the British officers by their bravery, whose country has been the source of our languages, our religions, and who represent the type of the ancient German in the Jat and the type of the ancient Greek in the Bramin (ibid.: 129–30).

Here the eloquent tribute Marx paid to the Indian people is another example to refute the charge that Marx was a racist Eurocentric of any kind.[24]

In the case of China, Marx closely linked the revolution in China with a possible revolution in Europe. 'Now, England having brought about the revolution of China, the question is how that revolution will in time react on England, and through England on Europe' (ibid.: 64). He predicted,

the Chinese revolution will throw the spark into the overloaded mine of the present industrial system and cause the explosion of the long-prepared general crisis, which, spreading abroad, will be closely followed by political revolutions on the Continent (ibid.: 68).

Therefore, when capitalism draws in its orbit all pre-capitalist societies, the consequences ensure that European capitalism and its colonies or semi-colonies mutually react on one another. Instead of a Eurocentric, we find the equal treatment of humanity in Marx. Indeed, he was never tired of emphasising the intrinsic relationship between the socialist struggles of the working class in more advanced capitalism and any anti-colonial struggle in less developed societies. From this standpoint, he considered colonialism as an accelerating element in the process of the collapse of capitalism in both capitalist West and its colonies. For Marx, any people that oppresses another people forges its own chains.[25] Hence, to become free of colonialism is a precondition for the English working class to emancipate themselves.

In conclusion, the geographical prefix of the AMP does not prevent it from being a scientific concept in comparative studies of different societies, because the concept does not carry negative connotation of any kind in Marx's writings. Although he insisted on the ultimate necessity of colonialism, Marx did not have a simple approach to the issue. First, Marx's analysis of colonialism is determined not by so-called Eurocentrism, but by his dialectical considerations of the world. For Marx, capitalism represents a culture that is both vulgar and civilizing. It is both destructive and constructive. By contrast, the AMP, like all other pre-capitalist modes of production, e.g. slavery and feudalism, represents a comparatively low level of productive forces, and hence will be replaced by capitalism.

Secondly, Marx's theory of colonialism, in its final analysis, is not to highlight what was good about European capitalism, but to point out what was wrong with it. It is one of the inexorable parts of Marx's critique of capitalism. It criticizes capitalist exploitation which has been built into European life and carried abroad to its colonies (Avineri, 1968).

Of course, scholars with different perspectives could give Marx a Eurocentric gloss. But this has nothing to do with Marxism, which will continue to apply the concept of the AMP in its analysis of diverse social and economic formations.

The following chapters will attempt to analyse the structural changes of ancient China in the light of the Marxist methodology discussed above.

3 The Myth of the Shang

Like other civilizations in the world, early Chinese history was mixed with legends and myths. According to the received chronology, the first dynasty was called Xia. It was placed between 2205 and 1766 B.C. Nevertheless, up to now no literature which could be ascribed to this period has been discovered. At the same time convincing archaeological confirmation of its existence is still lacking.[1]

The Shang (Yin)[2] is the first dynasty in Chinese history of which we possess both reliable literary records and massive archaeological evidence. There is, however, no consensus as to the chronology of this dynasty. Traditionally it is placed between 1766 and 1122 BC. But specialists who do not agree with this division have proposed many other dates.[3]

The nature of the Shang society has always been one of the most controversial subjects. Some scholars define it as either a feudal (Hu Houxuan, 1944; Cheng, 1960: 202–4; Eberhard, 1965: 22–4) or 'a proto-feudal and proto-bureaucratic' society (Keightley, 1969: 10; Creel, 1970), while others considered it as a slavery (Guo Moruo, 1976: 155–214; Fan, 1947; Li Yanong, 1954; 1955; Hou, 1955; Lu, 1962; Jin, 1983). In this chapter I shall examine the available contemporaneous records to see whether they warrant the above classifications. I shall argue that the first-hand evidence does not support either claim. Since available information on the subject is not sufficient, we are not in a position to discuss the nature of the Shang at the present stage. We have to wait for future archaeological discoveries which might enable us to penetrate the myth to a lesser or greater extent.

1 FEUDALISM OR SLAVERY?

In order to provide a sound analysis of the dispute over the nature of the Shang dynasty, it seems necessary first to highlight some major points of the available contemporaneous evidence. I shall then provide reasons to refute some interpretations offered by many scholars in China as well as in the West. I shall contend that both written records and modern archaeological discoveries are too scanty to permit a definite answer on the nature of the Shang.

Archaeological evidence suggests that the Shang was an agricultural society with hunting and fishing as supplements.[4] For example, in several

Shang ruins remains of crops have been found during excavations. Oracle-bone inscriptions[5] also reveal that millet, rice and wheat were the main agricultural products. One of the chief preoccupations of the Shang king was the promotion of agricultural prosperity through ritual intercession (Hu Houxuan, 1945: 134).

Since the agricultural implements of that time were mainly made of shell, wood, and sometimes bone, collective farming was practised to improve productivity. This has been confirmed by the oracle-bone inscriptions:

The king ordered the multitudes on a large scale... receive... (Qian, 7. 30. 2).[6]

The king ordered the multitudes (*zhongren*) and said: Cultivate collectively (*xie*) in the fields so that we shall receive good harvest! In the eleventh month (Xu, 2.28.5).

The *Xiao Chen* should order the *Zhong* to plant millet. The first month (Qian, 4. 30. 2).

We do not have any definite knowledge as to how the fields were specifically prepared. However, scholars agree that the most likely method was *ougeng*. According to historical literature, it was a practice of pushing and pulling the *lei* in pairs[7] (Zhang Zhenglang, 1973: 112; Shen Wenzhuo, 1977: 338).

The hypothesis of collective agriculture can also be supported by the archaeological finds of stone sickles in Yinxu sites. In pit B14 and slightly north of it, about 1000 stone sickles were excavated in 1928 (Guo Baojun, 1933: 594). Four hundred and forty-four stone sickles were also found in a square storage in pit E181, together with other 57 types of enormous objects such as pottery fragments, animal bones and bronze artefacts in 1932 (Shi Zhangru, 1933: 722–3). Obviously, these two stores could not have belonged to ordinary farmers. It is entirely plausible that the royal house might have owned those sickles and distributed them to the farmers at harvest-time (Chen Mengjia, 1956a: 548).[8]

Due to the lack of contemporary data, we are not able to calculate the average yields of that time. They must have been quite low before the introduction of iron tools and fertilizers (Ho, 1975: 83), but available sources indicate that the Shang farmers were capable of a surplus, thus releasing segments of the population to pursue non-agricultural activities (ibid.: 89; Chang, 1976: 56). This gave rise to a relatively high degree of social division of labour, which has been eloquently proved by both modern archaeological findings and literary records. For example, there were dramatic increases in sophistication and variety in the carving of marble during that period. Like other handicrafts in the Shang dynasty, marble productions originated in Neolithic times, but archaeological finds in the remains of the Neolithic period indicate that they were crude in fashion and that most of them were made merely for practical purposes. By comparison, Shang marble productions attained a much higher degree of professionalism with regard to both style and precision, particularly towards the end of the period (Cheng, 1957: 13–30; 1960: 102–25; cf Ito Michiharu, 1960: 36–57; 1975; Chang, 1980: 202–3).

Furthermore, the Shang made one of the most important technological contributions to Chinese civilization in the development of the bronze foundry, which provides us with what has become the most characteristic class of Shang artifacts (Cheng, 1960: 156–76). The pre-Shang people might have received their first knowledge of metallurgy from the loess highlands of China, but once the nature of metal was known, the Shang went on to invent a unique system of bronze casting with piece-moulds, which owed much to an existing and advanced ceramic technology (Barnard, 1961; Fairbank, 1962: 8–15). The Shang rulers well understood the importance of bronze and were able to mobilize labour and skills on a large scale to secure a sustained and rapid development. By the Late Shang period this industry had evolved into one of the world's great technological and artistic traditions.

Thanks to the mastery of casting techniques which characterized the Late Shang, bronze vessels were made with great assurance and self-confidence. Meanwhile there was a wide range of forms and styles from *yu* and *gui* bowls and musical instruments to ceremonial apparatus and fittings of all kinds.[9]

It seems that the Shang technological advances were chiefly directed towards sacrificial rites and conspicuous display. This can be proved by archaeological finds as well as oracle-bone inscriptions. Eleven large royal graves have been uncovered, together with 1232 small tombs at Xibeigang near Houjiazhuang of Anyang City, Henan Province. Although it has not been established beyond doubt that these were the Shang kings' graves, they were constructed on a large scale, presumably with elaborate ceremonial procedures. The earth-digging alone would require at least seven thousand working days for each of the large graves (Chang, 1986: 327). The best known of the tombs, no.1001, is shaped like a cross in the ground plan and forms a pit about ten metres deep. The mouth of the pit is 19 metres long, north to south, and 14 metres wide. The tomb was abundantly furnished with stone, jade, shell, bone, antler, tooth, bronze, and pottery artefacts, which represent the highest achievements of Shang technology and art (Liang and Gao, 1962; Chang, 1986: 327–31; Allan, 1991: 5–6). In 1975, another large tomb was excavated at Yinxu. It is known as Fu Hao Tomb because the inscriptions on the bronzes inside indicate that its owner was Lady (Fu) Hao, a consort of King Wu Ding (c. 1300–1242 BC). It is smaller than the cross-shaped grave mentioned above (only 5.6 by 4 metres at the opening). However, it is one of the most important archaeological finds in China, since it is the only tomb of its size which had never been plundered prior to excavation. It contains a complete complex of ritual artefacts. From the tomb chamber were recovered more than 1928 objects, including 460 bronzes, the largest being a pair of square cauldrons, weighing 117.5 kilograms or 258.5 pounds each, and hundreds of other precious ornamental objects (Anyang Gongzuodui, 1977: 57–98; Allan, 1991: 8).[10] We still know little about how society was specifically organized in the Shang, but there is little doubt that almost all technological progress was a response to the emergence of a social class whose primary concerns were with ritual and ceremony, and with conspicuous display in the interests of political and social prestige.

Both archaeological and written records also suggest that a system of kinship groups existed during the Shang period. This thesis can be confirmed first by the word *zu* (clan) in the oracle-bone inscriptions. Since the graph for *zu* is indicated by an arrow under a flag, scholars tend to agree that *zu* has been derived from a military unit of that time (Chen Mengjia, 1956a: 497; Ding, 1956; Hayashi Minao, 1966: 234–62, 1968; Zhang Zhenglang, 1973: 110–11). Many different *zu* have been identified by specialists. For example, Ding Shan claimed to have discovered more than two hundred *zu* (Ding, 1956: 111). K. C. Chang has confirmed Ding's argument through differentiation of possible clan emblems. As he has convincingly argued, different selections of decoration styles indicate that some of these *zu* might have been subdivisions of the same clans while others represented different lineages. In addition to military activities such as fighting with neighbouring tribes, *zu* had many other functions, e.g. reclaiming the farmland. *Zu* groups thus might have formed the most fundamental social units of the Shang people in small towns or small villages (cf. Shirakawa Shizuka, 1954, 1957; Chang, 1970: 239–315; 1980: 164–5).

Furthermore, the existence of kinship groups can be demonstrated by an analysis of the marriage system in the Shang.[11] According to specialists, both endogamy and exogamy were practised by the Shang (Hu Houxuan, 1944: 8a–b; Shirakawa Shizuka, 1951; Ding Shan, 1956: 55–6). The Shang kings seemed to marry not only female members of their own clan (presumably from the same lineage), but also female members of other clans (*zu*) or tribes. In the oracle-bone inscriptions it is not difficult to identify names composed of the character *fu* (lady) followed by a second character usually containing a 'woman' element. Scholars agree that the word *fu* refers to the 'royal consort' and that the second word represents the name of the clan from which she originally came. Hu Houxuan claims to have discovered 64 *fu* names. All of them are said to be wives of King Wu Ding (Hu Houxuan, 1944: 8a–b). This thesis seems to have been confirmed by the words '*duo fu*' (the multitudes of *fu*) in the oracle-bone inscriptions (Yicun, 321). It is very likely that the Shang expanded their territory and consolidated their power through arrangements of such marriages with other tribes or clans.

Finally, an analysis of the royal clans or lineages also confirms the existence of kinship groups in the Shang. According to Sima Qian (c.145-c.86 BC),[12] the royal house of the Shang came from a clan called *zi*. Within the *zi* clan, there was a *wang zu* (royal clan or lineage), from which kings were chosen. Other members of the *zi* clan served as king's loyal warriors (Hu Houxuan, 1944; Shirakawa Shizuka, 1954: 19–44; Ding, 1956; Sima Qian, 1972: 91–110; Chang, 1980: 165–88).[13] The available oracle-bone inscriptions indicate that the king would send them to some areas to carry out defensive activities.

The king orders the five *zu* (clans) to defend X (Cui, 1149).

Crack-making on the day ...*hou*. Five *zu* should be on garrison duty. Do not assemble the king's (*zhong*)[14] (Ye, 39. 10).

Furthermore, many inscriptions document the 'building of towns or settlements (*zuo yi*)'.

Crack-making on the day *gengwu*. The diviner Nei reads: If the king does not build a town here, *Di*[15] will agree. The diviner reads: If the king builds a town, *Di* will agree. The eighth month (Bing, 91 (iv) (vi)).

If the king builds a town, *Di* will approve that we should go to Tang (ibid.: 321 (i)).

Divining: I shall build a settlement here (Qian, 4.10.6).

According to Chen Mengjia, some inscriptions refer to as many as thirty *yi* at one time (Chen Mengjia, 1956a: 322).

On the other hand, archaeological excavations have verified the oracle-bone descriptions through the discovery of many Shang towns with *hang tu* (rammed-earth) foundations.[16] Detailed studies suggest the social complexity and stratification of that time. An excellent example is provided by the finds in Zhengzhou, the present capital of Henan Province. After many years of excavation, archaeologists are now able to identify a huge Shang town with a wall of roughly rectangular shape. The total length of the wall is more than seven kilometres long with an enclosure of 3.2 square kilometres. It was built by using the *hang tu* technique in successive compressed layers, each of which has as an average thickness of 8 to 10 centimetres. According to the estimation of some scholars, building the whole city wall would have required a labour force of 10 000 men working 330 days a year for approximately 18 years.[17]

Within the wall many large house foundations with *hang tu* method and human skulls were also found, presumably for sacrificial purposes (An Jinhuai, 1961: 73–80; Henansheng Bowuguan, 1974: 1–2). According to the oracle-bone inscriptions, the Shang kings not only ordered the construction of the city walls in the new territory, but were often personally involved in the building of houses, mostly palaces all over the country.

The king should build a residence (Zhu, 107).

Assemble the *ren*[18] at X and order them to build a house (Yi, 5906).

Build a royal residence at … (Qian, 4. 15. 5).

Remains of such buildings have been found in not only Zhengzhou, but also other Shang archaeological sites.[19] The purpose of constructing new towns (*zuo yi*) is obvious, namely, to open up new farm land to perform agricultural and other activities (Chen Mengjia, 1956a: 639) and hence to increase the size of the king's territorial control (Zhang Zhenglang, 1973: 114).

It is based on the above features that scholars with different persuasions have defined the Shang either as a feudal society (Hu Houxuan, 1944; Cheng, 1960: 202–4; Eberhard, 65: 22–4), or slavery (Guo Moruo, 1976: 171). However, as the preceding discussion has indicated, the available evidence clearly does not warrant either classification. Despite the differences in their specific interpretations, the same methodological mistake has been made in most researches; that is, scholars from both camps have been more than willing to project most of the essential features of later times into the Shang in order to substitute the missing but crucial evidence. It seems natural for them to think that since the Zhou, the second known dynasty in Chinese history, learned a great deal of its civilization from bronze-smelting to political and economic organizations from the Shang, the former must have inherited everything from the latter. Nevertheless, as Allan has convincingly argued, the transition from the Shang to the Zhou represented not only a continuation of the same culture in the broad sense of the word, but also a 'fundamental distinction between the Shang thought and that represented by surviving Zhou literature' (Allan, 1991: 13). The fact that the Zhou kings would send off their relatives to be heads of new clans in newly conquered areas does not necessarily imply that the Shang king had done the same (Ding, 1956: 158–99). Moreover, the possible existence of a kinship system in the Shang does not further our understanding as to how it functioned in practice. Therefore, it is premature to claim that a benefice system reminiscent of feudal Europe ever existed in the Shang, since no evidence unambiguously suggests that princes and queens of the Shang were granted benefice of any kind. Needless to say, no trace of a contractual feature in the vassal's obligation of fidelity to his or her feudal lord on the basis of militarism can be found in the Shang social organization. As indicated in the first chapter of this book, a strong sense of obligation on the part of the vassal and its military origin were two of the most important characteristics of medieval feudalism. In short, a feudal interpretation of the Shang dynasty is nothing but misleading.

On the other hand, scholars who seek to give the Shang a slavery connotation often stress the power of the Shang king to mobilize the labour force. Indeed, both archaeological finds and written records have confirmed that violence was employed in external relations as well as internal controls. The large graves at Yinxu and the wall encircling the ritual complex in Zhengzhou offer instructive illustrations of an increasingly sophisticated social organization in the Shang. The magnitude of those achievements is eloquent testimony to the concentration of ritual and political power achieved by one group of people represented by the king and his functionaries. This has been verified by oracle-bone inscriptions. for instance, many divinations indicate that the Shang king often gave commands to others to carry out his orders:

X and Ke will not carry out the king's affairs (Yi, 2882).

Crack-making on the day *jiyou*: The king should order Shan to be in charge of ... *kong*. Divining on the day *jiyou*: Shan will carry out the king's affairs (Shiduo, 432).[20]

Moreover, since the Shang economy was based on agriculture, one of the king's major concerns was inevitably about the weather and the success of harvest. Some oracle-bone records show that the king even took part in agriculturally related activities such as preparing the field and planting millet or inspecting the planting:

Divining: It will rain this evening (Chen Banghuai, 11).

Crack-making on *xinchou*, *Dui*: From today until *yisi* it will rain. On *yisi* it was cloudy; it did not rain (Heji, 20923a).

Approaching clouds will not rain. (They) really did not; it cleared (Heji, 21022). We shall receive harvest which Fu cultivated at Qi... (Bing, 381, (v)).

Crack-making on *bingchen*, X divined: Order to work in the fields at Zhi. We shall receive harvest (Heji, 220).

Cheng will protect my fields (Yi, 6389).

Order the Yin to make (work in or cultivate) the great field (Yi, 1155).

Work and cultivate at Shi (Qinghua, 11, 19).

Order: If we plant millet in the north, we shall receive harvest (Xu, 2. 30. 3).

The king should plant millet in the south (Xu, 1. 53. 3).

Crack-making on the day *jihai*: The king is going to offer libation and till. He should go (Jia, 3420 (i)).

Crack-making on the day *gengzi*: The king is to offer libation and till. He should go. The twelfth month (Hou, II, 28. 16).

Plant millet, we shall receive harvest (Yi, 7750).

The king should not go to inspect the millet planting (Puci, 492).

Do not inspect the fields at X, (for) it will rain (Heji, 28993).

It is chiefly based on the above evidence that Guo Moruo and others jump to the conclusion that all the land belonged to the Shang king who was the representative of a slave-owner class (Guo Moruo, 1976: 155–214; Fan, 1947; Li Yanong, 1954; 1955; Hou, 1955; Lu, 1962; Chang, 1980: 158, 223; Jin, 1983). No doubt the Shang king played an important role in the organization of many aspects of the society, since his primary duty was to determine and control the future through ritual sacrifices and divinations. But nowhere can we find a sentence suggesting that the king claimed to be the owner of all the land. A close review of the available oracle-bone inscriptions demonstrates that the relevant divinations about the weather and harvest in different directions were quite specific. They did not necessarily imply that those fields belonged to the king (Chen Mengjia, 1956a: 313-6, 532–3; Shima Kunio, 1967: 433–4). As our discussion on the concept of ownership in the first chapter clearly suggests, the existence of natural right is a necessary but not sufficient condition for the establishment of ownership. It has to meet its social requirements, namely, there must be a highly developed governmental system to enforce its existence. Furthermore, the owner must be aware of his or her exclusive rights over the control of his or her property. He or she should not be prevented from taking actions with his or her property such as selling it. No contemporary sources indicate that such a clear definition of ownership had been developed in Shang times. In absence of solid evidence, we are not in a position to provide a satisfactory answer to the question of landownership. Hence the thesis that the Shang was a slavery is also an arbitrary assertion which cannot be substantiated with empirical data.

2   THE STATUS OF *ZHONGREN*

Scholars in both the West and China agree that the main labour force of the Shang was called *zhongren* or *zhong* in oracle inscriptions. But opinions are in conflict about how to interpret this concept (or these concepts, because *zhongren* can be separated into two independent words in Chinese). Consequently, different statuses are assigned to it (or them). In this section I shall first examine the major arguments of those different schools and then I shall consult both the oracle inscriptions and archaeological finds to test their claims. Finally I shall propose what I consider as the right understanding of the status of *zhongren* in the Shang times.

Since *zhongren* is a compound in both classical and modern Chinese, most Chinese scholars regard it as one word which literally means 'the multitudes'. However, some specialists argue that *zhongren* was not a compound in the Shang oracle inscriptions (Chen Mengjia, 1956a: 610; Keightley, 1969: 72). They think that *zhongren* should be separated as *zhong* ('the multitudes') and *ren* (literally 'people') and that they belonged to two different groups of people. According to Keightley, *zhong* were state labourers, 'that is, workers permanently attached to the ruler, while the ren were public workers, members of the general population mobilized as the occasion demanded' (ibid.: 66). His main arguments, in brief, are: 1) grammatically speaking, we can separate *zhong* from *ren*; 2) 'no Shang usage supports *zhongren* as an independent term' (ibid.: 71).

On the other hand, Chen Mengjia, after a detailed analysis of many oracle inscriptions, concludes that there were three kinds of labour force in the Shang, namely, *zhong*, *ren* and *zhongren*. He argues that *zhongren* were connected only with the king while *zhong* were generally stationed on the border areas. Finally, although he considers *ren* as free men, he cannot explain their precise functions. Apart from their differences, Keightley's and Chen Mengjia's interpretations have much in common. For example, both admit that there were very few, if any, functional distinctions between *zhong* and *ren* (ibid.: 74, 89, Chen Mengjia, 1956a: 610).

It seems that these distinction are not necessary. Firstly, the pictograph for *ren* in the oracle inscriptions is the side-view of a standing man and hence can be interpreted as 'man' or 'men'. Many inscriptions suggest that the term *ren* was already a very general concept which did not have any specific meaning. It could be used in different situations. For instance:

Yu has been ordered to take the *ren* at Ge to attack Gongfang. There will be no misfortune (Jin, 522).

Crack-making on the day *dingyu*. Ke divined: We should not mobilize 3000 *ren* (Tie, 258, 1).

Order to collect *ren* in north Gong (Cui, 1217).

Ren at X should cut fodder at Jiao (Jia, 206 (i)).

Secondly, although we do not possess sufficient knowledge to exclude the possibility that *zhongren* can be separated, no oracle inscription indicates that we should not take them as a compound. Many inscriptions can be interpreted in this way without any loss in meaning:

In the next *xin* day, if Ya... San takes *zhongren* to X and Dinglu, order them to protect us (Qian, 7. 3. 1).

Crack-making on the day *jiyu*. Zheng divined: We should collect *zhongren* and order them to follow Qian to carry out the king's affairs (Qian, 7. 3. 2).

Thirdly, even if there were distinctions of a certain kind between *zhong* and *ren*, the incomplete nature of the contemporary sources does not permit us to draw a reliable conclusion. In fact, after some discussion on the different connotations between *zhong* and *ren*, Keightley reached a somewhat contradictory conclusion that 'the *Zhong* and *ren* were not functionally distinct' (Keightley, 1969: 74).

Finally, since the Shang diviners always sought to express their concerns in the shortest possible way, it is plausible to assume that sometimes they used either *zhong* or *ren* to convey the same message. For instance:

Do not pour out the *ren* at Tu, since the borderlanders will not come out there (Heji, 28012).

The king orders *zhong* to defend X... (Ye, 43. 6).

Do not order Qin to take *zhong* to attack Gong (Cui, 1082).

The *ren* in X should cut fodder at Jiao (Jia, 206 (i)).

Therefore, unless future archaeological finds provide more convincing evidence to support the separation of *zhong* from *ren*, it seems safe to conclude that they were the same people at the disposal of the king.

Does this mean that *zhongren* were slaves in the Shang society? Guo Moruo was probably the first modern scholar in China who gave an affirmative answer to this question (Guo Moruo, 1960: 211–15; 1976: 174–5). Since his conceptualization of *zhongren* as slaves in the Shang satisfied the requirement of orthodox Marxism in China, many people followed suit (Li Yanong, 1954; Lu, 1962; Jin, 1983). Different reasons are given to support the above claim, but the etymological one seems most interesting.[21] In the oracle-bone inscriptions the graph for the character of *zhong* symbolizes three men under the sun. According to this interpretation, it implies that *zhongren* were working together beneath the sun. For those in agreement with Guo, working in the field certainly means slave labour.

Ironically, based on the same evidence, another famous Chinese scholar, Ding Shan, reached exactly the opposite conclusion. He believes that the three people in the graph of *zhong*, instead of working in the field under the sun, were protected by it! Who else could have such a privilege in the ancient world if not the elites? Therefore, Ding claims that *zhongren* were nothing but free citizens, quite like those of the ancient Greek and Roman times (Ding, 1956: 38). This conclusion is shared by the famous Shang specialist Hu Houxuan, but he offers a different reason. Based on the 'Pangeng' chapter of the *Shang Shu* or the Book of Documents,[22] Hu contends that it is impossible to regard *zhongren* as slaves in the Shang times (1944, 3b–4b), because the speeches made by Pangeng reflect the close relationship between the Shang king and his subjects:

Previously, my predecessors together with your forefathers and fathers mutually shared both leisure and toil. How dare I administer unjust penalties on you? For generations the toils of your families have been confirmed, and I shall not conceal your goodness. Thus I present great sacrifices to former rulers, while your ancestors partake of those presents.... [Country's] welfare rests with you all. If it fails in prosperity, that must arise from me, the isolated man, having neglected the punishments. This is my declaration. From now on, each of you should devote yourselves to your business, fulfil the duties of your offices, and regulate your conversations, or punishment will extend to you personally, and your regret will be unavailing (*Shan Shu zhushu*, 9\5a–11a).

After the removal of the capital to the area of the present Anyang City, Henan Province, Pangeng not only exhorted the multitudes to work hard on the new land, but also demanded his officials to take care of the multitudes:

If you princes of the country, you officers in charge of all affairs, would but sympathise in my anxiety! I have continually aspired to be friend and to guide you, having regard for the respect of my people. I shall not support those who love wealth, but shall openly venerate the industrious. For those who nourish their multitudes, I shall employ and esteem (ibid., 9\11a; cf. Legge, 1865: 246–7).

As Hu points out, if the king's sacrifices to royal ancestral spirits were also shared by the *zhong*'s ancestral spirits, *zhong* could not have been slaves in the classical Greek sense (Hu Houxuan, 1944: 3b–4b).

It is obvious that each of the opinions presented above is supported by the author's strongly subjective interpretation of some available evidence while ignoring that of others. Therefore, it is incorrect to determine the status of *zhongren* through either an available abstract analysis of the pictograph for *zhong* in the oracle-bone inscriptions or the surviving historical documents of later dynasties.[23] The only solution to the problem seems to be a comprehensive analysis of the functions of *zhongren* in the oracle inscriptions.

In the first place, several thousand oracle-bone inscriptions document the military activities of *zhongren*. As indicated above, the basic social unit *zu* in the Shang was essentially a military organization, carrying out orders directly from the king. Since defending the frontier or expanding the territory was one of the king's major occupations, there were a great deal of divinations about the mobilization of *zhongren* for wars.

Divining on the day *dingmao*. The king orders Qin to collect *zhong* to attack the west bank of X (Xiaotun, T53. 2b: 111).

The king should assemble 5000 *ren* to attack Duofang[24] (Hou, II, 31. 6).

Crack-making on the day *gengzi*. Bin divined: If we do not assemble 3000 *ren* and order [them to attack] Gongfang, we shall not receive spiritual aid (Qian, 7. 2. 3).

Do not order Qin[25] to assemble the *zhong* to attack Gong (Cui, 1082).

Crack-making on the day *jiachen*. If Qin takes the *zhong* at X to attack Renfang, we shall receive spiritual aid (Cui, 1124).

Crack-making. The king shall not order Qin to organize the *zhong* to attack Gongfang (Hou, I, 16. 10).

Furthermore, there are divinations showing that *zhongren* were divided into left, right and centre units.

The king makes three divisions: right, middle, left (Cui, 597).

Order the *ren* of the centre (Hou, II, 8.6).

Should the *zhong* be assembled? The answer was auspicious. Should the *zhong* be organized on the left? The king read the divination and said: Greatly auspicious. Should the *zhong* be organized? The answer was auspicious. Should the *zhong* be organized in the centre? The king read the divination and said: Greatly auspicious. Should the *zhong* be organized? The answer was auspicious... (Qian, 5. 6. 1).

Crack-making on the day *bingshen*. Divining: Collect horsegroom, left, right, middle 300 people (*ren*) (Qian, 3. 31. 2).

The above inscriptions indicate that *zhongren* were an important source for the Shang army and that they could be summoned by the king for wars as well as garrison duties.

Secondly, *zhongren* were the main labour force of the Shang agriculture. Numerous divinations suggest that they took part in all the field work from opening up of new land to harvesting.

Crack-making on the day *wuzi*. Bin divined: Order *qunzhisu* to prepare the land at Hu (Jingdu, 281).

Crack-making on the day *kuici*. Bin divined: Order the *zhongren* ... to enter Yangfang ... and exploit the fields. Divination: do not order the *zhongren*. In the sixth month (Jia, 3510 (iv) (v)).

The king should go and take the *zhong* ... to plant millet in X (Qian, 5.20. 2).

[Order] the *zhong* to plant millet in X (Zhu, 788).

Divining: Xiao Chen should order the *zhong* to plant millet. The first month (Qian, 4. 30. 2).

Thirdly, *zhongren* were recorded to go hunting with the Shang kings.

Divining: Order ... *zhongren* [to catch] deer... (Jia, 3588).

Hunting at X, ..., take the *ren* of the right at Y, there will be no disaster (Jia, 2562 (i)).

Fourthly, in the oracle inscriptions *zhongren* are found to have many other functions from attending ceremonies to building city-walls. Although many inscriptions do not definitely indicate the exact task carried out by *zhongren*, the coercive nature of those works is beyond doubt.

...Qin assembles the *zhong* of X... at temple[26] ... to hold *yugao* ceremony (Jingjin, 1074).

Divining on the day *xinci*: Order the *zhong* ... (Qian, 1. 10. 2).

Order the *zhong* to carry out affairs (Qian, 1. 10. 2).

Since the king has issued formal order to the *zhong*, he should report it to (his ancestor) Fuding (Cui, 369).

Practise the *liao*-sacrifice and tell (the ancestors) the *zhong* ... have gone to Ding[lu] (Hou, I, 24. 3).

Hui should assemble the *zhongren*... to reinforce the city wall... (Heji, 30).

The king should not go and take the *zhongren* (Nanbei, Zhengming, 26).

Do not order our *ren* to go to Sui. Order our *ren* to go to Sui first (Yi, 6111).

Finally, no inscriptions suggest that *zhongren* were used as human victims (Guo Baojun, 1950: 1–61; Gu Derong, 1982: 112–23), as the Qiang[27] people and other war captives had been in the sacrificial rituals.

On the day *Jiawu*. Divining: The following day, perform the *yu* ritual to Zu Yi [and sacrifice] Qiang fifteen persons. Perform the *mou* ritual [and use] a kid. Perform the *yu* ritual and use one cow. In the fifth month (Yicun, 154).

Divining: [Perform ritual and sacrifice] Qiang four hundred, to *zu* X... (Nanbei, Shi, 1. 40).[28]

Moreover, we have not found any divination suggesting that *zhongren* could be sold or bought. It seems that the position of *zhongren* in the Shang was fixed (Zhang Zhenglang, 1973: 117; Zhu Fenghan, 1981: 59–69).

The above analysis demonstrates that *zhongren* were mobilized for most of the activities in the Shang times. From this perspective *zhongren* were what Marx called the 'general slaves' of the state. But strictly speaking, they were not slaves of the ancient Greek or Roman type, since the definition of a slave requires not only absolute control of the slave by the slave-owner in production activities, but also the right to transfer his ownership to another owner 'by sale, barter, gift, or in some other way' (Wilbur, 1943: 62). The Shang *zhongren* clearly did not satisfy the requirement of the above definition of a slave.

Furthermore, the concept of slave in ancient Greece and Rome was inextricably related to the concept of personal freedom. As Finley correctly argued, '[o]nly when slaves became the main dependent labor force was the concept of personal freedom first articulated (in classical Greece), and words were created or adopted to express the idea. It is literally impossible to translate "freedom" directly into ancient Babylonian or classical Chinese' (Finley, 1968: 308). Since they were not driven in leg-irons to the field-work, *zhongren* in Shang China clearly did not fit the image of slaves as we have come to understand the concept of slavery.

On the other hand, since it was obligation and duty rather than the legal concept of individual rights which dominated the whole Shang society, *zhongren* also did not meet the requirement of free citizens described by Finley.

Can we then define *zhongren* as serfs like labourers in medieval Europe? As indicated in the first chapter, serfdom was a particular phenomenon belonging to Western feudalism. Since there was no landlord in the Shang, it is difficult to define *zhongren* as serfs. Although no record of transfer of *zhongren* from one owner to another is found, oracle bones do reveal that they were mobilized from one area to another to set up new towns and that they were frequently organized to wage wars against other tribes to expand the Shang territories. As both labourers and fighters, *zhongren* were not permanently bound to their native places. The oracle inscriptions do not tell us if there was anyone who could provide protection for them, as happened to the serfs in feudal Europe. It is apparent that the term feudalism does not further our understanding of the Shang society and that *zhongren* cannot be classified as serfs.

3   CONCLUSION

The above discussion suggests first, that the Shang was chiefly an agricultural society with a mastery of many aspects of technology. Many industries such as stone, bone and bronze-making were all relatively highly developed and they provided one of the most fundamental preconditions for the transformation of ancient China from a primitive egalitarian community to a stratified society.

Second, although there are still many gaps in our knowledge of the real functions of the major labour force *zhongren* in the Shang times, the available oracle inscriptions reveal some of their basic features: 1) they were ordinary members of the Shang patriarchal clans. They were neither the free men of the ancient Greek and Roman type, nor slaves as we have come to understand the concept of slavery; 2) the Shang king had the power to order them for services of many kinds, but no evidence indicates that he owned them as private property and hence the concept of slavery would not have been readily comprehensible to the Shang society; 3) I have argued that it is not appropriate to categorize *zhongren* as serfs either, since their functions were quite different from those of the latter. Unlike the serfs in medieval Europe, *zhongren* were not bound to a particular place, but were ordered to build new towns or villages and to cultivate new lands in different places. Not surprisingly, a benefice system of any kind has not been found in the contemporaneous records. Therefore, there is no reason to classify the Shang as a feudal society.

Finally, through oracle-bone inscriptions we know that the Shang king showed great concern about the weather and harvest, and that production was often carried out on a massive scale. But no empirical evidence suggests that the king claimed to be the owner of all the land. Since all the available divinations about harvest in different directions were quite specific, they did not necessarily mean that those fields belonged to the king. As our discussion on the concept of ownership in the first chapter of this thesis clearly suggests, the existence of natural rights is a necessary but not sufficient condition for establishing landownership. Ownership has to meet its social requirements, namely, that there must be a highly developed governmental system and a complex legal system to enforce its existence. Furthermore, the owner must be aware of his or her exclusive rights over the control of his or her property. But no contemporaneous sources indicate that a clear definition of ownership had been developed in Shang times. In the absence of empirical evidence, we are not in a position to provide a satisfactory answer to the question of landownership. Hence the thesis that the Shang was a slave-owning society is also an arbitrary assertion and cannot be substantiated with convincing data at the present stage.

To sum up, with economic and technological developments, there was a tendency to concentrate power into the hands of the minority Shang dynasty. This undoubtedly promoted division of labour and hence differentiation of classes in the form of unequal access to both the means of production, surplus of labour and the power of control over ritual ceremonies. Apart from this impressionistic picture, we still do not have sufficient documentation to provide any detailed information on the nature of Shang society. We have to await further archaeological finds which might enable us to say something more concrete.

4 Economy and Society in the Western Zhou

The conquest of the Shang by the Zhou marked the beginning of the second known dynasty in Chinese history. The origin of this dynasty is obscure, shrouded in legend and fantasy (Creel, 1970; Wheatley, 1971; Hsu and Linduff, 1988: 33–67). The Zhou once lived under the shadow of the Shang dynasty,[1] but they gradually built up their power. By 1122 BC[2] King Wu led a coalition of tribes and successfully overthrew the Shang dynasty.[3] In the subsequent years numerous military expeditions took place, and the Zhou expanded its territorial control to the further south and east. Eventually it occupied approximately half the area of present China. As the longest dynasty ever (approximately 900 years), it fundamentally influenced the later developments of Chinese history. 'Its enduring influence is such that for historians it is often difficult to determine whether a characteristic under discussion is that of the Zhou or that of the Chinese' (Huang, 1988: 16).

Traditionally two periods are identified within the Zhou dynasty: the Western Zhou and the Eastern Zhou. At the beginning of the dynasty, the Zhou governed the country from the old western capital, Hao, not far from the present city of Xian, Shaanxi Province. It lasted until 771 BC when natural disasters and internal disturbances weakened its military strength, which enabled the non-Zhou people from the west to invade that area. This compelled the future King Ping to move the capital from Hao to Chengzhou, the eastern capital, in the present city of Luoyang, Henan Province.[4] Hence the period before 771 BC is known as the Western Zhou, and the period after that date as the Eastern Zhou.

In comparison with the Shang dynasty, we are in a better position to discuss the Western Zhou, especially its later period, because more information is available. In the first place, bronze inscriptions[5] will be used. Since they were written by contemporaries, they offer direct access to the ideas of that period, providing invaluable insights for our understanding of some important aspects of Western Zhou society, which edited texts of later times failed to record.

On the other hand, our knowledge about the bronze inscriptions is still very limited. Although epigraphic study of the ancient Chinese language has been developed to an unprecedented level in recent years, we still have

66

difficulties in interpreting some characters of the Western Zhou bronze inscriptions. I shall refer to different explanations of the authorities in this area to determine the specific meaning of a word when I intend to use it as possible evidence.

Furthermore, the authenticity of some bronze inscriptions has been doubted by Barnard (1958: 12, 39; 1965: 395–407) and Keightley (1969: 197). In this study, however, I shall only cite those regarded as true Western Zhou inscriptions by well-known scholars such as Guo Moruo, Tang Lan, Creel and Hsu.[6]

Second, many literary texts were traditionally considered to have been written during the Western Zhou period, but contemporary scholars believe that only few of them are untransmitted. I shall, therefore, use those chapters in the *Shang Shu* and some sections from the *Shi Jing*, which have been generally accepted as original Zhou materials (Keightley, 1969: 147–51; Creel, 1970: 448–63; Hsu and Linduff, 1988: XIX–XX). Since the *Zuo Zhuan* is also considered to contain massive authentic information on the Western Zhou, I shall cite it as one of the important sources for both this period and the subsequent 'Chun Qiu' ('the Spring and Autumn', 722–481 BC) period.[7]

Meanwhile, I shall exclude some works such as the *Zhou Li* or the Rites of the Zhou from my description of the Western Zhou society. Although it depicts an elaborate hierarchical structure, we do not know to what extent it reflects the actual conditions of that time.[8]

In the first section I shall investigate the level of productive forces, especially that of technology. I shall contend that during the Western Zhou there was no substantial improvement in either agricultural production or other major industries, from implement-making to bronze-manufacturing, in comparison with the Shang dynasty. The second section will be an attempt to define the specific nature of the *fengjian* system in that period. I shall seek to demonstrate that it is a misunderstanding to categorize the Western Zhou either as feudalism or as slavery, as some scholars want us to believe. With its distinctive features, the Western Zhou represented a particular mode of ruling a vast area when the productive forces were at a relatively low level. The essence of such a system was to govern the country through kinship. Consequently, the political and economic organizations were wholly assimilated to that of the blood relationship. Feudalism, with its well-defined rights and obligations between suzerain and vassals, did not exist in the Western Zhou.

In the third section, I shall argue that family farming, if it had ever existed during that time, was not the mainstream of production yet. The available evidence seems to suggest that lineage-based collective activities were predominant.

The final section will focus on how to define the status of the main labour force in the Western Zhou. A discussion of both contemporary records and the Zhou political philosophy is intended to illustrate the argument that different groups of the main labour force were unlikely to have been treated by the Zhou rulers as either slaves or serfs. Based on our distinction between different modes of production in Chapter 1, I shall define the Western Zhou as a society dominated by the AMP.

1   THE LEVEL OF PRODUCTIVE FORCES

To support their argument that the Western Zhou was a feudal society, some Chinese scholars seek to argue, first, that the Zhou was technologically better developed even before its conquest of the Shang dynasty. Thus it is the increase of the Zhou's productivity which explains its victory over the Shang (Lu, 1962: 130; Zhao Guangxian, 1980: 38). Secondly, they contend that iron tools had already been invented during the Western Zhou times. As a result, the level of the Zhou productive forces was qualitatively different from that of the Shang (Lu, 1962: 155).

However, archaeological evidence does not support the above contention. In all remains which have been dated to the pre-dynastic times, most Zhou implements are stone-made and the shapes are rough. Some implements are made of either seashell or bone, but they are relatively small in number. Agricultural tools are mainly comprised of spades and sickles, presumably for the preparation of soil and harvest. The spade has a rather broad cutting-edge and a narrow base that is to be tied to a wooden handle. The sickles are extremely similar to those found in the Shang remains (Zhongguo shehui kexue yuan kaogu yanjiusuo, 1962: 80–94).

In addition, fishing and hunting equipment is also identified. Arrowheads are made either of antlers or other animal bones. Since they are rather dull, they could have been used for other purposes such as killing small animals (Hsu and Linduff, 1988: 74–5). In summary, there is little evidence of Zhou technological innovation in their pre-dynastic archaeological remains.

The above archaeological findings are confirmed by the classical literature. Some poems in the *Shi Jing* describe the almost primitive conditions of the environment in which the ancestors of the Zhou struggled to survive. For instance, several verses depict the opening of roads and land reclamation, while others record cultivation of land, fishing and herding and so on (Legge, 1871: 441, 449–50). It seems perfectly plausible that the Zhou used those tools discovered in the archaeological remains to carry out such activities (Legge 1871: 307–8, 438, 457, 574).

Therefore, as some scholars have correctly argued, the defeat of the Shang by the Zhou is most likely due to the successful strategy of King Wu rather than to a technological superiority (Li Yanong, 1962: 666–9; Creel, 1970; Hsu and Linduff, 1988: 69–101). The productive capability of the Zhou was at most equal to that of the Shang. No significant advantages are visible from the available Zhou material.

Moreover, both archaeological and literary evidence indicate that there was no qualitative improvement in any field of technology during the whole period of the Western Zhou. In the first place, most agriculturally related implements resembled very much those of the Shang. Little change took place, since they were still made either of bone, stone, shell or horn. The fact that they could be found in the central area under Zhou control as well as in the outlying regions implies that the general level of technology was approximately the same everywhere (Beida Lishixi, 1979: 167). As Cheng correctly concludes, 'stone axes, adzes and spades for digging and knives and sickles for harvesting are standard finds, as well as whetstones for grinding and polishing and heavy perforated discs for pounding. Among the bone and horn artifacts are spades, chisels, awls, needles, arrowheads, spatulae and hair-pins as well as oracle bones. Shell artifacts include such common types as sickles, knives and saws' (Cheng, 1963: 184). In a bone workshop at Yuntang of Fufeng County, Shaanxi Province, archaeologists excavated about twenty thousand half-finished items. From storage pit no. 21 alone, there are approximately eight thousand pieces of raw bones which must have been taken from at least 1306 cattle and 21 horses. This shows that large workshops were probably monopolized by the royal court, very much like that of the Shang (Zhouyuan kaogudui, 1980: 29–35).

Secondly, no iron implement was found by the archaeologists among the identified Western Zhou remains. It is true that some tools were made of bronze (Guo Moruo, 1976: 199, 247–8), but we have reason to believe that they were not produced for the purpose of actual farming. First, they were very small in comparison with other bone-made implements. Second, they were beautifully decorated. Third, they were not discovered in massive numbers. Indeed, bronze was such an expensive material that it was far beyond the reach of common people in the Western Zhou. Thus farming tools were relatively simple and were mainly made of either bone or shell. In comparison with that of the Shang dynasty, they did not have any significant sign of improvement in both quality and shape (Hu Qianying, 1982: 62). Further differentiation and specialization to meet specific needs did not take place until the Eastern Zhou period, especially its later part (Beida Lishixi, 1979: 166–7; Hsu and Linduff, 1988: 338–41, 351–3).

Thirdly, jade-carving and pottery at the beginning of the Western Zhou seemed to have acquired new technologies from the Shang as well, since their products were almost always replicas of the Shang prototypes (Cheng, 1963: 185; Zou Heng, 1980: 304).[9] There were, of course, some improvements in their later development. In the case of jade, new styles in size, shape and decoration gradually became dominant, while in pottery there were two improvements: roof-tiles and well-rings. Both techniques were preserved in the following dynasties (Cheng, 1963: 205–6).

Fourthly, the manufacture of bronze was also greatly influenced by the Shang technologies. Some differences in shapes could be found between the Shang and Zhou vessels, but the Zhou bronze master cast his vessels in the same way as his Shang colleagues. The development of new styles in the later period was a natural continuation of the Shang tradition (Cheng, 1963: 221; Beida Lishixi, 1979: 160–70).

Since bronze industry needed not only huge investment, but also complex organization, it seemed to be largely monopolized by the royal court.[10] A huge foundry site of that period near the present city of Luoyang, the then eastern capital of the Western Zhou, was excavated between 1975 and 1979. The whole area of the workshop measured 700 metres east–west and 300 metres north–south. According to the report, the excavated area, which was approximately 2500 square metres, was only a small portion of the whole site. Many implements as well as foundations of houses, kilns, storage pits, several thousand fragments of clay moulds and other items were discovered. There can be no doubt that a large-scale workshop once existed there during the Western Zhou period (Luoyangshi wenwu gongzuodui, 1983).

Finally, archaeological findings reveal that chariots and harnesses were more widely spread in the Western Zhou times than during the Shang dynasty (Cheng, 1963: 59; 77). This means that there were more people engaged in many skilled handicrafts, related to chariot- and harness-making.

However, since they were used mainly for the purpose of war, those handicrafts were very much irrelevant to the general improvement of the well-being of the majority (ibid.: 265–9; Hsu and Linduff, 1988: 338–44). The Zhou kings' preoccupation apparently was to consolidate their power by suppressing the old Shang allies and expanding their territories further to the east and south. This perhaps is one of the main reasons that explains why the Western Zhou technology remained largely within the Shang tradition.

We are poorly informed about how the above activities were organized during that period, and to what extent those technologies were diffused over the huge area ruled by the Zhou kings. But archaeological findings indicate that many workshops required complicated coordination, which must have been managed by royal power, especially at the beginning of the dynasty. Since most workshops were located in areas near the two capitals of the Western Zhou, it seems likely that the royal power controlled a great deal both of the production and distribution of those industries.

2 THE NATURE OF THE *FENGJIAN* SYSTEM

Most scholars agree that the ownership rights of all the land in the Western Zhou belonged to the king. For instance, the 'Da Yu Ding' inscription documents the king's declaration that he was 'the one man' who ruled 'over the four quarters' (Tang Lan, 1986: 169–70).[11] This statement accords well with the descriptions in the literary sources. For example, a famous contemporary poem states: 'Under the heaven / There is nothing that is not the king's land... None who are not the king's servants' (the *Shi Jing*, 9/12a; cf. Karlgren, 1950b: 157–8).[12] But the implication of this poem is not the same to scholars working in different analytical frameworks or with various political orientations. In particular, opinions are deeply divided as to how to understand the crucial Chinese phrase *fengjian*. For some scholars, it is the Chinese equivalent of the concept of feudalism, while others argue that the phrase was fabricated in a much later time than the Western Zhou. Therefore, it by no means gives a true picture of the Western Zhou.

In this section, I shall first contend that both claims are biased. On the one hand, it is misleading to define the Western Zhou as feudalism. On the other hand, it is equally wrong to deny the *fengjian* phenomenon. Second, I shall suggest that the Western Zhou and feudal Europe were different in many essential aspects, despite some superficial similarities between the two systems.

As discussed in the last chapter, the Zhou shared the same culture with the Shang long before its final victory over the latter, although it undoubtedly kept some of its own regional features (Chang, 1980).[13] It is therefore not surprising to find the continuity of the Shang culture in the essential structure of the Zhou dynasty from the written system to social organization. The most important feature the Zhou inherited from the Shang was probably the latter's system of kinship groups or lineage (clan)[14] system, and its inextricably related activity – ancestor-worship. Although there were some changes in forms, the Zhou firmly believed that the lineage system and ancestor worship could guarantee not only their prosperity, but also their perpetuation (Chang, 1976: 59).

The existence of a system of kinship groups or lineage system in the Western Zhou has been confirmed by both archaeological and literary sources. For example, the style of burial and arrangement of things inside the graves in the Zhou archaeological remains are similar to those found in the Shang tombs. Lineage name inscriptions are also found on both the Shang and Western Zhou bronzes. According to Li Xueqin, approximately half of the discovered bronzes were inscribed with emblems. They are found not only on valuable vessels of the nobility, but also on objects found in many small tombs (Li Xueqin, 1985: 482). This is a clear indication that the lineage system was commonly practised.

Moreover, the word *zu* (lineage) is often mentioned as a basic unit of organization in the bronze inscriptions. The 'Ban Gui' records: 'The king orders Wu Bo: 'Lead your regiment to assist Father Mao from the left side.' The king orders Lu Bo: 'Lead your regiment to help Father Mao from the right.' [The king] gives the order: 'Lead your lineage members (*zu ren*) to follow your father and to protect your father's body in the fighting' (Tang Lan, 1986: 346–7; Tang, Lan, 1978: 19–24; Beida Lishixi, 1979: 191–6; Chang, 1980: 161–3; Li Xixing, 1984, Hsu and Linduff, 1988: 163–71; Xu Xitai, 1988: 106).[15]

Thus, in order to rule the country effectively, the Zhou kings had to parcel out territories to members of the principal lineage. The total number of people who received appointments from the kings is not known,[16] but the relationship between the kings and their appointees was that of kinship[17] rather than anything else. It is worth stressing this point, because it was the hallmark of the Zhou culture which dominated the whole society until it was replaced by the Qin dynasty (221 BC). The Zhou kings had great authority over others chiefly by virtue of the fact that they were the heads of the main branch of all the sub-lineages in the whole dynasty. In other words, it was their position in the lineage structure which determined the Zhou kings' power. Through this lineage system, both political and economic structures were closely interwoven with kinship ties.

In practice, the lineage system was manifested through a tight control of *Li*. It is very difficult to give a precise definition of the concept of *Li* in English. It can be regarded as a divinely ordained moral law, but it does not mean a religious ritual in its strict sense. In fact, it includes a proper conduct in all rituals. For example, the precise height at which one should hold a jade tablet in a court ceremony is clearly indicated in the *Zuo Zhuan* (CQZZZ, 1981: 1601). According to recent research, about twenty sumptuous forms of sacrificial rites to ancestors can be found in the Western Zhou bronze inscriptions (Liu Yu, 1989: 495–522). Thus the word *Li* denotes a code by which 'society was or should be governed' (Creel, 1970: 335–6). The integration of the ritual aspects of political subservience with a private religion, so to speak, enabled the Zhou rulers to mobilize the masses against any individual or group that did not follow their orders (CQZZZ, 1981: 86–9).

On the other hand, after being appointed by the king as the legitimate sources of authority within specific areas,[18] those granted power would be the heads of new lineages. It was through the institutionalization of this method that the Zhou kings expanded their territorial control and power. This system of organizing the country was known as *fengjian* in some classical Chinese sources.

The character *feng* is found in bronze inscriptions, referring to 'a mound', or 'the raising of a mound' (Wheatley, 1971: 197). In fact, the extended meaning of both *feng* and *jian* is 'to establish' in Chinese (Qiu Xigui, 1989: 206–9). The whole phrase appeared first in one of the poems of the *Shi Jing,* the 'Shang Song'.[19] The verse 'Zhou Song' also says: 'There are no establishments (*feng*) that are not your city-states; it is only the king who built them' (based on Karlgren, 1950b: 240). The *Zuo Zhuan* further explained this phrase in several places, and described how the Zhou kings granted different areas of the country to members of their own lineage (CQZZZ, 1981: 60–2, 93–4, 423–5, 1006, 1018–19).

According to Hou Wailu, it was Japanese scholars who first rendered the phrase *fengjian* to convey the Western concept of feudalism. Gradually it was accepted as the correct translation by most Chinese historians (Hou Wailu, 1955: 125). However, in order to support his argument that the Western Zhou was a slave society, Hou had to deny that the *fengjian* system ever existed. Since new archaeological discoveries and modern research have confirmed its existence during that period (Wheatley, 1971: 197–8), Hou's argument seems far from convincing.

At the same time, in an attempt to search for similarities between China and Europe, some scholars believe that the Chinese *fengjian* system is comparable with feudalism in Western Europe. This would mean that feudalism was already well developed three thousand years ago in ancient China. Many books have been written by scholars in both China and the West to justify the *fengjian* system as feudalism. Nevertheless, to meet their requirements, they have to exclude different variables of the concept of feudalism as applied to medieval Europe. For example, Creel defines feudalism merely as 'a system of government in which a ruler personally delegates limited sovereignty over portions of his domain to vassals' (Creel, 1964: 163).[20]

Such a definition has several defects. Firstly, whenever the word 'sovereign' is used in the authentic Zhou text of the *Shang Shu,* it refers only to the Zhou king (Legge, 1865: 168, 386, 396, 412, 416). Therefore, it is not correct to describe the power given by the king as 'sovereignty'. As I shall argue in the ensuing pages, the power of the appointees was not political but administrative. The *de facto* political sovereignty which the local lords enjoyed later on did not appear until the Chun Qiu period when the unitary kingdom was dissolved by the civil war.[21]

Secondly, as indicated above, the concept of feudalism refers not only to a system of political institutions, but also a special mode of economic organization.[22] But Creel admits that his definition of feudalism merely refers to the political features of feudalism, and thus its economic aspects are neglected (Creel, 1970: 320).

Thirdly, feudalism subsumes a range of essential variables which cannot be found in the AMP.[23] However, if we follow Creel's definition of feudalism, numerous fundamental differences between feudal Europe and Western Zhou China will be eliminated. For instance, the personal nature of the contract and its military origin in the former, and familism in the latter would disappear. Furthermore, the guild associations of all kinds, which are found in medieval European cities, did not exist in the Western Zhou. The cities were mainly centres of rituals and administration (Chang, 1976: 71);[24] the massive mobilization of forced labour, and the stress on social discipline and order in ethics and cosmology were also characteristics of the Western Zhou. Feudal Europe was certainly not comparable in those aspects.

Finally, Creel's conceptualization of feudalism is so abstract that it can be applied to many radically different societies. Such a broad categorization will not serve a rigorous analytical purpose.

This, of course, does not mean that there are no similarities between these two different societies. In fact, given a common agricultural background, it is not surprising to find some similar phenomena, although the reasons behind them may well be different. In comparison with feudal Europe, for example, the Zhou kings also entrusted local administration to the powerful lords. In return, those lords had to serve the king.[25] This does not, however, help us to answer the following questions: first, why did a highly centralized bureaucratic empire evolve out of the Zhou system in 221 BC? Second, why did this bureaucratic system have the power to dominate Chinese history for more than 2000 years, while feudalism in Europe was eventually replaced by capitalism?

Implicitly or explicitly, some scholars realize the weakness of their approach in the application of feudalism to the Western Zhou. Few even admit that Western Zhou feudalism was quite different from European feudalism in several important aspects. For instance, Hsu and Linduff draw our attention to the lack of militarism between the Zhou king and his appointees, which was at the heart of the relationship between a European feudal lord and his vassals (Hsu and Linduff, 1988: 185). As argued above, militarism is one of the most crucial elements to decide whether a society can be classified as feudal.

However, Hsu and many others do not think that this can seriously damage their definition of a possible Zhou feudalism (Lu, 1962; Fu Zhufu, 1980; Gao Heng, 1980b: 142). They seem to believe that other evidence they give about the Western Zhou is sufficient to categorize it as a feudal society.

In order to avoid a hasty judgement on this claim, it is necessary to investigate two prominent features of the Zhou *fengjian* system. They have been offered as definite evidence to suggest that feudalism of the Western European kind did exist in the Western Zhou.

The first feature is the *ceming* ceremony. Literally, the character *ce* signifies a written document, while *ming* means mandate. As a phrase,[26] it is correctly translated by Creel as 'command by reading a document containing orders' (Creel, 1964: 87). *Ceming* is a ceremony held by the Zhou king when he appointed one of his lineage members either to a new office or to rule an area of the country. Both bronze inscriptions and classical Chinese literature have confirmed not only that such a ceremony did take place in the Western Zhou, but also that it was an important part of the *fengjian* system.

According to detailed studies (Chen Mengjia, 1956c: 98–114; Qi Sihe, 1981: 51–65; Kane, 1981–2: 14–28), the ceremony would take place in the main hall of the palace or in the ancestral shrine of the royal temple where the king first gave the order of the appointment himself.[27] At the same time the appointees also received various gifts, such as chariots, horses, flags, bows, arrows and millet wine (Qi Sihe, 1981: 53–5). The *Zhou Li* contains a detailed description of the gradations of gifts. However, as indicated above, the book was written in a much later period, and its account of what had happened centuries before is so precise that it is unlikely to be very reliable.

Furthermore, since there were no strict ranks of aristocratic titles,[28] it is difficult to classify those gifts into different categories. But the numbers of gifts given were, in general, compatible with the position held by the appointee. This is confirmed by the available bronze inscriptions. For instance, the often-quoted 'Da Ke Ding' recorded the event in which Shan Fu Ke (Cooking Master Ke)[29] was appointed as Provisions Master. The relevant passage reads:

> The king... said: 'Ke, previously I have ordered you to promulgate our decrees. Now I appoint you a new title. I grant you... land at Ye and at Bei. I grant you farming households cultivating the land at Yong, to serve as your subjects and subordinates. I grant you land at Kang, at Yan, and at Fuyuan. I grant you service people, drums, bells... . Be diligent day and night and do not disobey my order.' Ke bowed and made obeisance, and humbly praised the virtues of the king... (Guo Moruo, 1958: 121a–b).

Presumably this is an important *ceming* ceremony, since Ke was given a large amount of land. Such generous bestowal is not commonly found in the available Western Zhou inscriptions. In many cases, only a few gifts were conferred upon the appointees. For instance, the 'Ling Ding' records that the king gives Ling and Fenchen thirty families only (Tang Lan, 1986: 232). In the 'You Gui' inscription, the king is satisfied with You's performance, but he gives You only three oxen (ibid.: 329).

Classical writings also confirm the above evidence in the bronze inscriptions. The 'Kang Gao' or 'Ordinance to Kang' in the *Shang Shu* documents the appointment of Kang Shu as the founder of the city-state[30] of Wei in the present Hebei Province. Apart from detailed instructions as to how to govern the newly conquered area, many gifts were given to Kang Shu (CQZZZ, 1981: 1538). In the *Shi Jing*, it is not difficult to find similar appointments. An excellent example is 'Jiang Han':

> On the banks of the Changjiang and Han rivers,
> The king ordered Shao Hu:
> 'Open up the four quarters,
> Divide my land and soil.
> ....
> Go and draw boundaries
> As far as the south sea'
> (based on Karlgren, 1950b: 234).

Gifts given by the king were mentioned as well:

> 'I give you a *gui* ladle,
> And a *yu* vessel of aromatic wine from black millet.
> Report to your ancestors;
> I give you hills and soil and fields' (ibid.).

The second crucial feature of the Zhou *fengjian* system is the direct involvement of the king in building settlements throughout the country. As described in the *Shi Jing* most conquered areas were still covered with wild growth in the Zhou times. Therefore, apart from places occupied by the Shang and Zhou people, the king's appointments meant setting-up new garrison-towns in remote areas. This has been confirmed by poems describing how the kings chose places, and organized people to build new cities. As the poem 'Song Gao' reads:

> The king ordered the lord of Shen
> To be a model of the southern garrison-towns:[31]
> 'Avail yourselves of those men of Xie to make your walls.'
> The king ordered the lord of Shao
> To make the statutory division of the lord of Shen.
> The king ordered the stewards
> To send henchmen.
> ....
> They started work on the walls
> And the ancestral temple was finished.
> ....
> The king sent to the lord of Shen
> A state carriage and its team of horses:
> 'I have planned for your residence,
> No place is better than the southern land;
> I confer on you a great sceptre
> As the symbol of your dignity.
> Go, my uncle,
> And protect the land of the south'
>
> (based on Karlgren, 1950b: 227).

Another poem, 'Zheng Min', also records: 'The king ordered Zhong Shan Fu to build a city in the eastern region' (Karlgren, 1950b: 230), while the poem 'Han Yi' says: 'Extensive are those walls of Han, they were built by the army of Yan' (ibid.: 232).

The available bronze inscriptions accord well with the above descriptions. For example, the 'Song Ding' records the event in which Song was appointed to be in charge of the construction of Chengzhou, the eastern capital of the Western Zhou. The king declared: 'Song, I order you to be responsible for Chengzhou. I shall give you twenty families. Supervise and continue the new construction' (Guo Moruo, 1958: 72a–b). Apparently, it was through this *fengjian* system that the Zhou kings expanded both their military and economic power. This was reflected in other essential aspects of the Zhou society.

In the first place, the king was personally in command of the military forces. Military victories of the Zhou kings were often the subjects of both bronze inscriptions and literary sources. Glorification of the kings' power was commonplace. The poem 'Chang Wu' describes how the king pacified the disobedience of the people in the area of Xu. The king's troops were said to be 'massive like a mountain, flowing like a river; / they were continuous and orderly; / they were immeasurable, invincible; / splendidly they marched against the state of Xu'. After the victory the king returned home (Karlgren, 1950b: 236).

Many bronze inscriptions record the kings' conquests of new territories. For instance, the 'Qiang Pan' inscription reads:

> In antiquity, King Wen reigned. God bestowed upon him virtues which allowed him to possess a multitude of states between Heaven and Earth. The powerful King Wu campaigned in four directions, took over Yin (Shang) people, and quelled the troubles with (nomadic) Di and the Yi peoples (on the east coast). The wise, sage-King Chang was assisted by strong helpers and consolidated the Zhou. The virtuous Kang was the one who divided the territory. The broad-minded King Zhao campaigned southward in the region of Chujing (Tang Lan, 1986: 150).[32]

Although some troops were usually under the command of the appointees, they undoubtedly had to obey orders from the king. In the 'Ban Gui' inscription, apart from the king's conferral upon him to be in charge of Guo Chenggun,[33] Mao Bo was also ordered to attack one of the eastern unsubmitted tribes (Tang Lan, 1986: 346–7).

Secondly, the king had the right to appoint not only high officials, but also officers of medium level. The inscription in the 'Tong Gui' records that the king appointed Tong to assist Wu Ta Fu: 'You will be the head of the gardeners, gamekeepers, foresters and herders, from the Biao east to the Yellow River, from its north to the Xuan river…' (ibid.: 432).

Thirdly, the king could order any of his appointees and their lineages to move from one place to another.[34] According to recent studies, all the Zhou city-states had moved from their original settlements at least once, and the distance over which they migrated was often as much as several hundred to a thousand miles (Chen Pan, 1969: 16–7; Hsu and Linduff, 1988: 158). A good example is the city-state of Xing. By the end of the Western Zhou it was located in the present Xingtai City of Hebei Province, but some bronze inscriptions inform us that its previous settlement was probably near present Baoji County of Shaanxi Province in early Zhou times (Chen Pan, 1969: 181–4; Hsu and Linduff, 1988: 161–2).

The 'Yi Huo Gui' inscription also records that land and people were given to a lord when he was transferred to a new place in the Changjiang valley (Li Xueqin, 1985: 13–16; Hsu and Linduff, 1988: 206). This happened to lord Shen and his lineage as well. According to Chen Pan, at the beginning of the Zhou, his lineage was located near Mount Song in the north. During the reign of King Xuan (827–782 BC), it was ordered to be moved to the present Nanyang City, Henan Province (Chen Pan, 1969: 153–4).[35] Although it is very difficult, if not impossible, to trace back the actual process of lineage movements, the available data do show that after receiving the appointment, an appointee had to lead his people assigned by the king to a new locality. The tendency was to move from Shaanxi or Henan to the east or south (Shirakawa Shizuka, 1973: 367–414, 422–4; Hsu and Linduff, 1988: 117–18).

Fourthly, all the appointees had to pay homage to the king by attending ceremonies and reporting on their local activities. According to some scholars, whenever they went to the court, the Zhou officials had to carry their jade token and to present it to the king. This was a symbol of their power, and it had to fit another piece of jade held by the king. The king would keep it until all ceremonies were satisfactorily performed (Wang Guowei, 1959: 50–70; *Meng Zi zhushu*, 2A\6b; cf. Mencius, 1984: 30–1). Some poems mention jade tokens of this kind among the king's gifts (Legge, 1871: 554; Karlgren 1950b: 227), and archaeologists have discovered jade tokens in the Western Zhou remains (Zhongguo shehui kexue yuan kaogu yanjiusuo, 1962: 102). The 'Shen Zi Gui' also records that Shen Zi[36] had to go to court regularly to perform different rituals (Tang Lan, 1986: 320).[37] It seems certain that the above events took place during the Western Zhou.

Fifthly, the king had a supervisory system to guarantee the obedience of those officials within his territory. Every year he would inspect different places.[38] At the same time, he ordered his trusted people to oversee every corner of the state to make sure that everything was done according to the Zhou regulations. As the poem 'Chang Wu' in the *Shi Jing* indicates, the king sent Master Yi to 'go along those banks of Huai, inspect the territory of Xu' (Karlgren, 1950b: 235). The *Zuo Zhuan* cites a minister of Qi in the seventh century BC as saying that, centuries before, the first Duke of Qi had been ordered to police the eastern portion of the Western Zhou (CQZZZ, 1981: 289–90, 1018–19).

The bronze inscriptions tally well with historical descriptions. For example, one inscription says that two officials were sent to various places to oversee the local lords (Chen Mengjia, 1955a: 144).[39]

If any official acted against the will of the Zhou king, he would be either removed from his position, or punished, according to the degree of his misconduct. Guan Shu was killed and Cai Shu was exiled because of their rebellion against the king (CQZZZ, 1981: 1540; Hsu and Linduff, 1988: 119). The lord of Qi was one of the most powerful city-state officials during the reign of king Yi. However, he was boiled to death in a cauldron, since he indulged himself, and did not perform his duty well (Sima Qian, 1972: 1481). The 'Shi Qi Ding' inscription records that Shi Qi had to pay three hundred *yuan*[40] of bronze as a punishment, because his people *zhong pu* refused to take part in a military campaign for the king (Guo Moruo, 1958: 26a; Tang Lan, 1986: 313). When King Xuan was ill, all the lords sacrificed to their local deities, and prayed for his early recovery (CQZZZ, 1981: 1476; Creel, 1970: 426). Some inscriptions indicate that troops were sent to 'tranquillize' different lords (Chen Mengjia, 1955b: 117, 119). Obviously, the Zhou king was so strong that nobody was able to oppose him.

Furthermore, the phrase *mie li* in the bronze inscriptions has long puzzled scholars. Recently Tang Lan suggests that it means 'to record merit'. This interpretation seems to work well for the term as it appears on bronzes. In fact, the 'Wu Gui' inscription says that after a military victory, 'wang *mie* Wu *li*' (the king records the merit of Wu) and conferred upon Wu clothes, 50 strings of shells, 50 fields of land at Han and 50 fields at X (Tang Lan, 1986: 480–1; Hsu and Linduff, 1988: 184–5). The 'Shi Yu Gui' also documents: 'The king went to Shanghou.[41] Master Yu went with him. The king examined Yu's records and bestowed upon Yu bronze' (ibid.: 265).[42] In short, all the evidence testifies the kings' tight control over their officials throughout the Western Zhou and the standard behaviour expected of those local lords was to follow the king's orders.

Finally, the increasing size of the Zhou territory encouraged the development of bureaucratization. In fact, approximately 900 Zhou official titles were found in both bronze inscriptions and literary sources of that period (Zhang Yachu and Liu Yu, 1986). Although they still have different explanations of the specific functions of those titles, scholars agree that the governmental system in the Western Zhou must have been much more sophisticated than that of the Shang. Otherwise, it would not have been able to maintain such a huge empire (Keightley, 1969: 154–74; Hsu and Linduff, 1988: 227–57). For instance, the reconfirmation procedure was well developed from the beginning of the Zhou. At the death of the old king, the officials in charge of certain areas had to be reconfirmed by the new ruler, while the new officials had to be reconfirmed by the king after the death of the old officials.[43] The new oath acted as a confirmation of the important relationship between the king and his appointees. Descriptions of such events can be found in chapters such as 'Gu Ming' and 'Kang Wang Zhi Gao' of the *Shang Shu*. In the enthronement of King Kang, all the officials were said to march in procession to present gifts as a token of their submission to the new ruler (Legge, 1865: 544–68). A bronze inscription also recorded a similar ceremony, in which numerous lords were ushered into the court as royal audience in the capital Hao (Chen Mengjia, 1955b: 111).

By the mid-Western Zhou there were not only regular departments or ministries such as the *San You Si* or the Three Ministries, but also signs of distinctions between the private aspects of the royal family and the public sector of the government. The specification of functions derived from the king's need to rationalize his control, but at the same time it also implied the king's increasing concentration of power. This process of differentiation of positions continued into the Eastern Zhou period, and eventually reached its apex in 221 BC when Qin Shi Huang Di built up the first empire in Chinese history through a highly developed bureaucratic system. Therefore, bureaucratization was one of the most important Zhou legacies which deeply influenced the development of Chinese history.

Based on some of the above features, some scholars argue that the *fengjian* system qualifies Western Zhou as a feudal society. First, according to their understanding, the *ceming* ritual resembles very much the investiture ceremony in feudal Europe (Qi Sihe, 1981: 50–2). When the king ordered a lord, it meant that 'a contract was made', and the reconfirmation of the new king was the renewal of the contract (Hsu and Linduff, 1988: 177). This does not seem to be a correct interpretation of the concept of *ceming,* because it fails to convey the specific meaning of the *ceming* ceremony in the Zhou context. In fact, the appointments of the king were no more than sacrally sanctioned introductions into the hallowed community of the Zhou nobility. As Wheatley has convincingly argued, there was no indication of 'contractually determined obligations on the part of the lord in return for a fief' (Wheatley, 1971: 121).

Secondly, it is true that the appointees were required to fulfil certain tasks, but almost every appointment in the world has requirements of some kind. It is certainly not permissible to classify all the appointments in economically and socially different systems as feudal. As repeatedly stressed previously, an important variable of feudalism is its personal nature of association and its military origin. Hence, investiture in medieval Europe chiefly implies a legal obligation between a feudal lord and his vassal.

By contrast, the Zhou *ceming* resulted from a system of kinship groups, and the appointments of the Zhou king were patriarchal by nature. It was nothing but a mode of social and economic organization, which was congenial to the spread of agriculture in Zhou times. The alignment with kinship relations explained the absolute power of the king and the stability of the society. Thus it is not the secular contractual arrangements but sacred family loyalty which constitutes the essence of the *ceming* ritual.[44] This meaning of the *ceming* only belongs to the Western Zhou *fengjian* system. From this standpoint, a Zhou official should be called a courtier, not a vassal, because he had only a certain degree of administrative, not political, autonomy. It is therefore misleading to say that the Zhou introduced feudalism in China. The complex contractual and legal concepts of European feudalism were absent or at best poorly developed (Wheatley, 1971; Gernet, 1982: 53; Huang, 1988: 16).

Thirdly, if the *ceming* is understood as feudal investiture, it will not reflect the proto-bureaucratic nature of the king's appointments. The appointees were certainly not professionals by modern standards, since they had not only administrative, but also military duties, such as the defence of territory. In addition, they were appointed not because of their ability, but because of their kinship relationship with the king. Notwithstanding, it will not be inappropriate to define them as functionaries,[45] since their responsibility was to carry out the Zhou rituals and the king's orders.

Fourthly, the idea of a feudal Zhou also comes from the belief that, as in feudal Europe, a strictly hereditary aristocracy existed in the Western Zhou. To make their arguments more plausible, some scholars often quote phrases from the bronze inscriptions, such as 'succeeding to the position of your ancestors' or 'have charge of the former colleagues of your father' (Chen Mengjia, 1956d: 113–14). Since all appointments were based on blood relationship, once the old official died it was possible that his son would resume his responsibility, for the king would like to give the position to those whose fathers had faithfully served him before. After all, they were the only people the king trusted. Nevertheless, there was no legal guarantee that they would definitely assume their fathers' positions, because the power of their entitlements was always in the hands of the king.

Moreover, if they held hereditary posts, it would be difficult to explain, first, why those officials had to pay homage to the king regularly; secondly, why the king kept the jade token during their visits until their missions were satisfactorily performed; thirdly, why the reconfirmation of appointments was compulsory. Many examples indicate that the king did reserve the power to revoke his previous appointments. Otherwise, it would not have been possible for the kings to maintain the Zhou empire for centuries (Creel, 1970: 396). The 'Qi Ding' inscription records that the queen Wang Jiang gave Qi three fields which previously belonged to a certain lord Shi Lu (Tang Lan, 1986: 225–6).[46] The 'Da Gui' documents that the king conferred upon Da an area formerly controlled by another official, Pei Kui:

> The king cried out to Master Hu to summon Da, bestowing him the area of Pei Kui. The king ordered Shan Fu Shi to tell Pei Kui: 'I (the king) order Da to be in charge of your area'. Kui answered: 'I dare not to be greedy' (ibid.: 434–5).

Pei Kui handed back the land immediately, according to the king's instruction. In the 'Da Ke Ding' inscription, among many fields given by the king to Ke there was a piece of land which previously belonged to a certain official called Jing (Guo Moruo, 1958: 121a).[47] It is, therefore, difficult to say that those conferrals were permanent.[48]

Finally, the temporary nature of the king's appointments was also reflected in the promotion system. For example, the 'Mian Zun' inscription records that the king went to Zheng.[49] After examination of Mian's record, the king was satisfied and appointed him to be *Si Gong* or the Minister of Works in the region (Tang Lan, 1986: 369).

We are fortunate to have two other bronze inscriptions which may well belong to the same family. The inscription on the 'Mian Gui' says that the king promoted Mian to be in charge of the western regiment (ibid.: 372), while the 'Mian Fu' inscription records that the king increased Mian's responsibility 'to succeed Zhou Shi to administer the foresters' (ibid.: 373). Although we do not have any other definite knowledge about these two people, the undeniable fact is that the latter was replaced by the former.

Another example of promotion can be found in the two bronze inscriptions associated with the Ke family. Previously Ke was only a chief cook, as the meaning of his name indicates (Guo Moruo, 1958: 88a; Li Yanong, 1962: 734; Keightley, 1969: 208). Apart from the 'Da Ke Ding' in which Ke was given a great amount of land with people, the 'Xiao Ke Ding' inscription also reveals that the same person was promoted again to be in charge of the eight regiments in Chengzhou, the eastern capital (Guo Moruo, 1958: 123a–b; Wang Guowei, 1959: 887–8; Hsu and Linduff, 1988: 231–2).[50]

In summary, first, there is little evidence in the *fengjian* system which exclusively relates to feudalism. The Western Zhou was a society in which the kings depended on rituals to reinforce mutual dependence among individuals. The kinship combined political and familial authority in the hands of the kings. This was confirmed by the elaborate ceremonies including conferrals of different gifts, from clothes and wine to land and people.

Second, the *ceming* ritual was nothing but an absolute order from the king to build and garrison new towns to increase his political and economic control (Yu Xingwu, 1964; Du Zhengsheng, 1979: 22–31; Li Zhiting, 1981). The power enjoyed by the Zhou king was much greater than that of the suzerainty in feudal Europe. Instead of constituting a contractual relationship between a lord and a vassal, both the appointment and supervision systems routinized by the Western Zhou king reflected an early beginning of bureaucratization in Chinese history. The idea that the country is an extension of the king's family[51] explains both the nature of the Zhou *fengjian* and its great influence on traditional Chinese mentality.

3   AGRICULTURE IN THE WESTERN ZHOU

How did the Zhou carry out their agricultural activities? Many scholars argue that individual farming had become predominant by that time (Fan, 1947; Eberhard, 1965; Hsu and Linduff, 1988). Since manorial economy was one of the important features of European feudalism, some even claim to have found evidence of its existence in the Western Zhou (Lu, 1962: 143–68; Zhang Yinlin, 1966: 21–36; Qi Sihe, 1981; Fu Zhufu, 1980: 67–85).

In this section, however, I shall contend that there is no evidence, either archaeological or literary, to suggest an extensive existence of individual farming in the Western Zhou. On the contrary, clan-based collective farming was the main form of production and evidence will be provided to indicate that collective farming implies communal landownership in the Western Zhou.

The argument that individual farming seemed impossible in the Western Zhou is supported, in the first instance, by the fact that the level of technology was still very low. As indicated in the first section of this chapter, metallurgical iron had not been discovered by that time, and the available material does not indicate that cattle or other draught animals were used in farming. Therefore, agricultural tools were merely one step beyond the primitive standard (Beida Lishixi, 1979: 167). Without further improvement in quality and variety, it is difficult to see how an individual farmer could feasibly carry out all the agricultural activities himself. It is even doubtful whether he could produce enough for his family's consumption, let alone pay tribute to the rulers.

Under these circumstances it seems likely that only the kinship organization enabled people to overcome natural adversities by working together in the fields. Anthropological studies reveal that communal agricultural activities, albeit in different forms, were still carried out among some of the Chinese minorities in pre-1949 China (Chen Zhenzhong, 1987: 54–78).

Secondly, almost all the classic literature unambiguously talks about large-scale collective farming. The most representative record can be found in the poem 'Yi Xi':[52]

> Oh, King Cheng
> Has given order to you (officers in charge of agriculture).
> He asks you to lead on those farmers
> To sow many grains of many kinds.
> Quickly take your implements (*si*)[53]
> To cultivate the land all over the (area of) thirty *li*.[54]
> Grandly perform your ploughing
> Ten times a thousand are the pairs (*ou*)[55]
>
> (based on Karlgren, 1950b: 244).

Other poems have similar accounts of the collective agricultural activities. For instance, the 'Cai Shan' says: 'Richly the grain is heaped up, / Myriads and hundreds of thousands, and millions (of sheaves) / We make wine and sweet unclarified wine; / We offer it to ancestors and ancestresses. / And so we consummate the many rites. / Fragrant is the food, / that is the glory of the state' (based on Karlgren, 1950b: 251). Similarly, the 'Feng Nian' says: 'What a harvest, we have plenty of millet and rice. / There are high granaries / for myriads and hundreds of thousands and even millions (of sheaves)' (based on Karlgren, 1950b: 245). These poems clearly indicate the existence of massive agricultural activities in the Western Zhou. An individual household definitely could not produce such a huge amount of millet and rice.

In addition, they also reveal that communal activities played an important role in the social life of that period. People not only worked together, but also performed rituals of ancestor worship for their blessings. Through regular ceremonies, solidarity was maintained within the lineage. This supports the explanation that each lineage could well be the basic unit of production in the Western Zhou. Collective farming itself does not necessarily mean that land must be collectively owned. But, if we take into consideration the fact that no contemporary documentation suggests the existence of either private landownership or any other form of ownership, it is highly plausible that the above literary record supports the thesis that land was practically owned by the kinship community in the Western Zhou. This argument is confirmed by the available bronze inscriptions. For instance, the 'Zai Gui' inscription reads:

The king said: 'Zai, I order you to be *si tu*. Be in charge of the *ji tian*. I bestow upon you a woven dark robe, a red apron, a banner with a jingle bell, and Chu and Zou Ma (officers). Take five *yuan* of bronze. Use them in my service' (Tang Lan, 1986: 448).

What is *ji tian*? Scholars agree that *ji tian*[56] may allude to the ceremony of the sacred field (Chen Mengjia, 1956a: 504; Yang Kuan, 1964: 225; Yu Xingwu, 1964: 153). It was originally a Shang tradition and a fertility ritual in which the whole lineage tilled the ground together. Oracle-bone inscriptions reveal that the Shang kings led similar rituals to symbolize the opening of the agricultural year.

Divining on the day *jihai*. Crack-making: 'The king is going to offer libation and till (*ji*). He should continue to go (Jia, 3420 (i)).

Three thousand people should till (*ji*) (Cui, 1299).[57]

The bronze inscription on the 'Zai Gui' indicates that the *ji tian* ceremony was practised by the Zhou as well. The 'Ling Ding' inscription further supports such a suggestion:

The king held a magnificent *ji* ceremony, and tilled in the field of Qi… (Tang Lan, 1986: 230–1).

This accords well with the descriptions in the *Shi Jing* and other classical literature. For example, the 'Chen Gong' says:

Oh, you ministers and artisan officers,
Be attentive in your tasks.
The king will give[58] you the achievement (of a good harvest).
He has come himself to scrutinize you.
. . . .
Thanks to the heaven,
There will be another harvest.
[The king said:] ' Order our *zhongren*;
Prepare your spades and hoes'.
(based on Karlgren, 1950b: 244).

The *Guo Yu* or the Discourses of States also confirms that the *ji tian* was practised in the Western Zhou (Guo Moruo, 1959: 8).[59] Therefore, it seems clear that the kings went to the field mainly for ceremonial purposes,[60] but the custom of the whole lineage working together was preserved as the main method of cultivation. Although the specific content of the *ji tian* is not known, the above evidence does reveal that the Western

Zhou agriculture was conducted under the control of the kings and their officers, namely, the so-called *si tu* in the above 'Zai Gui' inscription (Masubuchi Tatsuo, 1960: 301; Sato Taketoshi, 1962: 387; Keightley, 1969).

Who were those *si tu*? What were their functions? Both bronze inscriptions and literary sources indicate that they were 'ministers of land'.[61] When mentioned in the *Shang Shu* and the *Shi Jing, si tu* was placed directly below the prime minister (Legge, 1871: 322; Karlgren, 1950a: 46). Undoubtedly, they occupied an important position in the Zhou hierarchy. According to a recent study, the title of the *si tu* existed at the governmental level as well as at the local level (Zhang Yachu and Liu Yu, 1986: 8–10). They were responsible not only for the *ji tian*, that is, the organization of field work,[62] but also for other activities. For instance, some bronze inscriptions indicate that the king ordered different *si tu* to be in charge of his other properties. As the 'Mian Fu' records, the king appointed Mian to be *si tu* in charge of the gamekeepers, foresters and herders of the park of Zheng (Guo Moruo, 1958: 90a). Whenever there were land disputes, *si tu* would be asked to solve the problems. Two inscriptions on recently excavated bronzes mention the participation of two *si tu* in the land exchanges between Qiu Wei and other lords (Tang Lan, 1986: 459–63).

Moreover, *si tu* were also courtiers, assisting at the kings' appointments of others. The 'Wu Hui Ding' records that *si tu* Nan Zhong assisted at Wu Hui's appointment ceremony (Guo Moruo, 1958: 151a–b), while the 'Yang Gui' documents that *si tu* Shan Bo assisted at Yang's appointment as *si gong* ('minister of works') (ibid.: 158a).

Finally, some *si tu* were nominated as commanders of the king's troops. The 'Li Fang Yi' is a good example. The relevant part reads:

> The king... said: 'Have charge of the royal ranks of the six regiments and over the *san yu si:* the *si tu, si ma* and *si gong*.' The king ordered Li, saying: 'Have charge of the cultivation done by the six regiments and the eight regiments at the same time' (Tang Lan, 1986: 481–2).

Another inscription documents the king's appointment of Nangong Liu to be in charge of the herding of the six regiments in Yang and Da X as well as the agricultural affairs of Xi, Yi and Yang (Yu Xingwu, 1964: 152-5).

We are poorly informed as to how many troops of this kind existed during the Western Zhou, but the above appointments show, first, that it was one of the Zhou kings' great concerns to place those troops under the control of their trusted people. Secondly, in order to keep such a large territory, the Zhou kings had to ensure that, in addition to the defence of the country, the military forces should carry out farming, presumably to support themselves (ibid.: 155).[63] Therefore, clan-based farming was not the only collective activity. The agricultural production by military forces also played a crucial role in successfully maintaining the Western Zhou empire.

The often quoted evidence in support of a possible existence of individual farming is the poem 'Qi Yue':[64]

> In the seventh month the Fire Star possesses the meridian;
> In the ninth month clothes are given out....
> In the days of the third [month] we go to plough;
> In the days of the fourth, we take our way to the hills;
> All our wives and children carry food [to us]
> In those southern acres;
> The inspector of the field comes and is pleased...
> With the Spring days the worms begin;
> And the oriole utters its song.
> The girls take their beautiful baskets,
> They go along those small paths;
> They seek the soft mulberry [leaves];
> The days of Spring lengthen;
> In crowds they gather the white southernwood
> (based on Karlgren, 1950b: 96–7).

The poem gives a fairly detailed picture of farmers' year-round activities, especially that of agriculture. However, it cannot substantiate the claim that the farmers should be considered as serfs (Wu Qichang, 1966: 60; Hsu and Linduff, 1988: 349–50). First, the poem has been dated at either the end of the 'Chun Qiu' period or a much later time (Guo Moruo, 1957: 114). If it is true, it cannot be used to describe the Western Zhou.

Second, it seems closer to the meaning of the whole text, if we understood it as a description of lineage-based collective activities. Otherwise, it will not mesh with most evidence provided by both bronze inscriptions and other classical literature, which suggest an existence of massive collective farming in the Western Zhou.[65]

Third, since Hsu admits that *ougeng* was the standard method of farming during that period (Hsu and Linduff, 1988: 351), an individual farmer was not able to work by himself in the field, because there had been no substantial improvement in agricultural tools since Neolithic times. This clearly implies that each Western Zhou farmer did not have his own assigned piece of land, and that he could not make most of the decisions on production. Instead, he had to cultivate fields together with others. This has been confirmed by anthropological studies on the social and economic organizations in some pre-1949 Chinese minorities (Chen Zhenzhong, 1987: 54–78). Hence it is difficult to conclude that the verse adopts the point of view of a farmer (ibid.: 349).

A closely related question is whether the well-field (*jing tian*) system existed in the Western Zhou. Many scholars give an affirmative answer, but almost all their arguments are based on literary works of much later times such as the *Zhou Li* (Lu, 1962: 148–56; Yang Kuan, 1965: 114, 190, 124; Keightley, 1969; Guo Moruo, 1976: 243–48; Hou Jiaju, 1983: 11–30; Hsu and Linduff, 1988: 350).

Consequently, there is confusion about what this system was really like. Although much effort has been made, scholars still find it difficult to make their explanations compatible with the contemporary Western Zhou material. For example, Western Zhou literature used three terms to describe conditions of land: *xin, zi* and *yu*.[66] This three-year cycle within which lands were rested and cultivated is said to be closely related with two different descriptions of well-field systems in the *Zhou Li*. The first version reads:

> In case of the nonchanging land,[67] each [peasant] household should be given 100 *mu*; in case of the once-changing[68] land, each household should be given 200 *mu;* and in case of the twice-changing land, each household should get 300 *mu* (*Zhou Li zhushu*, 10/9a; Ho, 1975: 53).

However, according to the second version:

> In case of the upper-grade land, each male adult should be given 100 *mu*, together with 50 *mu* of *lai;*[69] any extra male adult [of the household] should be given the same amount. In case of the medium-grade land, each male adult should be given 100 *mu*, together with 100 *mu* of *lai*; any extra male adult should be given the same amount. In case of the inferior-grade land, each male adult should be given 100 *mu*, together with 200 *mu* of *lai*; any extra male should be given the same amount (ibid.: 15/9a; Ho, 1975: 53–4).

It is hard to believe that the above descriptions are sufficient to prove the existence of a well-field system in the Western Zhou. The reasons are manifold. In the first place, as indicated above, the *Zhou Li* is a very controversial work. Although it may contain elements deriving from antiquity,[70] it was probably first written by scholars in the second half of the Eastern Zhou period (771–221 BC). Later on it was tampered with by scholars of the Former Han dynasty (206 BC–25 AD) (Wheatley, 1971: 156–7). We certainly cannot rely on people to tell us what exactly was going on several centuries before.

Secondly, the discrepancy between these two versions seems to have paralyzed many scholars who seek to offer a satisfactory explanation. A seemingly plausible interpretation is that the first version might have existed in the highlands, while the second one may have been applied in the low plains of north China, 'where the soils are somewhat less fertile' (Ho, 1975: 54). This is a precarious statement, since there is no clear reason to believe that the soils in the low land of north China were less fertile than those of the highlands.

Thirdly, the problem is complicated by a further discrepancy between these two versions of land allotment and those of latter times.[71] Which version is closer to reality? Or which version was practised in which part of China? No definite answer has yet been given.

Fourthly, if well-field systems of any kind had prevailed in the Western Zhou, it would have been documented in one way or another in the contemporary literature. The Zhou rulers never failed to record other important aspects of their social and economic organizations. Nevertheless, no contemporary materials unambiguously indicate that such a land distribution structure ever constituted the economic basis of the Western Zhou society. It is not surprising, therefore, to find that scholars in favour of a well-field system cannot rely on the contemporary sources to support their argument. At this point, it is perhaps worth stressing that there are scholars who deny a possible existence of a well-field system in the Western Zhou: Fan Wenlan, (1947: 69), Wu Qichang (1966), Qi Sihe (1981). One of their main reasons against such a system is the confusion created by those different versions in the literature of much later times.

Finally, all versions used the word *mu* to describe the amount of land each household or male peasant should receive. If we turn to the Western Zhou sources, *mu* was never used as a measure word by that time. In most cases, the character *tian* (field) was used to indicate a certain amount of land. For instance, The 'Duo You Ding' reads:

> The king told lord of Wu: 'You have pacified the Jing Garrison. I enrich you, awarding you lands and fields (Shaughnessy, 1983–5: 55–6).

The 'Ke Xu' inscription also records that the king gave Shan Fu Ke 'fields and people' (Guo Moruo, 1958: 123a), while the inscription on the 'Bu Qi Gui' documents that Bu Qi received, among other gifts, 'ten fields' (ibid.: 106).

Obviously, *tian* was only a rough indication. It seems very likely that the Western Zhou still lacked a standard calculation system for land. Thanks to the expansion of the territory, the Zhou kings had plenty of land at their disposal, especially in the first half of that period. Under such a condition, it seemed unnecessary to have a precise division of land, and the concept of private property was certainly foreign to the individual members of the Zhou lineages. According to specialists, when the word *mu* appeared in the Western Zhou bronze inscriptions, it simply referred to 'flourishing field'. It was from the mid-Chun Qiu period (722–481 BC) that *mu* was gradually used as a measurement for land (Zhang Yinlin, 1966: 72). By that time, the increase in both population and technology intensified the use of land, which naturally required a smaller unit to draw clear boundaries.[72]

In conclusion, it seems that the well-field system existed only in the imagination of later scholars and became more precise with the passage of time. The mistake of scholars in supporting an extensive existence of family farming seems to lie in their misunderstanding of the unique features of the Western Zhou *fengjian* system. Moreover, they uncritically accept the descriptions of unreliable literature. Consequently they take fictions as reality. Unless future archaeology and further research provide definite evidence to suggest a substantial revision of the above arguments, it seems certain that most agricultural activities were carried out collectively either by kinship organization or military troops in the Western Zhou.

Does the massive-scale labour in the Western Zhou mean that it should be defined as a slave society? Orthodox Marxists in China such as Guo Moruo have no doubt about this. For them, collective labour of any kind in the ancient world must imply the existence of slavery. Is this contention plausible? I shall proceed to provide some preliminary arguments against the above claim in the next section.

4   THE STATUS OF THE LABOUR FORCE

Both bronze inscriptions and literary sources use many words to indicate different groups of people such as *renli*, *wangren*, *chen qie* and *shuren*. These people undoubtedly constituted the main labour force in the Western Zhou. For scholars who intend to meet the requirements of Stalinist Marxism, which demands a period of slavery in the development of every society, the above groups of people must be slaves. By contrast, for scholars in favour of a feudal interpretation of the Western Zhou, these people were serfs, albeit with Chinese characteristics.

This section will present contemporary evidence to examine the above two claims. I shall seek to argue that both fail to reflect the real status of those groups of people in the Western Zhou. Moreover, I shall contend that massive-scale agricultural activities do not necessarily mean that the labourers must be slaves. I shall finally propose that the concept of 'menial' seems to have characterized the common features of those groups of people.

The first group of the major labour force consisted of those non-Zhou peoples. They have been called 'racial slaves' by Guo Moruo (1954a: 13), and many others (Li Yanong, 1962; Yang Kuan, 1965: 73). According to these scholars, after each military victory, the Zhou would transform different subjugated tribal peoples into slaves, and compel them to carry out slave labour (Hou Wailu, 1955: 59–63; Guo Moruo, 1954a: 14; Jin Jingfang, 1983). The often-quoted passage to support this claim is from the *Zuo Zhuan*:

> After King Wu conquered Shang, King Cheng completed the establishment of the new dynasty, chose and appointed his relatives of intelligent virtue, to act as bulwarks and screens to Zhou.... Six tribes of the Yin people – the Tiao, the Xu, the Xiao, the Suo, the Chang Shao, and the Wei Shao clans – were ordered to lead the clans of the main branches, the remote as well as the near, to conduct the multitude of their connexions, and to repair with them to Zhou, to receive the instructions and laws of the duke of Zhou. They were then charged to perform duty in Lu. ... Lands were apportioned to the lord of Lu on an enlarged scale, with priests, superintendents of the ancestral temple, diviners, historiographers, all the appendages of city-state, the tablets of historical records, the various officers and ordinary instruments of their offices.... To Kang Shu[73] there were given ... seven clans of the people of Yin – the Tao, the Shi, the Fan, the Yi, the Fan, the Ji and the Zhongkui.... Both in Wei and Lu they were to commence their government according to the principles of Shang, but their boundaries were defined according to the rules of Zhou.... To Tang Shu, there were given nine clans of the surname Huai,... He was to commence his government according to the principles of Xia, but his boundaries were defined by the rules of the Jung (CQZZZ, 1981: 1538–9).

This is a fairly detailed description of the Zhou *fengjian* system. Kang Shu and Tang Shu were appointed to rule areas previously belonging to the Shang and the alleged Xia dynasties. Apart from the specification of their responsibilities, both were given land and peoples.

The reliability of this passage is confirmed by the 'Kang Hou Gui' inscription. It refers to the fact that Kang Shu was indeed ordered to establish a city-state in Wei after King Wu conquered the Shang dynasty (Chen Mengjia, 1955a: 161–4; Tang Lan, 1986: 33). Many other bronze inscriptions indicate that the Zhou kings gave people of different tribes to other appointees as well. For instance, the 'Shi Bei Gui' documents that the king conferred upon Bei 300 people from the Yi and the Yun tribes in recognition of his promotion (Guo Moruo, 1958: 139b). The 'Jing Hou Gui' records the king's bestowal upon Jing of people from three places: Zhou,[74] Dong and Jong (ibid.: 39a).

The above records reveal no more than the fact that people were assigned to follow the kings' appointees to set up new city-states. There is no clear indication that people in the newly conquered regions were condemned to slavery. If they had become slaves, as some scholars want us to believe, why were Kang Shu and Tang Shu instructed to govern their areas according to the principles of the Shang and Xia respectively instead of the Zhou rules? A slave-owner is expected to impose his will on his slaves, not vice versa.

Furthermore, an investigation of the Zhou political philosophy will reinforce my argument that those non-Zhou peoples were unlikely to have been treated as slaves by the kings' appointees. As indicated in the previous section, the Zhou was a relatively small tribal state when it overthrew the Shang which had dominated a much larger area with more population than that of the Zhou.[75]

After the establishment of the new dynasty, the Zhou soon realized the importance of political propaganda in pacifying the subjects of the former Shang who refused to obey their rules. A theory was, thus, formulated to legitimize the replacement of the previous dynasty. It was known as the Mandate of Heaven (*Tian Ming*).[76] According to their theory, the law of the human world derived from Heaven (*Tian*) who created the human beings (Legge, 1871: 505).[77] The Shang were able to build an empire, because their founder, being a leader of ability and virtue, had received a mandate from Heaven.

However, the Mandate of Heaven must be justified by continued good government. Since the last king of the Shang did not care about his people, he failed to meet the requirements of Heaven. The Zhou Kings Wen and Wu, because of their virtues and good conduct towards their people, received the Mandate of Heaven.[78]

It is obvious that the Zhou did not regard themselves as conquerors of an alien people but inheritors of a common culture[79] and a Central Kingdom or *Zhongguo*.[80] To restore the Mandate of Heaven, the Zhou had to fight against the last vicious Shang king, not his people. From this perspective, the Zhou considered their reign as a natural continuation of the Shang level of domination over the whole of China.[81]

If we follow this philosophy, it is difficult to believe that the Zhou had any intention to put heavy chains on their conquered people to work for them as slaves. In fact, they adopted very flexible, sometimes even tolerant policies towards the non-Zhou peoples. As the king claims in the *Shang Shu*:

> When I think clearly of the people, I see they are to be led to happiness and tranquillity. I think of the virtue of the former wise kings of Yin (Shang), whereby they tranquillized and regulated the people, and rouse myself to realize it (based on Legge, 1865: 395–6).

Consequently, when Kang Shu was appointed to rule over the Shang population, the king urged him to use the Shang elites in the local administration. According to the king, this was the best way to set up an example of respecting the people, which would eventually lead them to 'the enjoyment of plenty and peace' (Legge, 1865: 386, 416).

The employment of the former Shang elites has been confirmed by both bronze inscriptions and archaeological findings. As the 'Qiang Pan' inscription indicates, the ancestor of Qiang was a scribe-historian in the Shang court. Even after the fall of the Shang, Qiang family members continued the job for the Zhou kings.

> Our ancestor recited in Wei, at the time when King Wu conquered the Shang. Our great-grandfather was the historian of the Wei state and came to the court of King Wu. King Wu ordered the Duke of Zhou to assign him a residence at the Qizhou. Our great-grandfather served the king and the reign enjoyed his confidence. Our great-grandfather Zuxin gave birth to many of the descendants of many branches. He brought them blessings and happiness. To him we should offer sacrifices. Our father Yigong, wise and virtuous, engaged in farming and managed well, for no one uttered criticism of him. I, Shiqiang, who love my parents and my brothers, work hard all day and night. Qiang received grace from the king to cast this precious vessel. It is the fortune built by my forefathers that gave the Qiang their land. May good luck and blessings last until my hair turns white and my skin becomes white. May we serve our king well. May the vessel be treasured ten thousand years (Hsu and Linduff, 1988: 115; cf. Xu Zhongshu, 1978: 144; Tang Lan, 1986: 150).

At the Western Zhou remains of Chengzhou, the present city of Luoyang, archaeologists discovered approximately twenty Shang burials. The style of their tombs, the accompanying objects, and types of sacrifices, and so on, suggest that the Shang elites still practised their own customs (Guo Baojun and Lin Shoujin, 1955).

Furthermore, the Zhou allowed the Shang people to practise their old traditions such as the excessive drinking of wine, while the Zhou people would receive heavy punishment if found drunken (Legge, 1865: 412; Tang Lan, 1986: 448–50; Hsu and Linduff, 1988: 186). Even after the suppression of the famous Shang rebellion,[82] the Zhou king still appointed members of the deposed Shang royal lineage to be in charge of their people in the present eastern part of Henan Province (ibid.).[83]

A similar policy was adopted by the Zhou to manage other local tribal peoples, although they did not follow the exact model for cultural diffusion with these peripheral groups as they did with the Shang people. It is true that there were more differences between the Zhou and those outside groups, but the Zhou were not keen on showing their cultural superiority. In general, their strategy was to join hands with the local people, and to introduce the *fengjian* system to modify the local political and economic structures. It seems that confrontation and high-handed suppression took place only when there were no other options (Hsu and Linduff, 1988: 191–2). Unsurprisingly, through intermarriages and cultural influence, the local leaders were gradually assimilated into the power elites, and their peoples were incorporated into one nation. From this viewpoint, the Zhou rule resulted from a coalescence of all the peoples in China. In this process the theory of Mandate of Heaven definitely played a great role in accommodating both the conquerors and the conquered. As Hsu and Linduff correctly point out, 'the differences between the Zhou and those whom they conquered were overcome through toleration and shared values, the result of acculturation – the Hua-Xia culture base – developed and continued' (ibid.: 152–3). Therefore, it is groundless to classify the non-Zhou peoples as 'racial slaves'.

The second group of people who have been defined as slaves were *chen* and *qie* (Hou Wailu, 1955: 64–7; Li Yanong, 1954: 50–6; Guo Moruo, 1954a: 67, 94, 96; 1976: 175–6).

Chen has two meanings in Shang oracle-bone inscriptions. First, as a noun, it refers to the king's high officials, who carried out the king's orders.[84] Second, as a verb, it means 'to be subject to' (Chen Mengjia, 1956a: 505). Bronze inscriptions from the beginning of the Zhou or shortly after confirm that *chen* had the same functions in the Zhou court (Keightley, 1969: 192–7). At the same time *chen* acquired the new meaning of a captive or prisoner (Li Yanong, 1964: 66–7; Keightley, 1969: 197). For instance, the 'Zhong (Fang) Ding' reads:

The king conferred on the grand scribe Xong the land of Ke. The king said, 'Zhong, these people of Ke were sent in to perform services. They were given to Kong Wu to be *chen'* (Guo Moruo, 1958: 16a).[85]

From the first half of the Western Zhou, *chen* is mentioned together with another word, *qie*. The earliest inscription in which the two words are connected is found on the 'Fu Zun' (Li Xueqin, 1985: 473). The 'Da Ke Ding' also contains such a phrase: 'I give you the households of Jing and the fields of Bu on mount Chun, together with their *chen qie*' (Guo Moruo, 1958: 121a). The 'Shi Hui Gui' records that the king ordered Shi Hui to be in charge of, among others, '*chen qie* of the eastern and western Pian'[86] (Guo Moruo, 1958: 114a).

It is very difficult to tell the exact meaning of *qie*, since we are poorly informed about their specific functions. Judging from the context, there can be no doubt that they were the female equivalent of *chen* who were servants of the Zhou officials. The fact that they could be given to others shows that the transfer of people did happen in the Western Zhou. Nonetheless, this is not a sufficient condition to define those *chen* and *qie* as slaves. First, nowhere can we find any indication that they could be killed at will.[87] Secondly, there was no convincing evidence to testify that a slave market existed by then.[88] Thirdly, all the inscriptions seem to show that the *chen* and *qie* refer to people of different areas, and probably there were even different degrees of status among them. As Keightley suggests, the geographical origins of those households may imply that they belonged to various regions before being given to a new official (Keightley, 1969: 97–9). If this is true, the *chen* and *qie* were no more than a general concept, which may have a wide range of meanings, since they were used in a variety of different situations. Hence it will be arbitrary to categorize them all indiscriminately as slaves.

It is more plausible to assume that the *chen* and *qie* were in a similar situation to the junior members of the Zhou sub-lineages. In fact, they would all be assigned to the new administrators, when the king appointed his relatives to start a new settlement. Therefore 'menial' seems to be the nearest possible word to indicate their identity with the provisos discussed above.[89]

Moreover, there are many other groups of people who have been classified as slaves, such as *ren, shuren, zhongren, li, renli, baigong, wangren* and *pu* (Li Yanong, 1954: 50–6; Guo Moruo, 1954a: 16, 19, 67, 94, 96; 1976: 237, 239, 243, 250). Two bronze inscriptions are perhaps the most famous among the often-quoted examples: the 'Da Yu Ding' and 'Yi Huo Gui'. The former records a promotion of Yu. Apart from giving numerous gifts such as wine, clothing, chariots and horses, the king said:

'I confer upon you: *bangsi*, 4 *bo*; *renli* from *yu* to *shuren*, 659 *fu*. I confer: *yisi wangchen*, 13 *bo* and *renli*, 1050 *fu*' (Guo Moruo, 1976: 241).

The 'Yi Hou Gui' documents the king's appointment of Ze as the administrator in charge of the area of Yi:[90]

> The king…said: 'I order you to be in charge of Yi. I award you… land and forests 200;… I give you *wangren* 17 [?] surnames to live in Yi. I give you *bo* of Zheng, X [and their] *fu* 1050 [?]. I give you *shuren* of Yi 616 [?] *fu* (Tang Lan, 1986: 152).

It is extremely unlikely that most of the people mentioned above can be qualified as slaves. Scholars still disagree about the specific functions of each group, although different interpretations are proposed. In the first place, we do not know whether there is any difference between *li* and *renli*. Some scholars think that *renli* should be read separately as *ren* and *li,* while others consider it as one concept. Consequently, they are defined as either bondsmen, or registered labourers, or prisoners of war.[91] We are not in a position to decide which one of the above versions is correct, since each interpretation undoubtedly comes from a different understanding of the same sources.

Secondly, what is the meaning of *wangren*? Some scholars take them as 'descendants or retainers of the Shang king' (Barnard, 1958: 24; Keightley, 1969: 218), while others regard them as belonging to the Zhou people (Xu Fuguan, 1974: 10; Li Xueqin, 1985: 14).

Thirdly, we are not better informed about the status of the *pu*. They have been translated as chariot-drivers (Legge, 1865: 583; Keightley, 1969: 221). However, Hsu believes that they were servants at the beginning of the Zhou, but they acquired the function of military officers later on (Hsu and Linduff, 1988: 232–3).

Fourthly, the concept of the *shuren* has been defined as serfs or commoners (Barnard, 1958: 33; Lu, 1962: 146; Hsu, 1965: 11; Eberhard, 1965: 22–3; Keightley, 1969: 219, 232, 253; Wheatley, 1971: 125; Fu Zhufu, 1980: 52–67), while Guo Moruo classifies them as slaves (Guo Moruo, 1954a: 95–6). Zhao Gongxian even argues that the *shuren* belonged to the Zhou aristocracy (Zhao Guangxian, 1980: 76).

Fifthly, the most arbitrary decision is perhaps to regard the *bo* as slaves, since there is no suggestion, from either bronze inscriptions or historical literature, that their status could be so low. *Bo* seemed to be heads of some tribes or clans during Shang times (Chao Lin, 1982). As mentioned above, even after the conquest of the Shang, Zhou kings recruited the Shang people with either governmental skills or writing abilities to serve the new regime. This implies that former Shang tribal or clan heads could be well-respected by the Zhou. The inscription on the 'Yi Hou Gui' confirms that it was not unusual for the Zhou kings to assign the Shang *bo* to help his appointees, presumably, to manage the new garrisons in some remote areas. It is, therefore, unlikely that the *bo* would have been treated as slaves by the Zhou (Lu Wenyu, 1991: 25; cf. Shirakawa Shizuka, 1973: 3-68; Hsu and Linduff, 1988: 254–5).

Finally, if we follow the theory of the Mandate of Heaven, it is unlikely that the Zhou rulers would have treated most of the above people as slaves.[92] Since it was based on a moral obligation to bring about prosperity, peace and happiness to the people through good government, one of the most crucial features of this theory was the Zhou's belief that the appointment of Heaven was not constant. Thus Heaven was difficult to rely upon, and its appointment was subject to dismissal, if dereliction of duty and crime occurred. The fear of losing their Mandate of Heaven was reflected repeatedly in both the *Shang Shu* (Karlgren, 1950a: 59), and the *Shi Jing*. For example, the 'Wen Wang' verse reads:

> The Heaven is not constant.
> ....
> Always striving to accord with the will of Heaven.
> So shall you be seeking for much happiness.
> Before Yin lost the multitudes,
> Its kings were the assessors of Heaven.
> Look to Yin as a beacon,
> The great Mandate is not easily preserved.
> ....
> Do not cause your own extinction.
> Display and make bright your righteousness and name
> (based on Legge, 1871: 430–1).

On the one hand, it is obvious that the Shang lost their right to rule, because they had lost the trust of their people. As the final judge, Heaven, who wishes the people to have a happy life, appointed the virtuous Zhou king to take away the Shang's Mandate (ibid.: 505–7).

On the other hand, the poem also suggests that it was possible for the Zhou to maintain their power, if only they could follow the will of Heaven. From this point of view, human effort became the ultimate determining factor in the theory of the Mandate of Heaven.[93] The will of Heaven is nothing but the will of the people, which is manifested in the interaction between the ruler's performance and the support of the ruled. The 'insight' and watchfulness of Heaven are expressed through the 'insight' and watchfulness of the people. Therefore, the best way to preserve the Mandate of

Heaven for the Zhou rulers was to act in accordance with the interests of the people. Otherwise, people would have the right to overthrow them. In short, the theory of the Mandate of Heaven gave people equal political status. If this is true, there is no reason to believe that the above groups of people were all treated as slaves by the Zhou rulers.

Equally, the speculation that some groups of the above people, such as the *shuren*, *shumin* and *zhongren*, should be defined as serfs cannot be substantiated by the available evidence. First, we are not able to identify precisely their functions in Zhou society. The contemporary materials can be interpreted so differently that any definite conceptualization seems impossible at the present stage. For instance, the *shuren* is usually thought to refer to the Zhou masses (Karlgren, 1950b: 196–7), but some evidence suggests that it also includes recently conquered non-Zhou peoples (Guo Moruo, 1958: 34a).

Secondly, as indicated in the preceding section, the low level of technology rendered it impossible for individuals to cultivate the land by themselves. According to the above investigation, collective farming was still predominant in the Western Zhou. Lineage members were working together for themselves as well as for the whole community represented by the king and his administrators.

Finally, since they had to move from one place to another at the decree of the king, those people did not have permanent places to stay, and hence there was no customary right to protect them. They were merely tools of the Zhou king to carry out his expansionist schemes.

To summarize: first, there can be no doubt that the transfer of different subordinate groups of people did take place in the Western Zhou. Most were assigned to the king's appointees together with other gifts, as either rewards for their military victories or part of the conferrals. This was one of the prominent features of the so-called *fengjian* system, and the introduction of such a social and economic organization into the conquered regions was probably the best way to spread the Zhou's control. Therefore, to a great extent, the success of the Zhou expansion lay in its ability to intermingle with the local people. Through intermarriage and mutual cultural influence, the non-Zhou people were gradually integrated into the Zhou social, political and economic system. Consequently, the Zhou established a vast empire from an obscure Neolithic background, and a common identity of Chineseness or *huaxia* also evolved out of this process.

Secondly, there is no clear indication that those transferred people could be traded freely in slave markets, once they were given to the officials. This implies the latter's lack of the full power of a slave-owner. Thirdly, both the limitation and ambiguity of the original sources prevent us from reaching a conclusive agreement about the specific status of each group of those people. Unless future archaeology provides more substantial materials, discussions at the present stage seem unlikely to yield fruitful results.

However, we do know that all the labourers in the Western Zhou were certainly not free, because the concept of freedom as understood by the ancient Greek citizens did not exist. Moreover, they must have occupied different points on the spectrum of servitude, depending on their skills and social positions. But it is hard to find a precise English concept to define those subordinate groups of people, since their functions uniquely belonged to the Zhou *fengjian* system. The concept of 'menial' is suggested to characterize the most common aspect of those people, although it is far from satisfactory.

Of course, we cannot exclude the possibility that some transferred people were treated as domestic slaves, but domestic slaves of different kinds existed throughout Chinese history until the fall of the last dynasty, the Qing (1616–1911). This is definitely not a sufficient condition to classify a society as being dominated by slavery. If some scholars insist on using the concept of slavery to refer to the organization of labour in the Western Zhou, its meaning has to be redefined. It should refer to a hierarchical system in which people, based on kinship relations, work both for the community and the state.

Not unexpectedly, this brings us back to what Marx had called the 'general slavery' of the state (Marx, 1964: 95). In most cases, it was the Zhou king who had the power to assign the subordinate people to his own kinsmen. To be sure, this 'slavery' is obviously different from the one in ancient Greek and Roman times. Therefore, it is a misunderstanding of the Zhou *fengjian* system to define the main labourers in the Western Zhou as slaves.

Fourthly, the existence both of political suppression and economic exploitation in the Western Zhou is beyond question, but the method used by the Zhou was much subtler than that of the slave-owners in ancient Greece and Rome. The Zhou must have realized that it would be much easier to mobilize the masses to carry out corvée labour of all kinds, if they could convince the people that their interests and the king's were the same. From this perspective, there was probably no better invention than the theory of the Mandate of Heaven, which could disguise the real purpose of the Zhou ruling class. The theory was hypocritical by nature, since it was created to justify the rule of the Zhou over the Shang and other indigenes. However, its humanistic face compelled the Zhou not to enslave their conquered people through sheer brutality. People were told to work for the benefits of the whole community as well as for themselves, but their fruits were reaped mostly by the few who claimed to be the heads of their lineages.

Finally, there is no convincing reason to believe that some groups of people such as *shuren* can be considered as serfs, since their functions were quite different from the serfs in feudal Europe. They not only worked in the fields on a massive scale, but were also ordered to move from one place to another to carry out the Zhou kings' expansionist schemes.

5 The Great Transition in the Making: the Eastern Zhou

The Eastern Zhou refers to the period which began with the first year of the reign of King Ping (771 BC) and ended with the death of King Nang (256 BC). However, most scholars extend this period to 221 BC when China was reunited by Qin Shi Huang Di (the First Emperor of Qin, 259–210 BC). Within the Eastern Zhou two distinctive, though not chronologically connected, periods can be located. They are known as the Chun Qiu period (the Spring and Autumn period, 722–481 BC) and the Zhan Guo period (the Warring States period, 476–221 BC),[1] to confirm the time-span of two classical history books: the *Chun Qiu* (the Spring and Autumn Annals) and the *Zhanguo Ce* (the Strategy of the Warring States).[2]

Scholars agree that great changes took place in all aspects of Chinese society during the Eastern Zhou period, but their interpretations of those changes are radically different. Some believe that the period symbolized a transition from slavery to feudalism (Guo Moruo, 1976: 254, 313; 1978: 24), while others claim that a new political system based on a centralized government replaced the feudal relationships by the end of the Chun Qiu period (Du Zhengsheng, 1979; 1984; Yang Kuan, 1980; Hsu and Linduff, 1988: 180–1; Bodde, 1990: 27–8). This chapter and the next, however, seek to demonstrate that those changes represented a transitional stage from a society dominated by the AMP to a new social and economic system in which different modes of production coexisted. The first section of this chapter will contain a brief discussion of the political developments during that period, and I shall argue that the dissolution of the traditional clan system took place much more slowly than scholars have maintained. The second section will focus on the major technological developments of that period with the purpose of supporting the argument that political changes can be chiefly accounted for by changes in technology.

In comparison with the previous times, a much larger quantity of literature written by the Zhou contemporaries is available to us. For the Chun Qiu period, the *Zuo Zhuan* will be used as the main source. In addition, I shall cite some materials from other works such as the *Guo Yu* or the Discourses on the States.[3] For the Zhan Guo (the Warring States) period, there is less dispute about the authenticity of some important classics. Nevertheless, explanations will be given, whenever these sources are used as evidence.[4]

Furthermore, since archaeological discoveries have their own unique value, they will be utilized as much as possible to support my arguments.

1 THE DISSOLUTION OF THE *FENGJIAN* SYSTEM

As indicated in the previous chapter, the original purpose of the *fengjian* system, that is, the establishment of city-states throughout China, was to support and protect the Zhou empire. Political stability was achieved through the practice of *li* or the traditional moral codes and the *ceming* system during the Western Zhou period. Nevertheless, the diffusion of technology from the Wei centre to the periphery increased the strength of local lords who had both political and economic obligations to the Zhou king. After the removal of the capital to Luoyang in 771 BC the Zhou king gradually lost his control over the local lords and was eventually reduced to a position similar to that of the weaker city-states. Consequently, the system was no longer regulated by rituals. The whole empire became a stage on which the strong city-states competed to subjugate the neighbouring weak and small ones. The *Zuo Zhuan* documents about 540 wars in approximately 259 years (Lewis, 1990: 36, 261). By the mid-Chun Qiu period (around 600 BC), the old social order of the Western Zhou had already started to crumble, but it took several centuries to disappear completely (Qi Sihe, 1981). In this process the small city-states at first tried to preserve their identities by making alliances with the powerful ones, but were eventually conquered by the latter.[5] The territorial appropriation and state extinctions are well documented in the historical literature. There were about 140 city-states at the beginning of the Chun Qiu, but no more than 13 states[6] of any importance survived the wars by the beginning of the Zhan Guo period (Gu Donggao, 1888; Walker, 1950: 20). The city-state of Qi is said to have conquered 35 others, while the city-state of Chu destroyed 51 (Sima Qian, 1972: 509–758; Guo Moruo, 1976: 302; He Hao, 1982: 55–62; Li Xueqin, 1985: 170–88). Interstate relationships became a pure power struggle. The old ethical code was invoked only when it might give a semblance of legality to power politics (CQZZZ, 1981: 465, 1018). In 403 BC there were only seven large states waging wars against one another for the control of the whole of China. By 221 BC the state of Qin eliminated the rest and established the first centralized bureaucratic empire in Chinese history. It laid a solid foundation of a new type of society for the subsequent dynasties.

What are the dynamics behind all these changes? In order to provide a definite answer to the question, I should start the investigation from the changing nature of the political structure during the Eastern Zhou. At the beginning of the Chun Qiu period the whole society was still organized within a ramified kinship structure which provided a conventionalized pattern for all social relations (Hsu, 1965: 1). This was particularly true in the clan-based style of government. Broadly speaking, there were two grades of ministers, the *qing* and the *daifu*,[7] within the ruling class of each city-state. They were almost exclusively relatives of the local lords and were designated to certain areas to form new sublineages. They had the right to impose taxes in the areas under their control. In the course of time, the improvement in cultivation methods, the growth of population, and the relative geographic isolation[8] encouraged a desire for independence by the heads of sublineages. As a result, the most powerful clans sought to secure not only solid economic bases, but also the loyalty of their junior branches in their struggles to expand their domains.

Eventually some became strong enough to contend for power with their local lords. Although all originally came from the same lineage, this did not prevent them from fighting with each other. The *Zuo Zhuan* faithfully documents many such examples. The first year entry of the book tells us that Duke Zhuang in the city-state of Zheng gave an area with fertile land to his younger brother Gung Shu.[9] However, when the latter thought that he was strong enough, he initiated a war in order to replace his elder brother and ended in failure (CQZZZ, 1981: 10–14). In the city-state of Jin, Marquise Zhao conferred upon Heng Shu the area in Qu Wu (ibid.: 93–5).[10] Together with his children, Heng Shu built up his power which enabled his grandson Wu Gong to successfully replace the previous Jin ruler within 67 years (ibid.: 203, 240, 1237). Therefore, ministers became powerful not because they held a position in the government, but because they were the heads of important sublineages, who controlled part of the territory within each city-state (Hsu, 1965: 78). For example, Jisun Shi was in control of governmental affairs in the city-state of Lu, not because he was the chief minister, but because he was the head of the most powerful clan (Yang Kuan, 1965: 192; CQZZZ, 1981: 1502).

As a result, while in theory they were the subjects of the Zhou king, all the local lords enjoyed a *de facto* political sovereignty over their territories. It was not the case in the previous times, because no contemporary records indicate that the local lords in the Western Zhou had the power to disobey the order of the kings.[11] Inevitably, many old noble clans underwent decline in the process of constant wars. New clan leaders usurped the power of different city-states for a while before they, too, were replaced by the heads of other clans. The interrelationships among different ministers were complicated. Sometimes they formed alliances for their preservation; sometimes they fought one another, to increase their own power (Hsu, 1965; Tong Shuyie, 1980; 1987). But the overall tendency was the transfer of power from the hands of the rulers to those of powerful ministers. For example, in the city-state of Lu[12] three clans (Ji shi, or Ji clan, Meng shi, or Meng clan, and Shusun shi, or Shusun clan) shared the power to manage the government affairs at the beginning of the Chun Qiu period (CQZZZ, 1981: 986–7, 1261–6). Later on, power was monopolized by Ji shi alone (ibid.: 1487, 1658).

Meanwhile, in the city-state of Jin, the Marquise of Jin conferred upon each of his three sons a large area. This eventually brought the state into a long period of civil war over the problem of succession (ibid.: 240–1; Maspero, 1978: 234–6). For some time six clans became powerful, but only three survived the mutual exterminations by the beginning of the Zhan Guo period (Wen Wu, 1976: 94; Tong Shuyie, 1980: 329–30; CQZZZ: 1981: 1167–9, 1237, 1493–4). In the city-state of Zheng governmental affairs were interchangeably controlled by the Han clan and Si clan (CQZZZ, 1981).[13] Therefore, the centre of the political stage was occupied by the competitions between clans in the Chun Qiu period.

Under such conditions, political reforms were not only necessary, but inevitable for the local lords to preserve themselves. One after another new political institutions were introduced in some city-states and gradually replaced the old. Traditionally, Guan Zhong (d. 645 BC)[14] is believed to have been the first Legalist or *fajia* in ancient China to have implemented some reforms, but we do not have reliable sources to confirm to what extent his policies had changed the old system in the city-state of Qi (the *Guo Yu*: 1959: 77–86). According to the *Zuo Zhuan*, Zi Chan[15] was the first statesman in Chinese history to introduce a set of laws, into the city-state of Zheng in 536 BC (CQZZZ, 1981: 1274).[16] Twenty-three years later the city-state of Jin made its own law codes on the tripods (CQZZZ, 1981: 1504). In 501 BC the city-state of Zheng put into effect a new system of law written by a person named Deng Xi (ibid.: 1571). Since the *Zuo Zhuan* does not give further information, the content of those codes are not known to us. It is plausible that they belonged to a code of penal laws, which were created at will and served as the coercive tools of the state (Needham, 1956: 544; Ames, 1983: 125–41).[17]

Consequently, the process of expansion and consolidation of a strong power called for the creation of new administrative offices, while the filling of these offices with new trustworthy officials in turn promoted more concentration of the rulers' power. From this viewpoint, the tendency of the time was by and large a movement from a government based on customary morality toward a state with rulers possessing absolute power (Feng Youlan, 1952: 312). The old clan ties began to disintegrate.

Some scholars maintain that this process was completed by the end of the Chun Qiu period. Since then, China entered a period of feudalism (Guo Moruo, 1976: 316; 1978: 24). However, this assertion is not correct, because it oversimplifies the complicated nature of this transition. The transition of political control from the clan-based system to a growing bureaucracy could not take place in ancient China in such a short span of time. There were many complex factors determining the speed of change. For example, a considerable progress in technology would have had to occur to support the increasing expenses of state apparatus (Walker, 1950: 26). As will be indicated in the next section of this chapter, the economic conditions before the Zhan Guo period were still not sufficient to provide for such a financial burden.

Therefore, despite the ups and downs of different clans in the fierce struggles for power, the traditional kinship organization was still functioning as the basic social foundation of most activities throughout the Chun Qiu period. This hypothesis is borne out, in the first instance, by the fact that *zu* (clan) was still one of the most, if not the most, commonly used word to refer to a group of people as a unit in the *Zuo Zhuan*.

Secondly, there is much evidence indicating that even towards the end of the Chun Qiu period, when ministers killed their opponents, very often they would slaughter all the latter's clan members. For instance, in 547 BC Qing Feng, the Minister of the Left in the city-state of Qi, took advantage of dissensions within the Cui clan and exterminated them all (CQZZZ, 1981: 1137–8). Nevertheless, this did not save him from danger. Only one year later, several other clans formed an alliance and killed all his clan members when he was hunting. He immediately fled to the city-state of Wu after hearing of the news (ibid.: 1148–9). In 515 BC following an order from Zi Chang, Yan Jiangshi killed all the members of three other clans who were considered the best men in the city-state of Zheng. Later Zi Chang had Yan Jiangshi and Fei Wuji as well as all the members of their clans killed to please other clans (ibid.: 1488).

Finally, ancestor worship and sacrificial ceremonies are two of the most important features of a clan-based society. According to the *Zuo Zhuan*, they still played a crucial role in both social organization and people's lives during the Chun Qiu period (ibid.: 860–1). The blood relationship was often emphasized, although the purpose became increasingly political (ibid.: 1175, 1180).

The destruction of the time-hallowed clan society did not take place until China entered the Zhan Guo times. The process was accelerated chiefly through the radical reforms introduced by the so-called Legalists.[18] Li Kui, who was the Chancellor in the state of Wei around 400 BC was the first well-known person to have taken strong measures to implement Legalist ideas.[19] In addition, he is said to have written *Fa Jing* (The Book of Law) containing six statutes. None of them has been preserved, but scholars agree that this Legalist tradition was enriched and supplemented by Shang Yang, or Lord Shang[20] who was in control of the state of Qin from 361 to 338 BC (Duyvendak, 1928: 14–15).[21] From 359 BC onwards, Shang Yang introduced a series of radical reforms.[22] One of his successful reforms was to divide the state into new administrative units known as *jun* (prefecture) and *xian* (counties) (Sima Qian, 1972: 2232).[23] In contrast with the old *fengjian* system, the king now directly appointed governors and magistrates to manage those units, and the selection of the functionaries was largely based on the ability of the people rather than on their blood relationship (Hsu, 1965: 92). They were paid by the central government and could be dismissed at the will of the king.

This inevitably increased social mobility. It now became possible for commoners to climb the ladder and become ministers or senior officials.[24] It is difficult to detect the changes of speed in every state during the Zhan Guo period, but there was a perceptible trend which definitely encouraged both bureaucratization and the recruitment of able people regardless of their origin (Yang Kuan, 1980). Consequently, the kinship system lost its relevance as the basis of organizing every aspect of society.[25]

Moreover, there is little doubt that such development must have called for order and discipline, although we cannot draw an accurate picture of how such a system functioned in reality. The archaeological discovery of Qin law strips at Shuihudi in Hubei Province in 1975 throws some new light in this respect. As many bamboo strips explicitly indicate, inspection, merit ratings and annual reports on the conduct of officials in almost every field of administration had been developed to a highly sophisticated level in the state of Qin (Hulsewe, 1985; Shuihudi, 1990).[26]

In retrospect, the Qin system by the end of the Zhan Guo period was the logical continuation of a pattern which had been developed since the beginning of the Eastern Zhou. Its new model of state administration represented a threshold in Chinese history.[27]

Therefore, the establishment of the *jun xian* system throughout China after 221 BC symbolized the end of the transition from a clan-based society to a territorial one at the national level. One of the chief reasons for this political change was undoubtedly the self-interest of the autonomous sublineages in the Zhou city-states. The ramification of the kinship system not only created a multi-level society, but also developed to an extent beyond the expectation of its inventors. The heads of the new sublineages were eventually powerful enough to challenge the authority of their rulers, and not surprisingly, they expanded their power at the expense of the old aristocratic clans. From this point of view, the Zhou empire offers one of the best examples in which familial relationships caused its initial territorial expansion as well as its final destruction.

But, what enabled the autonomous sublineages to promote their own interests? In the ensuing section I shall seek to argue that the political development in the Eastern Zhou was deeply rooted in technological changes.

2   THE ADVANCE OF TECHNOLOGY

In this section I shall provide evidence to demonstrate that the dramatic technological[28] advance accounted for the emergence of the new political system in the Eastern Zhou. Since the emergence of iron[29] is one of the most crucial factors that improved productivity in ancient world, I shall first examine the gradual process of popularization of this important metal in China. Second, I shall discuss several other technological changes brought about, directly or indirectly, by the wide use of metallurgical iron. They include the development of irrigation projects, and the invention and popularization of the iron plough.[30] Finally, an attempt will be made to calculate population growth in the Eastern Zhou. I shall contend that demographic changes by the end of the period can be considered as evidence testifying to the fact that technological progress had greatly transformed the whole society.

Guo Moruo argues that iron had already been discovered during the Shang dynasty, and by the end of the Chun Qiu period iron tools had replaced other primitive implements made of shells, stone, wood and bones. Since then, China entered a period of feudalism (Guo Moruo, 1976: 254, 313). This argument has been generally accepted in China (Yang Kuan, 1980).

On the other hand, some scholars outside China believe that iron tools were not extensively used before the Han dynasty (Hsu, 1965: 130; Chang, 1968: 316), while others contend that iron implements became available to the majority of peasants only after the mid-Zhan Guo period. As Ho argues, 'there had been no basic changes in agricultural techniques' from Neolithic times to about 400 BC (Ho, 1975: 82–3). Although he claims elsewhere that he does not intend to project the Zhou system backwards to remote antiquity (ibid.: 51), Ho has no doubt that 400 BC was a true watershed in the development of technology in Chinese history (ibid.: 83). According to him, the fact that many iron-made farming tools were discovered in the tombs of the mid-Zhan Guo period seems merely a coincidence. However, I shall argue that the above hypotheses do not account for the slow but steady spread of iron tools in ancient China.

As described in the previous two chapters of this book, the Shang and Western Zhou represented the great Bronze Age in Chinese history. But four pieces of bronze artefacts have been found to be inlaid with iron (Gettens *et al.*, 1971; Beijingshi wenwu guanlichu, 1977: 1–8). That is why iron is believed to have been discovered in the Shang dynasty.

Nevertheless, Guo and others fail to make clear that all four artefacts have been scientifically proved to be made merely of meteoritic iron (Li Xueqin, 1985: 317). Undoubtedly, this discovery demonstrates that the Chinese had a considerable understanding of the nature of iron long before the Europeans. But, irrespective of this remarkable achievement, those iron blades were not the result of iron metallurgy. Thus it is difficult to imagine the wide use of this technology before the Western Zhou.

The earliest melted iron artefact was found at Shangcunling in Sanmenxia City of Henan Province in May 1990. It is an iron sword with a bronze handle, a jade face-guard and a set of inscribed bronze-ware. Many believe that it was made in Western Zhou times (Xiao Tong, 1991: 34; Wang Min, 1991: 34; Jiang Tao, 1992: 9–13), but it seems more likely to belong to the early Eastern Zhou period. The first reason is that archaeologists are still not able to identify the person who was buried with the iron sword in the tomb. It is, therefore, premature to conclude that it must have been a tomb of Western Zhou times only because the city-state of Guo, in which the iron sword was found, existed from the Western Zhou (c. 1015 BC) to the mid-Chun Qiu period (655 BC) (CQZZZ, 1981: 307–8). We certainly cannot exclude the possibility that the sword was produced in the latter period. Second, the styles of most archaeological finds in the same remains are quite similar to those discovered in other tombs dated to the early Eastern Zhou period. Unless iron artefacts which can be dated with certainty back to the Western Zhou are found in the future, it is reasonable to presume that metallurgical iron was only discovered around the early Chun Qiu period (Yu Yi, 1959: 64–5; Yu Weichao, 1991; Li Xueqin, 1991b).[31]

Although we are not able to date the iron sword precisely, this new discovery has great significance in helping us to resolve the controversy over the authenticity of some ancient texts. Previously, due to the lack of archaeological confirmation, scholars who believed the existence of cast iron in the Chun Qiu period often quoted a passage from the *Zuo Zhuan* to support their argument. It explicitly indicates that in 513 BC tripods inscribed with penal laws were cast with iron in the city-state of Jin (CQZZZ, 1981: 1504). The passage is traditionally accepted as the first reliable text in which the word *tie* (iron) is clearly used.[32] Li Xueqin even suggests that casting such tripods must have required very high skills (Li Xueqin, 1985: 318). This implies that people in Jin, if not in other city-states, must have had a long history of making simpler cast iron artefacts before 513 BC.

Nevertheless, this thesis had been challenged by some scholars since the Song dynasty (906–1279 AD). They believe that the word *tie* (iron) in this passage is not the original correct character. Quoting from another Zhou source, which happens to have a similar passage, they contend that another word *zhong*[33] should be in the place of *tie* (Li Xueqin, 1985: 318). Thanks to the latest finding in Sanmenxia City, this controversy has lost its relevance. For the very first time we are able to conclude with confidence that the Chinese had a definite knowledge about metallurgic iron before the mid-Chun Qiu period, without referring to this famous passage.[34]

Does this mean that the ancient Chinese were able to replace other relatively primitive implements with iron tools in both agriculture and other fields of production by the end of the Chun Qiu period? As far as we can tell from present archaeological finds, there is no convincing reason to believe that the above hypothesis advocated by Guo Moruo is well grounded (Guo Moruo, 1976: 254).

First, unless there is a compelling reason, people are generally not well motivated to spread new ideas or technologies, and this is particularly true for less developed societies. Among the most conspicuous examples are Chinese cast iron which antedated European cast iron by more than two thousand years and the Chinese crossbow which was never heard of in Europe for more than a millennium after its invention in China (Needham, 1958: 6; Ho, 1975: 366). Thus it seems not surprising that metallurgic iron artefacts which can be dated to the Chun Qiu period are found only in a few archaeological sites. Apart from their smallness in number and shape, they also lack variety (Huang Zhanyue, 1976: 68).[35]

Second, only a few tools can be classified as agricultural implements among the small amount of iron artefacts. The rest are mostly swords and knives (Li Xueqin, 1985: 320–2). In the context of the political situation of that period,[36] it is only natural that cast iron was at first mainly used to make weapons, since the rulers of all the city-states were preoccupied either with expansion or preservation of their territories. Although Li Xueqin, by citing other recent archaeological discoveries, argues that 'wrought iron, cast iron, and steel all existed' in the late Chun Qiu period (ibid.), the aggregate archaeological evidence so far is still meagre. It does not indicate unambiguously that iron tools were already widely used in agriculture by the end of the period.

Finally, if we turn to contemporary texts, it is not difficult to notice that the word *tie* is only sporadically used.[37] It must be more than coincidental that scholars in the Chun Qiu period paid so little attention to the development of iron technology. A plausible explanation of this phenomenon is that iron implements had not replaced other tools yet.

By contrast, the importance of iron implements is stressed by every contemporary scholar in the Zhan Guo period. For example, the 'Qingzhongyi' (the Light and the Heavy, Part B) chapter in the book the *Guan Zi* explicitly indicates that

> A peasant must have a plough, a spade, a sickle, a hoe, a mallet, and a bill hook. Then he becomes a peasant. A cartwright must have an axe, a saw, naves or hubs for the wheels, an awl, a chisel, a gouge, and an axle-tree. He then is able to make a cart. A woman must have a knife, an awl, a short needle and a long needle, then she can be (called) woman (The *Guan Zi*, 24: 2a–b).[38]

The above description indicates that iron tools became important not only in the process of production, but also in the daily life of ordinary people. This has been confirmed by the increasing archaeological discoveries of the recent decades. As Lei Congyun correctly summarises, 'the number, variety, and distribution of locations of iron artifacts all increased' from the beginning of the Zhan Guo period (Lei Congyun, 1980: 92; Li Xueqin, 1985: 323). They include objects of every kind, but most are implements of agricultural production. Spades, sickles of different types, digging sticks, rakes, picks, hoes, plough-shares and so on can be seen in most archaeological remains of that period throughout China. As Li Xueqin has illustrated in considerable detail, the aggregate excavations in the state of Yan, which was the weakest among the so-called 'Seven Strong States',[39] have indicated that iron metallurgy was surprisingly highly developed. The quantity, quality and variety of those artefacts, especially that of the agricultural implements, are far beyond previous expectations (Li Xueqin, 1985: 323–8).

What is more striking is that a large quantity of iron objects were found not only in the remains of big cities, but also those of the remote areas. An excellent example is the discovery of more than eighty artefacts, mostly farming tools, at a small settlement site of Lianhuabao in Fushun of Liaoning Province. Interestingly, the shapes of the iron implements there are identical with the Yan tools found in Hebei Province. The writer of the report is certainly correct in his conclusion: 'Unless the iron industry had become widely used, it would have been difficult to imagine that at a small site such as Lianhuabao there could have been found such large numbers of iron agriculture implements' (Wang Zengxin, 1964: 286–93; Li Xueqin, 1985: 326–7).

The recent discovery of the bamboo strips at Shuihudi of Hubei Province further supports the above conclusion. It clearly indicates that, first, iron tools were extensively used in agriculture in the areas under the control of the state of Qin (Shuihudi, 1990: 23, 38). In some cases the government even lent iron tools of all kinds to the commoners (ibid.: 44). Second, the government had officials in charge of both iron mining and implement production.[40] Specific regulations were made to control the quality and quantity of the production. Officials would be punished if they failed to meet government requirements (ibid.: 84–5; cf. Hulsewe, 1985: 112). Thirdly, the old and worn iron tools had to be recast (Shuihudi, 1990: 40; cf. Hulsewe, 1985: 53).[41]

In short, even if we cannot give a precise date as to when iron tools supplanted other primitive implements on a large scale, the above discussion does suggest that iron products were no longer rare and expensive by the mid-Zhan Guo period. Undoubtedly, this resulted from a gradual accumulation of knowledge and experience which had lasted for centuries.

The diffusion of metallurgical iron on an extensive scale was accompanied by great improvements in many other fields of technology. It is impossible to give an account of all technological changes brought about, directly or indirectly, by this 'magic' metal in ancient China. However, two important aspects warrant our special attention. They are the increased scale of irrigation projects and the utilization of iron ploughs in the Eastern Zhou period. Both are directly connected with the diffusion of iron technology.

According to the *Zuo Zhuan*, a reform was initiated by Zi Si who was the Chancellor of the city-state of Zheng in 563 BC. It was related to 'laying out the ditches through the fields' (CQZZZ, 1981: 981). This is probably the earliest documentation of irrigation in Chinese history. Soon afterwards, Zi Si was killed by members of five other clans, because the project is said to have damaged their interests. Therefore, it is not clear to what extent the project was carried out (Ho, 1975: 47).[42] Although other projects related to irrigation are also recorded in the *Zuo Zhou* (CQZZZ, 1981: 1107), it seems obvious that all of them were fairly small and easy to implement. Presumably they could have been done with rather primitive tools made of stone, wood, or even bamboo.[43]

Reliable evidence strongly suggests that the first large-scale irrigation network was carried out around the mid-Zhan Guo period. But it was the

third century BC which witnessed a dramatic increase of large-scale irrigation projects in China. One of the most famous examples is *Dujiangyan*
(Dujiang Dam). It was a great water-control system accomplished by Li
Bing when he was the governor of Shu[44] in the middle of the third century
BC (Chi, 1963: 66–9, 75–7; Sima Qian, 1972: 1407). This network established the basis of prosperity in the Chengdu plain. The complete system,
only slightly modified later, is still functioning today and the area has been
credited as 'paradise on earth' since then.[45] It is certainly not a mere
coincidence that large-scale irrigation projects were not only encouraged
by scholars, but also carried out since the mid-Zhan Guo period.
Technologically speaking, it was not feasible to organize such projects
unless highly sophisticated implements, most of which must have been
made of iron, were widely used by the peasants (the *Xun Zi*, 1979: 129).[46]
The scale of irrigation and flood-control projects was therefore largely
decided by the development of iron technology in ancient China. In short,
the Zhan Guo period witnessed an acceleration in the process of diffusion
of iron technology.

The same is true of the invention and spread of the iron plough. But,
since it is inextricably related with the utilization of draught-animals,
especially oxen, I shall discuss them together.

According to one legend, the plough was invented in remote antiquity
by a person named Shu Jun. He is said to be the grandson of Emperor
Yao's minister Huo Ji (the Lord of Millet) (Duyvendak, 1928: 4).[47] Based
on this assumption, some scholars argue that the use of the plough started
in Neolithic times in China, and that farmers in the Shang dynasty must
have used ploughs to till their fields (Guo Moruo, 1976: 188; Bray, 1984:
161, 164). Furthermore, oxen are said to have been commonly used in
farming by the end of the Chun Qiu period (Guo Moruo, 1976: 315; Yang
Kuan, 1980: 55; Qi Sihe, 1981: 85–94). There are two reasons to support
this argument. First, some Chun Qiu texts document that there were
people whose names were associated with both ox (*niu*) and tillage (*geng*).
For example, Confucius (551–479 BC)[48] had a disciple with such a name
(Confucius, 1983: 108–9; Yang Kuan, 1980: 56; CQZZZ, 1981: 1503).
Second, based on a single discovery of an ox sculpture with a ring through
its nose at Ligu Village in Hunyuan County of Shanxi Province, Yang
Kuan believes that the sculpture is a reflection of the popularity of oxen
being used for agricultural purpose (Yang Kuan, 1980: 56–7).

It is plausible that ploughs of some kind might have existed since the
beginning of Chinese civilization,[49] but it seems unlikely that they were
pulled by draught-animals before the end of the Chun Qiu period. First, it
is questionable to depend on such unreliable sources as legends alone to

support any argument unless it is borne out by archaeological discoveries. In this respect, the massive finds have not yet yielded solid evidence.

Second, since the Shang dynasty, oxen, among other animals, were chiefly used in different ritual ceremonies as sacrifices. According to the *Zuo Zhuan*, this tradition continued to exist in the Chun Qiu period (CQZZZ, 1981: 963, 972, 983).

Third, after a systematic study, etymologist Xu Zhongshu has convincingly argued that the semantic element for 'ox' does not occur in any of the characters associated with tillage in the Chun Qiu period (Xu Zhongshu, 1930: 11).

Fourth, the only archaeological evidence used by Yang Kuan is not definite enough to support his thesis, since it is subject to different interpretations. Therefore, we have to wait for further archaeological discoveries to determine whether Yang Kuan's speculation is correct or not. To treat the evidence as generously as possible, we can conclude that even if oxen had been used in agriculture, it must have been sporadic before the end of the Chun Qiu period.

Finally, as carefully examined in the preceding two chapters, the *ougeng* (pair cultivation) constituted the main, if not the only, method associated with field-work in both the Shang and Western Zhou. People tilled land with tools made of stone, shell, wood or bones, etc.[50] Evidence indicates that this traditional cultivation was still practised in different parts of China towards the end of the Chun Qiu period (the *Li Ji*: 14\12a; 17\13a; the *Guo Yu*, 1959: 218; CQZZZ, 1981: 1379–80; Confucius, 1983: 184). As will be discussed in the ensuing pages, the method of *ougeng* lost the precondition of its existence only after the oxen-drawn iron-ploughs began to be used extensively.

The above lengthy discussion about the ox-plough is necessary, because scholars agree that the way it spread must have been closely related to the development of iron technology (Sun Changshu, 1964: 72). Though we cannot exclude the possibility that oxen might have been used incidentally in farming before the invention of iron plough-shares, the massive utilization of oxen does not seem to have occurred until the peasants could afford iron plough-shares. Soon after that, or at the same time, the importance of oxen must have been realized by the peasants, since the iron plough-shares were much heavier than the previous tools. That could be crucial in motivating them to encourage the wide adoption of oxen for cultivation.

When did this process of diffusion finish? Many classical texts explicitly tell us that oxen and iron ploughs were extensively used from approximately the mid-Zhan Guo period onwards. As Mencius (372–289

BC) confirms, it was quite common for peasants to employ 'iron imple-ments for ploughing the fields' in the state of Teng[51] (*Meng Zi shushu,* 5B\1b; cf. Mencius, 1984: 102). It is worth stressing that Teng was only a small and weak state struggling for survival by that time. It seems reason-able to assume that all the powerful states of that time must have been at least as technologically developed as the state of Teng (the *Guan Zi,* 23\1a–7a).

However, classical works have not convinced every scholar. Some maintain that the ox-plough did not play any important role in Chinese agriculture until the later Han dynasty (Hsu, 1965: 130; Chang, 1968: 316).[52] They were certainly correct to cast serious doubt on the reliability of some historical accounts, since archaeology had not provided sufficient evidence for a sound confirmation by the time they wrote. But the increas-ing amount of recent archaeological finds has verified the authenticity of the related literary sources. For example, iron plough-shares dated to the second half of the Zhan Guo period have been discovered in many parts of China. Moreover, the Shuihudi bamboo strips have offered the most con-vincing evidence to end the controversy. They unambiguously indicate first, that oxen were extensively used for the purpose of agriculture towards the end of the Zhan Guo period (Shuihudi, 1990: 19–31, 38).[53] Second, draught-animals were privately owned by peasants (ibid.: 51, 130). Third, the government seemed to possess a great number of oxen, and detailed regulations were set up to check the physical conditions of oxen and other animals. Inspections by the government agencies were carried out four times a year. The responsible officials would be punished if oxen were found too thin, and rewarded if the conditions of oxen satisfied the requirements of the government (ibid.: 22, 86–7). Such sys-tematic management must have resulted from long government experi-ence. It was an indication that draught-animals had already been used in agriculture in the state of Qin well before its unification of China in 221 BC.

Therefore, the wide use of iron plough-shares by the mid-Zhan Guo period symbolized a breakthrough in the development not only of plough-ing technology, but Chinese agriculture in general.

There were many other concomitant changes in agricultural techniques largely resulting from the accumulation of experience. For example, one may first cite that evidence clearly indicates that green and other fertilizers were commonly used in the second half of the Zhan Guo period (Chen Liangzhuo, 1973: 20–1; the *Xun Zi,* 1979: 146–7; Bray, 1984: 293).[54] Second, contemporary literature identifies different soils and informs people about how to improve the quality of land. Some works repeatedly

emphasize the advantages of ridging and furrowing to control soil mois-
ture (the *Xun Zi*, 1979: 146). Third, the timing of planting and harvesting
is clearly stated and many famous scholars strongly advised rulers of different states not to interfere with the busy agricultural seasons (the *Guan
Zi*, 23\16b–17a; 188; the *Xun Zi*, 1979: 128). The *Lushi Chun Qiu* or
Master Lu's Springs and Autumns[55] even contains a detailed discussion of
how to plant cereals in properly spaced rows (Wang Yuhu, 1981: 11,
29–31). This is confirmed by the Shuihudi strips, which indicate how to
preserve the grains and the amount of seeds to be used for grains of different kinds (Shuihudi, 1990: 29; cf. Hulsewe, 1985: 41–2). Finally, double-
cropping is definitely referred to for the first time by Xun Zi (c. 298–238
BC) (the *Xun Zi*, 1979: 147)[56] and crop rotation is also said to have existed
around the same period (Wang Yuhu, 1981: 22). Both improvements
demonstrate the intensification of cultivation (Mencius, 1984: 8). In short,
it is no exaggeration to say that the great technological changes in the
Eastern Zhou period, especially those of the Zhan Guo times, are comparable with those of ancient Greece.

Is there any way of measuring the results of those changes? One of the
best indicators certainly is the output of grains per acre. However, the earliest reliable documentation comes from the Yinqueshan strips, which can
be dated to approximately the mid-Zhan Guo period.[57] It shows that the
average production of one medium-quality *mu* was about two piculs[58] of
grains (Yinqueshan, 1985: 146). There is some difference between this
figure and the one preserved in the *Han Shu*, which offers an estimate of
1.5 piculs of grains per *mu* in around 400 BC. But these figures have little
significance for present purposes, since there is no reliable data for the
average yields per *mu* in pre-Zhan Guo times for comparison.[59]

It is difficult to quantify the increase in material wealth, but evidence
from available sources does reveal an overall qualitative improvement of
standards of life by the end of the Eastern Zhou. There is much evidence
to support this thesis, but I would like to concentrate here on one single
aspect: population growth. No serious scholar will disagree that increase
of population results, in most cases, from progress in technology.

However, as an allegedly Polish joke goes: 'Only the future is certain,
because the past is always changing.' As in any other research subject in
Chinese history, opinions have been divided on the number of people in
ancient China ever since scholars first attempted to give a definite answer
to the question. No doubt the subsequent discussion will not be the last
one on the subject, but I shall be more than happy if it can convince the
reader that dramatic demographic changes did take place in the Eastern
Zhou period.

How dramatic was the increase in population? Chinese scholars believe that there were about four and half million people in the Chun Qiu period, while the population at the end of the Zhan Guo times is said to be 30 million (Ning Ke, 1980: 3–19; Chen Zhongyi and Zhao Wang, 1983: 116). Nonetheless, a careful examination of the available historical texts will reveal that the population during the Eastern Zhou was much smaller than scholars want us to believe.

According to the *Zuo Zhuan*, at the beginning of the Chun Qiu period, the capital of each city-state was approximately two square kilometres, and within the control of each city-state there were so-called 'big cities'[60] that were about one-third the size of the capital. A medium-size one is said to be only one-fifth the size of its capital, while a small one should not exceed one-ninth the size of the capital (CQZZZ, 1981: 11–12). Archaeologists have identified some ancient city remains as capitals of the Chun Qiu period. One of them is near the present village of Niu in Houma of Shanxi Province. It was once the capital of Jin in the early Chun Qiu period and had a quadrangular enclosure with sides of 1340, 1100, 1740 and 1400 metres (Zhang Shouzhong, 1960: 11–14; Wheatley, 1971: 138). More city remains, believed to be the capital of Jin in the late Chun Qiu period, were also discovered by archaeologists in a place not far from the previous one. The original form of the inner enceinte is said to be a square with a side of 1100 metres. The outer enceinte was about two to three kilometres (Shanxisheng wenwu guanli weiyuanhui, 1959: 222–8; Wheatley, 1971: 140). These finds indicate that the real size of a capital was slightly smaller than is described in the classical texts.

It is unfortunate that archaeologists are still unable to provide an estimate of the population living in those cities, but it is possible to establish an upper limit to the number of people, depending on the size of those cities. Taking into consideration the area occupied by the rulers' palaces and ceremonial centres of all kinds, it seems plausible to presume that a Chun Qiu capital could accommodate no more that five to ten thousand people. This judgement is substantiated by historical sources, which indicate that some cities contained a population of a thousand families (Confucius, 1983: 38), while others reached approximately a hundred families (CQZZZ, 1981: 898).

Moreover, the number of towns each city-state possessed varied. While the stronger city-states might have more than ten, the smaller ones such as the city-state of Wei[61] possessed only two settlements apart from the capital (ibid.: 265–7). In 660 BC, when the city-state of Wei was defeated by a non-Chinese army, only 730 people survived the massacre. Under the help of the rulers from the city-states of both Song and Qi, Wei claimed to be a city-state again in a place named Cao.[62] By then the total population of the new Wei was merely 5000 (ibid.).

The above information gives the impression that most of the city-states were thinly populated, but this does not mean that there was no increase in population during the period in question. In fact, along with the technological development, more cities were built in formerly wild areas. As indicated in the previous section of this chapter, some ministers regarded their cities as being strong enough to challenge the authority of their rulers (ibid.: 1328–9). But this did not fundamentally change the overall situation in the first half of the period. For example, the southern part of the city-state of Jin is said to be a place where 'jackals dwelt and wolves howled' (ibid.: 1006), while in the powerful city-state of Chu much of its territory was still covered with wild grass (ibid.: 1339).

Furthermore, the scarcity of population is verified by the small number of armies in each city-state. The Wei army is said to have consisted of only 30 chariots[63] after being defeated by the non-Chinese. Several years later it regained its strength of 300 chariots (ibid.: 273). In 666 BC, the city-state of Chu waged a war on Zheng with only 600 chariots (ibid.: 241). With 700 chariots, Jin won a battle over a combined army from Chu, Chen and Zai in 632 BC (ibid.: 459–62). In 626–7 BC the army of the city-state of Qin wanted to make a surprise attack on Zheng. The soldiers were seen for the first time in a place not far from Zheng by a certain merchant, who was on his way to the Zhou (Luoyang) for business. The fact that the Qin army had travelled several hundred kilometres before being found by the Zheng shows that the area between the two city-states was sparsely populated (ibid.: 489–96). This can be supported by another episode, which says that nobody had lived in an area between the city-state of Song and that of Zheng[64] since ancient times. However, from around 495 BC Zheng built three settlements there (ibid.: 1599). This caused a war between the two city-states, which eventually neutralized the area again (ibid.: 1673–6).

But the most striking evidence seems to be the constant movement of those city-states from one place to another in the Chun Qiu period. The small city-state of Xu[65] is one of the best examples. Feeling unsafe near the city-state of Zheng, it first moved to a place named Yie, to the west of the present Ye County of Henan Province in 576 BC (ibid.: 872). A little more than four decades later, it moved eastward to the present Bo County of Anhui Province (ibid.: 1306). Within several years, it came back to Ye (ibid.: 1348). In 524 BC it moved again to the present Xishan County of Henan Province (ibid.: 1393). In less than twenty years it moved to the present Lushan County of Henan Province (ibid.: 1533). It is inconceivable for us to imagine how a city-state could keep on moving five times in seventy years, but what seems even more incredible is that the distance of its movements was well over one thousand kilometres. Moreover, nowhere are we informed that it was prevented from settling down in the new places. A plausible explanation is that few, if any, people lived around those areas. It is worth stressing that the region in which Xu moved about belonged to the so-called core area of the Zhou civilization.[66]

Finally, irrespective of the poor information, a rough estimate of population can be derived from the number of military forces recorded in the *Zuo Zhuan*. Towards the end of the Chun Qiu period, the strong city-states were known as 'the city-states of a thousand chariots' (ibid.: 716). However, this figure cannot be taken literally. In fact, Jin, once the strongest city-state (ibid.: 1353), is said to have had 4000 chariots, while Chu had a similar number (ibid.: 716). Since the total number of chariots throughout China was about 25 000, this means that there were about 500 000 people in the whole military force.[67] If we presume that one person in five had to serve in the army, which is a very high ratio, the population in China cannot be more than two and a half million.[68] In summary, although we are not able to calculate the exact population, the overall impression of the above account should leave no doubt that China was relatively thinly populated in the Chun Qiu period.

A great increase of population did not take place until the Zhan Guo period. According to Mencius, 'a city of three li on each side and outer walls measuring seven li' was commonplace in the mid-Zhan Guo period (*Meng Zi zhushu*, 4A\1a; cf. Mencius, 1984: 72).[69] Linzi, the present city of Zibo, is said to have had 350 000 people (Zhang Hongyan, 1988: 210).[70] Han Fei (c.280–233 BC), the great Legalist philosopher, says that it was normal to have five sons in a family and that a man usually had at least 25 grandsons before his death (the *Han Fei Zi*: 19/1a). This is compatible with the descriptions in the Yinqueshan bamboo strips, in which a family with five people is regarded as small (Yinqueshan, 1985: 145). The state of Qi was so densely populated that the 'sound of cocks crowing and dogs barking can be heard all the way to the four borders' (Mencius, 1984: 52; cf. Du Zhengsheng, 1984; Zhang Hongyan, 1988: 208–9).

The contemporary descriptions about the average size of a city is confirmed by archaeological discoveries. The city wall of Xia Du, the ancient city of the state of Yan near Yi County in present Hebei Province is said to be 8300 metres from east to west and 3930 metres from north to south (Huang Jingluo, 1962: 10–19, 54). In Qu Fu, the hometown of Confucius, archaeologists discovered the capital of the state of Lu. Its walls measured some 3.5 kilometres from west to east, and about 2.5 km from north to south (Zeng Shaoyu and Yi Huanzhang, 1959: 54). In the newly developed areas such as the present Changzhou of Jiangsu Province, a city wall is said to have been six kilometres long (ibid.: 146). All this indicates that the sizes of the cities in the Zhan Guo period were much larger in general than those of the previous period. Therefore, cities in the Zhan Guo increased significantly in number, size and complexity of plan.

Moreover, the number of soldiers each state possessed had dramatically increased. The strong states were by now known as 'the states of ten thousand chariots' (*Meng Zi Zhushu,* 2B\3b; 3A\2b; *Shang Jun Shu,* 4\5b; the *Guan Zi,* 1954: 185; the *Xun Zi,* 1979: 105; Yinqueshan, 1985: 127). It is not surprising that the scale of wars also became much larger in comparison with previous times. According to the *Xun Zi,* if an army of 40 000 to 50 000 soldiers won battles, it was not because of its strength, but because of the bravery of its soldiers (the *Xun Zi,* 1979: 259). The famous strategist Wei Liao[71] informs us that most states had at least 200 000 troops (Wei Liao Zi, 1979: 9; cf. Sima Qian, 1972: 2339). Given the aggregate evidence, it seems plausible that there were approximately four million soldiers, that is, at most 25 million people in all toward the end of the Zhan Guo period (cf. Wang Yumin, 1990: 41–2; Lewis, 1990: 60–1, 271).

It need scarcely be said that the rapid expansion of population can only be explained by the rapid increase of material wealth. Wealth in turn derives from the improvement of technology, that is, the development of the forces of production, which provides the possibility to increase productivity. Therefore, demographic changes in the Eastern Zhou period were facilitated, in the final analysis, by the development of the iron industry, which eventually revolutionized the whole of society.

But what specific changes did this technological revolution bring about with regard to economic relations? How did it affect traditional communal landownership in particular? The next chapter will seek to offer preliminary answers.

6 The Dynamism of Ancient China

As has been argued in Chapter 5, the advance of technology in the Eastern Zhou promoted economic development. As a result, dramatic changes took place in all aspects of relations of production. However, in this chapter I shall concentrate on the changing forms of landownership, because it was one of the most crucial factors in determining the economic development of ancient China. Inevitably, received understanding of many historical events will be critically reexamined, and new interpretations will be proposed whenever necessary. For example, I shall argue that the process of the emergence of private landownership in China was much slower and more complicated than has been described by scholars. The purpose of this chapter is to see whether the changes in the forms of landownership can indeed be accounted for by the improvement of technology in ancient China. The first section will be focused on the form of landownership in the Chun Qiu period. I shall argue that communal landownership still persisted throughout the period, although changes were already taking place in some city-states. In the second section I shall investigate how the process of transition from communal landownership to private landownership was accelerated in the Zhan Guo period. I shall contend that private landownership was eventually established and that the AMP ceased to be the dominant mode of production by the end of the period. From then on, China entered a new era in which different modes of production coexisted.

1 THE FORM OF LANDOWNERSHIP IN THE CHUN QIU PERIOD

Many scholars believe that private landownership had become predominant by the end of the Chun Qiu period. According to their analysis, this implies that slavery was supplanted by feudalism (Guo Moruo, 1976: 254; Yang Kuan, 1980: 130; Yang Bojun, 1981: 200). On the other hand, some scholars assert that the Chun Qiu period represented the end of Chinese feudalism (Hsu, 1965: 108; Du Zhengsheng, 1986). Nevertheless, I shall contend that both interpretations failed to reflect the reality of that period. As indicated in the previous chapter, iron tools were still rare and certainly beyond the reach of the majority of peasants during the Chun Qiu period. This is borne out by the *ougeng* method of cultivation documented in the historical literature.[1] Therefore, it is reasonable to presume that communal landownership was still prevalent by that time. In fact, the introduction of iron implements into peasants' life is the precondition for the majority of people to cultivate the land individually. This did not take place in the Chun Qiu period.

Moreover, the concept of private property seems unlikely to have existed during the Chun Qiu period, because land was abundantly available to a relatively small population. This also enabled different city-states to constantly move from one place to another, while continuing to adopt the same 'slash and burn' farming system inherited from their ancestors. As long as there was land available for free cultivation, there was no need for the concept of private property to arise.

Finally, a brief discussion of the taxation system in that period will also indicate that land was not yet privately owned. The evolution of different forms of taxation in ancient China is a complicated problem,[2] and scholars dispute on almost every relevant issue. However, no one seems to disagree that the Shang and Western Zhou rulers supported themselves out of the tribute from the local lords, who received their shares through a system known as *ji*.[3] According to the available sources, *ji* was still extensively practised by the end of the Chun Qiu period. For example, the *Zuo Zhuan* flatly tells us that 'the people of Yu[4] cultivate together (*ji*) on the public lands' in 524 BC (CQZZZ, 1981: 1397). Forty years later, from one of Confucius's remarks we know that the taxation system formulated by the Duke of Zhou was still in existence in the city-state of Lu (ibid.: 1667–10).[5] If the land had already been privately owned by then, such a method of both cultivation and taxation would have disappeared and Confucius would not have referred to it. Thus the establishment of private property must have been very gradual and complex. No simplification will reveal the dynamics of this process.

Nevertheless, three historical events have been regarded by scholars as evidence to prove the existence of private landownership in the Chun Qiu period. I shall, however, contend that the traditional interpretations of those events in their specific historical contexts cannot stand up to a critical analysis.

The first event is related to the capture of Duke Hui of Jin by the Qin troops during one of their battles in 645 BC. To save face, the Duke accepted others' advice and agreed to be succeeded by his son as the ruler of Jin. After that, according to the *Zuo Zhuan*, '*Jinzuo yuantian*' (CQZZZ, 1981: 361). The crucial word in the sentence is *yuan*, which means 'exchange'. The literary meaning of the sentence can be rendered as 'Jin makes exchange of land.' The ambiguity of the sentence has created diverse interpretations, but four of them are worth noting in this context.[6] First, some scholars believe that before this event the so-called well-field system[7] was the dominant form of landownership in Jin. According to their understanding, the sentence implies that Jin had carried out land reform, which abolished the old boundaries between different fields. After that, the well-field system no longer existed in Jin (Maspero, 1978: 197; Yang Bojun, 1981: 362).

Ironically, the second interpretation is the opposite of the first. It claims that the reform introduced the romanticized well-field system into Jin (Xu Xichen, 1983: 272–6).

In the third case, the sentence is understood as giving land to people. For proponents of this view, peasants before the reform worked on the communal land and a rotation system was practised.[8] Pieces of land of different qualities were said to be rotated among peasants periodically in order to prevent inequality. But nobody knows how these rotations were organised in practice. After the reform, however, the rotation system is believed to have been abandoned (Li Yanong, 1956: 171; Guo Moruo, 1976: 325; Zhang Jinguang, 1983: 30).

Finally, the word *yuan* in the sentence is understood as *shou* (to receive), because these two characters are said to be closely related in ancient form and meaning (Duan Yucai: 1971, 4\5b–6a; Kusuyama Shusaku, 1973: 70–87; Koga Noboru, 1980: 411–35; Lewis, 1990: 57). The purpose of this association is to identify the *yuan* field as the earliest form of the *shoutian* system in China.[9] It is worth noting that despite their different interpretations about what was going on before the reform, the first and the last two interpretations of the above sentence 'Jinzuo yuantian' share a similar conclusion. Both, explicitly or implicitly, admit that land began to be owned by the individual peasants in Jin from 645 BC onwards (Yang Kuan, 1980: 129; Yang Bojun, 1981: 361–2).

Nevertheless, none of the above theses seems plausible. First, no solid contemporary source indicates the existence of a well-field system in Jin both before and after the reform. Second, given the low level of technology at that time, it is unlikely that a rotation system could be predominant, if it ever existed. As will be argued in the next section, Guo Moruo and others, without providing firm evidence, have projected a rotation system which existed from the Zhan Guo period into Chun Qiu times.

Moreover, such a system is not necessary, unless people cannot cope with a dramatic population growth. But, according to my previous account, the whole of China was thinly populated by the end of the Chun Qiu period.

Third, the last hypothesis is unlikely to be correct, because it is not supported by contemporary evidence and the link of the character *yuan* with *shou* is by no means definite. We do not have a thorough understanding of the relationship between the two words concerned in their ancient forms.

Finally, utilization of land became the central tenet in the thought of both scholars and statesmen only in the Zhan Guo period. As far as historical record can reveal, such an idea was carried out for the first time in the state of Wei in approximately 400 BC. The *shoutian* system was one of the most crucial components of such a policy to encourage the cultivation of land as much as possible since the mid-Zhan Guo period.[10] Hence there is no convincing reason to believe that the *shoutian* system was adopted anywhere before the Zhan Guo period. At the present stage of our knowledge, the identification of the character *yuan* as *shou* seems anachronistic and one-sided. In short, the above interpretations of the quoted sentence from the *Zuo Zhuo* failed to penetrate the gloss of scholars of a much later period, especially Han scholars (cf. Ban Gu, 24A/2b–3a).

What then, is, the correct implication of this sentence? It seems to imply that Jin officially allowed free exchange of land among different sublineages.[11] It is not difficult to find the reason.

As indicated in Chapter 4, exchange of land had come into practice among different local lords towards the end of the Western Zhou,[12] but transactions had to be reported to the Zhou court, since the land was theoretically owned by the king. However, from the beginning of the Eastern Zhou, the king started to lose his power. Consequently, exchange of land no longer required any report to the Zhou court by Chun Qiu times. For example, in 711 BC the Duke of Zheng secured an area of land in a place called Xu[13] from the city-state of Lu with a piece of jade (CQZZZ, 1981: 58, 74, 82) and the Zhou court was not informed of the exchange.[14]

Nevertheless, it seems that within each city-state land was still under the tight control of each local lord. He had the power to give any area to his favourites, just as the previous Zhou kings had to their relatives (ibid.: 1078, 1085, 1239, 1289, 1307, 1606).[15] No firm evidence from the available sources suggests that exchange of land took place within each city-state, at least before 645 BC in the city-state of Jin.[16]

Why does the *Zuo Zhuan* inform us that the nobles warmly welcomed the reform? Presumably, the heads of the sublineages in Jin had long dreamed of controlling more fertile land in order to expand their power.[17] The order to allow free exchange of land legally opened this possibility for them. Therefore, they became willing to provide more contributions to strengthen the power of the city-state in order to protect their own interests (CQZZZ, 1981: 362–3). In short, the above analysis indicates that the reform was unlikely to have anything to do with opening up the old boundaries between different fields.

The above interpretation fits well with the historical context, because it presupposes a slow but steady process of the emergence of private landownership in ancient China. Free exchange of land is undoubtedly an important step towards the final dissolution of the old communal system, but it is a gross simplification to claim that land was already owned by individual peasants in Jin after this reform. It cannot be correct, because it fails to reveal the real relationship between the majority of people and the land on which they earned their living. In fact, land was still owned by the Zhou king in theory, as a passage towards the end of the Chun Qiu period unambiguously informs us:

> The dominion of the Son of Heaven extends everywhere; the local lords have their own defined boundaries. This is the ancient rule. Within the empire, what ground is there which is not the king's? What individual of all whom the ground supports is there that is not the king's subject (CQZZZ 1981: 1284; cf. Legge, 1872: 616)?

The rhetoric certainly cannot be taken seriously, because the real control of land as well as people had been transferred into the hands of the local lords by then. Nevertheless, this is only one side of the picture.

On the other side, since all the land within each city-state was cultivated through clan organizations, it also seems correct to say that the land belonged to the community in practice. To be sure, each community was still under the actual control of its patriarchal leaders. Such a complicated issue cannot be summarized in one sentence. Therefore, the reform in Jin represented a step towards the emergence of private landownership, but the process is far from finished.

The second event which has been used by scholars to support their thesis that private property existed in the Chun Qiu period took place in the city-state of Lu. According to the *Zuo Zhuan*, in 594 BC Lu '*chushuimu*' (starts to impose taxes according to the amount of *mu*) (CQZZZ, 1981: 766). Like the previous instance, this event is described in a short and ambivalent sentence. No further explanation is given to inform us of what it was really about. But many scholars maintain that it symbolized the end of the well-field system in the city-state of Lu. Since then, private landownership is said to have come into existence there (Yang Bojun, 1981: 766; Jin Jingfang, 1983: 130–7). Guo Moruo even regards the event as the starting point of feudalism in Chinese history, although we are not told what elements this feudalism consists of (Guo Moruo, 1976: 326).

There are several reasons why the above hypothesis is not well grounded. First, nowhere can we find solid evidence from the contemporary sources suggesting the existence of a well-field system in Lu before 594 BC. If so, there was nothing to be abolished.

Second, a brief investigation of the terms referring to taxation in ancient China will not give any support to the above argument. The first term is known as *zheng*[18] (CQZZZ 1981: 361–4, 987). It seems to refer to the traditional tribute (*gong*) system (ibid.: 290–1, 367).[19]

The second term is *shui*. Since it has a graph for grain, it must have originally implied land taxes (Yang Lien-sheng, 1969: 98). Presumably, the rulers received tribute from their communities in the name of offering contributions to the expenses of the rites and festivals in the ancestor shrines. Hence, this is another word to express the same idea of taxation through payment in kind.

The third term is known as *fu*. It is comprised of two graphs: the left-hand one is a shape of 'cowrie', while the right-hand one means 'military'. It seems to refer, originally, to a contribution[20] closely related to military purposes (ibid.: 104–6). Traditionally, it has been understood as mere military tax. However, much evidence from the contemporary sources indicates that there was no fundamental difference among the above three terms in the Chun Qiu period. In fact, they were already used interchangeably. For example, in 484 BC the *Zuo Zhuan* informs us that a minister in the city-state of Zheng imposed a tax (*fu*) on his conferred land[21] to supply the expenses of marrying one of the duke's daughters (CQZZZ, 1981: 1661). Obviously, the word *fu* does not refer to a military tax of any kind here. Rather, it has the same meaning of the second term *shui*. Therefore, it is hardly surprising that the two words *fu* and *shui* became synonymous in the Zhan Guo period. After that, they are often used together to refer to taxation in general (Li Jiannong, 1957: 117–21; Yang Lien-sheng, 1969: 106–7).

This lengthy discussion should lead us to the conclusion that the imposition of a new tax on land initiated in the city-state of Lu in 594 BC most likely implied an increase in the general level of taxation.[22] As indicated in Chapter 4, there was no strict division of land in previous times. Different fields were marked by natural boundaries such as trees, rivers and mountains (Li Xueqin, 1983). Under such conditions, taxes could be levied merely on the basis of a rough estimation of a certain area. With the reform, a new unit of measurement, *mu*[23] came into effect and it is plausible that the new *shui* (tax) was levied accordingly.

Finally, a brief discussion of the political background seems to confirm my thesis that the reform did not bring about the existence of private landownership in Lu. As a second-rate city-state, Lu was engaged in a struggle for survival among more powerful city-states. Since it needed more revenues to strengthen itself, the best solution was to increase taxation. Consequently, the economic situation of the peasants deteriorated. At the same time, hardship compelled them to improve their cultivating techniques in order to obtain higher yields. In retrospect, this interaction must have accelerated economic development, which would have eventually provided the possibility for the emergence of individual farming. But, for the time being, the conditions to establish private landownership were still premature. For example, nowhere can we find a definite passage from the reliable materials revealing that most land was already in the hands of individuals. Confucius himself condemned the increased taxation in Lu, but he did not mention any change in the landownership system. On the contrary, when he said that the regulations made by the Duke of Zhou still existed, he seemed to imply that communal landownership was still predominant in Lu towards the end of the Chun Qiu period (CQZZZ, 1981: 1668).

Undoubtedly, the reform in Lu represented a step forward in the transition from communal landownership to private. Moreover, it indicated that the process had occurred not only in Jin, but also in other places around the same period. Due to different circumstances, the specific measures taken by the two city-states were different, but both had similar effects in shaping the future economic development in Chinese history.

Therefore, the purpose of the reform in Lu was to increase its taxation and there was no confirmation that it was exclusively related to the establishment of private landownership (Tong Shuyie, 1980: 340). Needless to say, no trace of feudalism can be found in Lu after 547 BC.

The last event which I shall refer to took place in the city-state of Zheng. As indicated in the second section of the previous chapter, in 543 BC Zi Chan[24] carried out such reforms as grouping houses by five, responsible for one another,[25] and marking out all the fields by banks and ditches (CQZZZ, 1981: 1181). Guo Moruo claims that these measures imply the legalization of private landownership in the city-state of Zheng (Guo Moruo, 1976: 350), while Yang Kuan holds that they symbolized a restoration of the so-called well-field system, and that the purpose was to protect slavery there (Yang Kuan, 1980: 130–1). Both arguments seem to be misleading. But, to determine the most plausible interpretation of these measures, we have, in the first place, to ask why Zi Chan wanted to define the exact boundaries between the fields. Obviously, he intended to measure the exact amount of land each sublineage had for the convenience of taxation.[26]

This is confirmed by another event which took place in 538 BC. Five years after these measures were introduced, Zi Chan started to levy a new tax (CQZZZ, 1981: 1254).[27] Though we are poorly informed about how Zi Chan divided the land, it seems beyond doubt that there was no strict division of land before the reform. Thus there is no evidence to support Yang Kuan's thesis that a well-field system ever existed in Zheng. If so, there was no such system to be restored by Zi Chan. Therefore, the argument that Zheng was once a society dominated by slavery is not well grounded.

What, then, was the form of landownership in Zheng after Zi Chan's reform? Much evidence in the *Zuo Zhuan* strongly suggests that land was still under the actual control of the sublineage communities. But the best confirmation of this thesis seems to be Confucius's comments on Zi Chan. Confucius spent his life preaching the idea that the best government is the one modelling itself on the past. In other words, everything should be done in accordance with the rules set up by the Duke of Zhou (CQZZZ, 1981: 1341, 1504, 1668; Confucius, 1984). When he heard of the death of Zi Chan, Confucius shed tears and said, Zi Chan 'afforded a specimen of the love transmitted from the ancients' (CQZZZ, 1981: 1422).[28] This remark is perhaps the best appraisal a person can expect to get from Confucius. In fact, for him, Zi Chan represented the ideal with which he identified himself.

A careful examination of Zi Chan's lifelong activities, as transmitted through the *Zuo Zhuan*, justifies Confucius's comment. Much evidence suggests that Zi Chan would seek to follow the Zhou tradition whenever possible. For example, Zi Chan was almost killed by a certain Feng Juan, presumably the head of another sublineage, in 543 BC. Instead of taking revenge, Zi Chan kept Feng Juan's properties in a good condition, while the latter was expelled from Zheng. Three years later, Zi Chan invited Feng Juan back and returned everything to him including his three-year tributes (ibid.: 1181–2). Indeed, nowhere can we find that Zi Chan was interested in giving land to individual peasants. Otherwise, he would not have received such a eulogy from Confucius. Therefore, it is unlikely that there was a well-field system in Zheng after Zi Chan's reform.

Moreover, if we put this reform against the background of the political environment in that period, it is not difficult to find that, being a weak city-state between the strong and powerful Jin and Chu, Zheng constantly faced the threat of extinction. The only way to preserve its existence was to increase taxation. Hence, Zi Chan's reform must have resembled what had happened in the city-state of Lu.

The above analysis demonstrates that new measures were taken by different city-states either to permit free exchanges of land or squeeze more surplus out of people's income in the Chun Qiu period. The ultimate purpose of these reforms was to increase the wealth and power of the city-states to support their struggles for hegemony or survival. These measures in turn brought about changes in people's relations to land and production. Although no contemporary sources inform us about what was going on in many other city-states during the Chun Qiu period, the reforms in Jin, Lu and Zheng seemed to be representatives of an overall trend. In other words, the specific interaction among different factors might have had its own variations in different city-states, but the above measures did symbolize the initial stage of a transition from communal to private landownership in Chinese history. Consequently, the traditional rules were replaced by the new ones and the seeds of private landholding were planted, which would have brought private landownership into actual existence in due time.

To be sure, notwithstanding all the changes, the land was still owned in practice by different sublineages within each city-state in the Chun Qiu period, and this communal landownership would not have been finally broken down until Chinese history entered a new era, known as the Zhan Guo (the Warring States) period.

2 THE ESTABLISHMENT OF PRIVATE LANDOWNERSHIP IN CHINA

It is still a controversial question whether or not private landownership was established during the Zhan Guo period. Some scholars argue that land was still in the hands of the state (Wu Shuping, 1981: 80–1; Luo Zhenyue, 1985; Zhang Jinguang, 1983; 1991). Based on a different interpretation both of historical texts and recent archaeological discoveries, I shall argue that the establishment of the Qin dynasty symbolized the end of communal landownership as the dominant mode of production. From that time, private landownership came into existence and the AMP was replaced by the coexistence of different modes of production in Chinese history.

The importance of agriculture was greatly stressed by every scholar in the Zhan Guo period, which had not been the case in previous periods, but the reliable texts do not contain anything explicit on the subject of landownership. Therefore, we are not well informed about whether land was privately owned or not. Inevitably, my discussion will suffer from the lack of precise knowledge, and most of the ensuing arguments have to be based on a number of assumptions. Nevertheless, I shall seek to provide as much evidence as possible to support them. I shall contend that an analysis of the aggregate information will substantiate my argument that communal landownership was indeed replaced by private landownership by the end of the Zhan Guo period.

The earliest evidence related to landownership in the Zhan Guo period is transmitted to us through the *Han Shu*. It indicates that individual farming already existed in the state of Wei in about 400 BC. A man was allegedly able to cultivate 100 *mu* of land to support a family of five persons (Ban Gu, 24A/6b–7a; Swann, 1950: 140–2). Since this information is preserved in a work written approximately 400 years later, we are not absolutely sure to what extent this account can be trusted. As discussed above, there are cases in which the information in the *Han Shu* about early China has proved to be either inadequate or misleading, such as in its description of the *jingtian* (well-field) system.

However, since it is the only evidence we have about the mid-Zhan Guo period, almost no scholar casts any doubt on its authenticity (Hsu, 1965: 109; Ho, 1975: 84–6; Guo Moruo, 1976: 5–6). If it is true, it demonstrates that the method of cultivation had dramatically changed from the traditional *ougeng* (pair cultivation) to individual farming by mid-Zhan Guo times. This hypothesis is supported by contemporary evidence. First, the phrase *ougeng* almost disappeared from the Zhan Guo texts on agriculture. When it is occasionally mentioned, it refers to events which occurred in the past.

Second, as has been argued in the last chapter, a preliminary examination of both bronze and iron farming tools in archaeological remains shows that they were available to the individual farmers towards the mid-Zhan Guo period (Li Xueqin, 1985: 323). Moreover, greatly improved cultivation techniques, such as the widespread use of different manures and the introduction of draught-animals for farming purposes, further encouraged the independence of peasants.

Third, as the name Zhan Guo (the Warring States) unambiguously suggests, frequent wars between states continued to dominate the political scenario throughout the period. Hence, the destructive effect of war also contributed a great deal to the dissolution of the communal-based system of cultivation into individual farming. Previously, people were conscripted through communal sublineages, the lowest level of administration. They had no choice but obey the order to fight for the interests of the ruling class. But it is entirely plausible that people would have sought to escape the war if the improved technologies provided an alternative for them to move to remote areas to cultivate land individually. We cannot trace back who was the first person to leave his old community to start a new life with his family, but this seemed to have been a perceptible trend during that time. It is clearly reflected in every contemporary work. Regardless of their different political ideals, all scholars showed great sympathy for the miserable conditions of the peasants. They travelled from one state to another, proposing solutions to bring peace to the people.[29]

The final evidence to support the argument of a widespread existence of individual peasants in the Zhan Guo period is closely related to the government policies of that period. Agriculture had always been important for the ruling class in ancient China, but the available sources reveal that it was from the mid-Zhan Guo period that different states began to pay special attention to the opening up of new land and to the efficient use of labour. For example, Li Kui[30] is said to have initiated the policy to cultivate as much land as possible for the first time in the state of Wei (Ban Gu, 24A\6a–b; Swann, 1950: 136–8; Hsu, 1965: 226). The purpose was to increase its revenues and hence its ability to compete with other states. According to other contemporary sources, similar policies were adopted by many other states (the *Xun Zi*, 1979; Mencius, 1984; the *Guan Zi,* 1986).[31] It is no coincidence that measures of this kind were taken at this time in Chinese history, if we set them against the background of my previous discussion on technological progress. They testify to the fact that agricultural implements had developed to an unprecedented level by then. In other words, it would have had little significance to adopt such policies if cultivation methods were still as primitive as Ho wants us to believe (Ho, 1975: 83). Therefore, it was the improved technology which explained the implementation of the above new policies. As a result, the number of individual farmers must have greatly increased by the mid-Zhan Guo period.

However, does this mean that the process of transition from communal landownership to private landholding had already finished by then? This interpretation is accepted by most scholars (Hsu, 1965: 112; Bodde, 1986; Yang Zuolung, 1989: 1–13). But a closer examination of the authentic sources reveals that the above contention is not tenable, because it fails to reflect the intricate process of the emergence of private landownership. As indicated repeatedly, the evolution of the concept of private property in ancient China is much more complicated than most scholars presume. This thesis is borne out by taking into consideration the wide adoption of the *shoutian* (land-bestowal) system in different states during the mid-Zhan Guo period.

What is the *shoutian* system? According to the bamboo strips discovered at Yinqueshan[32] in Linyi of Shandong Province in 1972, land was divided into three categories: fertile, medium-grade and poor.[33] People were given pieces of land of different qualities for cultivation each time, and they had to change their fields every three years. For example, a single family in the first three years was given fertile land, in the second three years medium-grade, and in the third three years poor.[34] This system was designed to prevent inequality among peasants. Since the government had the power to redistribute the land, it is difficult to say that the land was owned by the peasants at this stage.

This account is compatible with the available contemporary documents. For example, the chapter 'On Riding the Horse' of the *Guan Zi* indicates:

> In every prefecture and district, the fertile land should be given to a certain number of peasants; the medium grade land to some of them, and the poor land to others. Being definitely settled on lands, though of different qualities, the people will not move away. Those who suffer from poverty should be given relief, and those who suffer from low production subsidized. The people will then be pleased with their sovereign, if the surplus yielded by the best soil may be used to subsidize the peasants who work on the inferior soil (the *Guan Zi*, 21\20b–21a).

It seems certain that the *shoutian* system was practised in the state of Qi. Moreover, some contemporary sources indicate that similar policies were also adopted in other states at approximately the same time. For example, on different occasions Mencius indicates that the *shoutian* system was carried out in several other eastern states. In his advice to King Hui of Liang, Mencius says:

> If the mulberry is planted in every homestead of five *mu* of land, then those who are fifty can wear silk; … if each lot of a hundred *mu* is not deprived of labour during the busy seasons, then families with eight mouths to feed will not go hungry (*Meng Zi zhushu,* 1B\4a; cf. Mencius, 1984: 21).

In another place, Mencius informs us that Duke Wen of Teng implemented similar policies (*Meng Zi zhushu,* 5B\1a–2b; cf. Mencius, 1984: 103). One statute in the Shuihudi strips in Hubei Province seems to indicate that the state of Wei also practised the shoutian system (Shuihudi, 1990: 174; cf. Hulsewe, 1985: 208).[35] Obviously, the change in cultivation methods from communal-based *ougeng* to individual farming does not necessarily mean that the land was already privately owned by the peasants. In fact, according to the above analysis, along with the political concentration, land was increasingly under the control of the states, and the peasants had only the right of usufruct.

Some recent archaeological finds indicate that the *shoutian* system of a kind was carried out in the state of Qin as well. Based on a different interpretation of the reliable evidence, some scholars argue that land was also owned by the state in Qin by the end of the Zhan Guo period (Wu Shuping, 1981: 80–1; Zhang Jinguang, 1983; 1991). Among the often-quoted examples is a Qin statute on the bamboo strips discovered at Shuihudi of Hubei Province in 1975. It suggests that the Qin government was very much concerned about almost every aspect of agriculture. For example, it required reports from local officials about the rain that had benefited the crops and the grains in ear, as well as the number of *qing*[36] of cultivated fields and areas without crops. Similar reports were also required if there were drought and violent wind or rain, floods, hordes of grasshoppers or other creatures which had damaged the crops (Shuihudi, 1990: 19; cf. Hulsewe, 1985: 21). According to these scholars, this passage is a clear indication that land must have been owned by the Qin state. Otherwise, the government would not have had such specific demands from the local officials.

However, the strongest evidence to support their thesis is another statute from the same set of the Qin bamboo strips. It informs us that the delivery of hay and straw per *qing* had 'to be done according to the number of fields bestowed (*shou*)'. Irrespective of whether the fields were cultivated or not, the delivery per *qing* was three bushels[37] of hay, or two bushels of straw (Shuihudi, 1990: 21; cf. Hulsewe, 1985: 23). It seems to be an undeniable fact that the *shoutian* system must have been practised in the state of Qin, because the word *shou* in the passage is exactly the same as the one we find in the texts about other states. But I would like to argue that the *shoutian* (land-bestowal) system in Qin is different from those adopted in other states.

In the first place, both contemporary works and archaeological sources do not explicitly tell us that the land belonged to the Qin state. As to those detailed reports on the conditions of agriculture, it is very easy to find a more plausible explanation. Since Qin was an agricultural society, taxes from peasants provided the major financial support for its existence. It is not surprising that the Qin government was so anxious to know as much as possible about the conditions of all crops. But nowhere are we told that this is inextricably related to the specific forms of landownership. Indeed, as evidence shows, the government of the Han dynasty also required similar reports from its local officials, and no one seems to disagree that private property was already well established by that time (Li Jiannong, 1957: 242–6; Bielenstein, 1980: 7–17; Du Zhengsheng, 1985: 12–44). Therefore, the regulations for agriculture demonstrate Qin's unique feature of economic organization which was inherited by subsequent dynasties. It was those strict Qin statutes which guaranteed a constant flow of taxation.

Consequently, the increasing wealth of the state provided a solid economic foundation for Qin to reunite China in 221 BC.

Secondly, scholars are greatly impressed by the detailed descriptions of different punishments in the Qin law on the bamboo strips discovered at Shuihudi of Hubei Province. Indeed, the approximately 1155 strips indicate that Qin had already established a complicated system of institutions to carry out its policies.[38] It is not an exaggeration to say that Qin had built up one of the most sophisticated legal systems in the world before the end of the third century BC.

Not surprisingly, a large number of those Qin statutes are inextricably related to peasant activities, and there is even a specific section known as Statutes on Agriculture (Shuihudi, 1990: 19–22; cf. Hulsewe, 1985: 21–5). If the same *shoutian* system adopted in the eastern states had also been implemented in Qin, some of its most general features should have been indicated in one way or another. For example, there must have been, at least, some hints as to how much land was given to each family, how long it would have taken to rotate the land among the bestowed peasants, and possibly how many grades the land was divided into. Information of this kind was found in a somewhat less significant discovery at Yinqueshan in Shandong Province in 1972 (Yinqueshan, 1985). Why does no Shuihudi statute even indirectly suggest the existence of a periodical rotation with a fixed amount of land managed by the state? The most plausible explanation is that this system did not exist in Qin. It is extremely unlikely that the Qin law-makers would have been so careless that they had forgotten to write such a regulation, if the system had existed by then.[39]

Thirdly, a brief discussion of Shang Yang's reform will further prove that the *shoutian* system in Qin was different from those adopted in other states during the Zhan Guo period. According to the *Shi Ji,* Duke Xiao of Qin (c. 382–338 BC) was convinced by Shang Yang to reform Qin in about 359 BC.[40] This is not the place to offer a comprehensive analysis of all the measures taken by Shang Yang,[41] but there are three distinctive features worth our special attention, for they are closely related to the present discussion.

First, in order to cultivate as much wasteland as possible, Shang Yang initiated policies to attract more people from other eastern states to come to Qin (*Shang Jun Shu,* 4\2a–b; cf. Duyvendak, 1928: 268). He understood not only that the nature of people was to have more 'fields and houses' (*Shang Jun Shu,* 4\1a; cf. Duyvendak, 1928: 267), but also that generous conditions must be offered to the newcomers. Thus he promised not to levy any taxation[42] on them for three generations (*Shang Jun Shu,* 4\4b; cf. Duyvendak, 1928: 274). The state of Qin badly needed those people, because its 'population is ill-proportioned to the territory' (*Shang Jun Shu*, 4\1a; cf. Duyvendak, 1928: 266). According to Shang Yang's estimation, less than two-fifths of its land had been cultivated before the reform (ibid.). Since no reliable sources suggest that there was any limit to the amount of reclamation, it is likely that Shang Yang granted the new-comers the right to cultivate as much as possible.

Second, for both political and economic purposes, Shang Yang first doubled taxes on families having two or more adult males living together (Sima Qian, 1972: 2234).[43] In 350 BC he issued a new order forbidding fathers and sons, elder and younger brothers to live together in the same house (Duyvendak, 1928: 18; Sima Qian, 1972: 2232). Both measures indicate that the people of Qin were living in a patriarchal society in which the communal landownership was very likely predominant before Shang Yang's reform. Politically speaking, the new policies represented a step in the direction of breaking up the old social system, but from the economic point of view, they demonstrate Shang Yang's eagerness to encourage people to bring more land under cultivation.

Finally, Shang Yang set up the first hierarchical ranking system in Chinese history. It is worth stressing that this system was different from that of medieval Europe, because it was based exclusively on military merit such as the number of enemy heads a person had cut off (*Shang Jun Shu*, 4\5a–7a, 5\1a–3b; cf. Duyvendak, 1928: 274–5, 296–303). Its purpose was merely to honour military bravery (ibid.: 14–15, 61–5; Shuihudi, 1990: 55; cf. Hulsewe, 1985: 83).[44] We are not well informed about whether all ranks were heritable, but some evidence unambiguously indicates that it was the case at least with some ranks. For instance, one Qin statute from the Huihudi of Hubei Province informs us that if someone died after having been given an aristocratic rank, but before having received the reward, his successor-son would have the right to receive the reward (Shuihudi, 1990: 55, 110; cf. Hulsewe, 1985: 83, 139–40). Another Qin strip discovered at the same place also made crystal-clear that when a person died in battle for the service without sur-rendering, a rank should be bestowed to his successor-son (Shuihudi, 1990: 88; cf. Hulsewe, 1985: 117). These statutes certainly represent a continuity of Shang Yang's policy to reward brave soldiers (Kroll, 1990: 69).

Was there any material benefit attached to those ranks? Again, we do not possess systematic knowledge on the subject. However, some frag-mentary sources seem to suggest that there was a quantitative correspon-dence between the ranks and the size of the bestowed land and other advantages. As Loewe has convincingly argued, such a correspondence existed in the aristocratic bestowal system of the Han dynasty (Loewe, 1960). For example, when the tenth aristocratic rank was conferred upon Bu Shi, he was given 10 *qing* of land at the same time (Ban Gu, 24B/13a; Swann, 1950: 284). Furthermore, scholars seem to have no dispute over Dong Zhongshu's comment that the Han dynasty inherited almost all the major policies of the Qin government (Ban Gu, 24A/15b; Swann, 1950: 182–3; Qiu Xigui, 1981: 239, 299).

To further support the above thesis, some quotations from the *Shang Jun Shu* are instructive. At one point we are told that if a soldier captured the head of a man of rank, he would be given one *qing* of land and nine *mu* of estate in addition to a reward of one degree of rank and a bodyguard for each rank (*Shang Jun shu*, 5\2b; cf. Duyvendak, 1928: 299–300). A few lines later it clearly indicates that the number of trees on the grave of a rank-holder 'should be one for each degree in rank' (ibid.).

Moreover, the above description coincides with the comments made by the famous contemporary philosopher Xun Zi. He says that if someone killed five enemy soldiers in Qin, he would be given five families under his control (the *Xun Zi*, 1979: 234).[45] It seems reasonable to presume that there was at least 100 mu of land difference between each rank in Qin and that the higher a person's rank was, the more land he would receive.

Finally, was the bestowed land in Qin heritable or not? Based on the information in the *Han Shu*, scholars presume that the received land had to be returned to the Qin state when the receiver reached a certain age (Ban Gu, 24A\3a; Swann, 1950: 122). But there are two reasons why this is unlikely to have happened in Qin. First, nowhere in the massive contemporary literature and recent archaeological discoveries can we find any sentence suggesting that land had to be returned to the Qin state. Hence what is described in the *Han Shu* is at most a reflection of the situation in the eastern states during the Zhan Guo period. Second, since the Qin ranks were heritable, it is entirely plausible that its material benefits would be inherited by the successors of the rank-holders (cf. Loewe, 1960: 154–5; Moriya Mitsuo, 1968: 3–69; Koga Noboru, 1980: 325–410, 557–8, 568; Yu Haoliang and Li Junming, 1981: 163–8).

The above analysis should lead us to the conclusion that different policies were initiated by Shang Yang, because they were designed to resolve Qin's own problems. Therefore, the content of the *shoutian* system[46] in Qin was not the same as those adopted in the eastern states. Since Qin had much wasteland for people to reclaim, any restriction in the amount of cultivation would have been against the main principles of Shang Yang's reform.

However, does this imply that Shang Yang established the concept of private landownership in Qin? Many scholars both in China and the West believe so (Duyvendak, 1928: 53; Hsu, 1965: 112: Guo Moruo, 1978: 15; Bodde, 1990: 37). Two historical texts have often been used to support their argument. The first evidence is a comment allegedly made by the famous Han philosopher Dong Zhongshu at the beginning of the second century B.C. According to the *Han Shu*, Dong maintains that Shang Yang abolished the well-field system and that people were allowed to sell and buy from then on (Ban Gu, 24A/15a; Swann, 1950: 180). But there are three reasons to believe that Dong Zhongshu's remarks do not reflect the real situation of Qin in the mid-Zhan Guo period. First, as argued above, no contemporary sources indicate that Shang Yang gave people the right to sell and buy land after his reform.

Second, the *Shang Jun Shu* informs us that Shang Yang did not even permit the merchants to buy and the peasants to sell grain (*Shang Jun Shu*, 1\4b; cf. Duyvendak, 1928: 177). Therefore, it is difficult to believe that he would encourage people to make land transactions. On the other hand, since there was so much land available, it is strongly doubtful whether most people had any motivation to engage in such activity, although occasional exchanges of land could have taken place in reality (cf. Li Jiemin, 1981: 59).

Third, a brief review of Shang Yang's tight administrative control of the whole population also points to the same conclusion. Shang Yang modified and strictly carried out the mutual responsibility system. He divided people into groups of five families and did not allow them free movement (*Shang Jun Shu*, 5\11a–b; cf. Duyvendak, 1928: 287, 296, 321). Hence it is unlikely that he would allow people to buy and sell land.

As indicated above, the invention of a golden past in the remote antiquity in which a well-field system was adopted, reached its apex in the imagination of the Han scholars. There is no solid reason to believe what they said in this respect. In fact, as some scholars have correctly argued, Dong Zhongshu's accusation of Shang Yang indicates his discontent with the great disparity between the rich and poor in his own time. It served as a justification for his proposal of a redistribution of landholding in the Han dynasty (Swann, 1950: 179–81; Lin Jianming, 1981: 74–6).

The second piece of evidence to support the argument that Shang Yang brought about private landownership in Qin comes from the *Shi Ji*. In Shang Yang's biography, Sima Qian says that Shang Yang 'weitian kaiqianmo fengjiang'[47]. The sentence means that Shang Yang broke the old *qianmo* (the east–west or north–south roads between fields)[48] and initiated a new *qianmo* system.[49] This has been confirmed by the recently discovered Yinqueshan strips, which clearly indicate that the size of one *mu* had changed from 1 × 100 paces to 1 × 240 paces in some of the eastern states before Shang Yang's reform. Moreover, another recent important archaeological discovery in a Warring States cemetery in Qingchuan County of Sichuan Province[50] indicates that Qin indeed enlarged the size of one *mu*. The size of the new *mu* was approximately the same as that in the state of Jin (Yang Kuan, 1982: 83; Huang Shengzhang, 1982: 72; Sichuansheng bowuguan and Qingchuanxian wenhuaguan, 1982: 11; cf. Hulsewe, 1985: 212–13). Although it seems certain that Shang Yang did replace the old *mu* with the new *mu* for the purpose of reducing taxation,[51] it is not clear whether he was inspired by the reforms in other states or not.

Consequently, the measure to increase the size of one *mu*, together with many others discussed above, definitely served the purpose of breaking down the traditional organization of the clan system in Qin. At the same time, it also represented a crucial step towards the final establishment of private landownership. Nevertheless, it is far from true to claim that Shang Yang legalized the existence of private landownership in Qin. First, no reliable evidence explicitly informs us that Shang Yang had made such a declaration. Second, as indicated above, the concept of private landownership does not make any sense to a person who is able to cultivate as much land as he wants. Hence the thesis that Shang Yang established private landownership fails to reflect the precise meaning of Shang Yang's reform in its specific context. In short, most land must have been in the hands of the state, although a growing amount came under actual control of the individual peasants as a result of the reform.

However, from the time that Qin carried out radically different measures from those adopted in the eastern states, it embarked on a new road leading to the final emergence of private landownership. In other words, the purpose of Shang Yang's reform was simple, that is, to bring as much wasteland as possible under cultivation in order to strengthen Qin's power. Therefore, he implemented what he believed to be the most suitable measures for this purpose, but the fact that they eventually brought about the institution of private property was not his immediate concern. We may reinterpret his policies from the perspective of our own interests, but we shall never know for certain whether the result is what he wanted at the beginning.[52] A tentative conclusion seems to be that Shang Yang's reform consolidated peasants' right of usufruct rather than symbolizing the establishment of private property in Qin.

Social progress is always slower and more complicated than people are willing to admit. Hence, it must have taken a considerable time for the individual peasants to fully realise their rights over what they had, even if the Qin government had unconsciously adopted the right policies to encourage them to possess more. But it took even longer for those rights to be acknowledged by the state. This only happened about 150 years after Shang Yang initiated his first reform in 359 BC.

It is unfortunate that no contemporary scholars have written anything on how the above process took place in practice. We are not able to trace back who was the first person in Chinese history to declare exclusive ownership[53] over his land, but we do possess an increasing amount of evidence unambiguously indicating that private landownership was indeed formally established.

It is not difficult to find evidence from the historical sources to support the above argument, but the most authoritative confirmation seems to be the Shuihudi bamboo strips found in Hubei Province in 1975. They provide us with much invaluable information strongly suggesting the existence of private landownership towards the end of the Zhan Guo period. This is not the place to discuss all the details related to this subject, but it is hoped that a brief review of some crucial evidence should be sufficient to convince the reader.

As indicated in Chapter 1, the concept of private property refers to a person's exclusive rights over his property such as selling and buying of land, and it must be protected by law. These features can be observed through an analysis of two relationships defined by the Qin law. The first one is the relationship between the state and individuals. One statute says:

> If persons have to pay debts to the government and those [owing] fines and redemption fees live in another county, documents to charge them should be sent to the county where they are living. If the government has not paid debts to commoners,[54] the county concerned should also be informed; the county should repay them (Shuihudi, 1990: 38; cf. Hulsewe, 1985: 48).

It is evident from the above description that both the state and individual peasants were independent and well-defined financial units. If the land was still owned by the state, it would not have been necessary to make such precise legal obligations between the two. According to my previous discussion, the relationship between the government and peasants in the state of Qi, where a certain fixed amount of land was given by the state to each family, was quite different from that of Qin. Evidence shows a harmonious as well as cooperative picture in which the state took great care of the peasants. Nothing suggests a clear division of responsibility, including the financial one between the state and individual peasants in such a society.

There are many other specific regulations in the same set of statutes, distinguishing different obligations between the government and individuals. For example, another statute clearly states:

If those repaying their fines, redemption fees or debts through statute labour return [home] to work in the field at the time of sowing and at the time of weeding, they are allowed to have twenty days respectively (Shuihudi, 1990: 53; cf. Hulsewe, 1985: 67).

There are at least two points worth our special attention in this passage. First, although we are not quite sure about the exact nature of the punishments, some must have been derived from the peasants' failure to pay enough taxes to the state. No strict regulations of this kind have been found in those states where everyone is supposed to stay with his family to cultivate a piece of land. Indeed, it is very doubtful whether such heavy punishments were necessary under a system in which equality was the great concern of the government. This point is important, because it implies that the Qin law must have been based on a totally different form of landownership. Second, the permission for those peasants working off their debts etc. to return home for agricultural work also explicitly indicates that each of them had his own land.[55] This can be supported by another regulation which tells us:

If commoners having fines, redemption fees or debts, and they have a male or female slave,[56] or they have a horse, or an ox, with which they wish to work off the [above obligations], this is to be permitted (Shuihudi, 1990: 51; cf. Hulsewe, 1985: 69).

It is not clear how commoners got their slaves,[57] but this passage unambiguously suggests that some people had more land than others. Otherwise, it would have been very difficult, if not impossible, to support both their families and their slaves if they had only a small plot allotted by the government.[58] Moreover, since the *shoutian* system in other states must have been based on an egalitarian principle, it is extremely unlikely that the commoners were allowed to possess slaves there. In fact, we are not informed of the existence of slaves in those states. On the other hand, it is plausible that some commoners in Qin had their own male or female slaves, because Qin law protected the existence of private property.[59] Otherwise, the above statute would not make any sense.

The second relationship which is well defined by the Qin law is the relationship between individual farmers. One statute tells us of a case in which a person's horse ate another person's grain. Since the owner of the horse had not reached the height of six feet,[60] he was not warranted to be sentenced nor to repay the grain (Shuihudi, 1990: 130; cf. Hulsewe, 1985: 165). Obviously if he was taller than six feet he would have been sentenced as well as having to repay the grain. Another article says that if a person had stealthily picked another person's mulberry leaves and that the illicit profit was not more than one string of cash coins, he still would be sentenced to thirty days' statute labour (Shuihudi, 1990: 95; cf. Hulsewe, 1985: 122). All these strict punishments demonstrate that private property was strongly defended by the Qin government.

But the most convincing evidence is from one statute explicitly indicating that if a local official who had levied taxes on the 'fields of commoners' did not report it to the government, he would be accused of 'hiding fields'[61] (Shuihudi, 1990: 130; cf. Hulsewe, 1985: 164). Hulsewe seems correct to say that this is merely indirect evidence suggesting the existence of private landownership in Qin, because it does not explicitly define the concept in modern terms (Hulsewe, 1986: 217).

Nevertheless, if we relate it to another two Qin codes, it will be very difficult to escape the conclusion that land was indeed privately owned in Qin. The first code is from the Qingchuan strips. They inform us that all the fields must be marked by border-mounds which were four feet high and that their size must correspond to their height. Between the border-mounds there must be partitions which were one foot high and two feet thick at the bottom.

> In Autumn, in the eighth month, the border-mounds and the partitions must be repaired. The borders and field limits must be corrected. Moreover, the tall grass on the East–West and North–South roads must be cut. In the ninth month both the roads and the dangerous passages must be thoroughly cleared. In the tenth month, bridges must be made, embankments and dikes repaired, fords and bridges cleared and weeds cut. [Although] it is not the time for clearing the roads, whenever there are holes and bad places, making it impossible to proceed, (clearing) must be undertaken (Sichuansheng bowuguan *et al.*, 1982: 11; cf. Hulsewe, 1985: 212).

Why did the Qin government make such detailed regulations to guarantee that all the fields were strictly marked? Apparently this was closely associated with the evolution of different forms of landownership.[62] As indicated above, under the communal landownership, no strict rules were required to divide land into fields of the same size.

Furthermore, the thesis that land was privately owned by the end of the Zhan Guo period is borne out by my second example. It is a statute from the Shuihudi bamboo strips indicating that if a person had secretly shifted the border-mounds between the fields, he would be punished by a redemption called 'shaving off the beard'. However, it clearly states that this was not a heavy punishment (Shuihudi, 1990: 108; cf. Hulsewe, 1985: 164). If the land had belonged to the state and been redistributed periodically, it would not have been necessary for people to secretly move the border marks between the fields. For they knew that several years later it would have been their turn to cultivate the land presently occupied by someone else. Under such a condition the Qin government would not have made such a well-defined statute. Obviously, the purpose of these articles is to protect the right of the landholders.

Finally, the consolidation of private property by the end of the Zhan Guo period can also be detected through the development of commercial activities. The widespread use of coined money towards the end of the Zhan Guo period has long been recognized by scholars (Yang Lien-sheng, 1952; Hsu, 1965: 116–19). It is an important indication that commercialization was relatively highly developed by then. In recent years Chinese scholars have made systematic studies of the latest archaeological finds. They provide even more detailed evidence to confirm the above thesis. For example, they have convincingly proved the widespread existence of both government and private workshops and their deep involvement with commercial transactions of all kinds. These activities must have been based on an acknowledgement of private property (Li Xueqin, 1980b: 25–31; 1982: Qiu Xigui, 1980: 289, 295; 1981: 274–9; He Qinggu, 1981: 15–22; Hulsewe, 1985: 231).[63]

Moreover, land became the object of transactions. There were many reasons to encourage people to buy land, but one of the most important seems to be the social contempt for merchants, a contempt that was created by the state. Much contemporary evidence suggests that the governments of all the states during the Zhan Guo period showed great concern over agriculture at the expense of commercial development. Inevitably, traders were regarded as inferior to peasants (the *Guan Zi*, 15\14b–15a). Although it did not stop people trading, this policy had a crucial impact on Chinese economic development. In order to acquire social status, the best investment for the merchants was to buy more land.[64] Therefore, it is not surprising to find that the merchant class used its wealth to gain political power towards the end of the Zhan Guo period. The most successful merchant, named Lu Buwei (290–235 BC), eventually became the Chancellor of the state of Qin.[65]

Although we are not well informed about the extent of the phenomenon of buying and selling land by that time, the fact that it existed seems beyond doubt (the *Han Fei Zi*, 11\8a). Consequently, the process of the emergence of private landownership was dramatically accelerated (Hulsewe, 1985: 227–33).

The above analysis indicates that private landownership had replaced communal ownership by the end of the Zhan Guo period. But it was not formally recognized until 216 BC when the first emperor ordered that: 'the black-hair people[66] must voluntarily declare their holdings' (Sima Qian, 1972: 251). Since then, there were, in broad lines, three major property systems regulating the use of land in Chinese history: state ownership,[67] small peasant ownership and landlord ownership.[68] They coexisted, supplemented one another, and formed different combinations at different times.[69]

Moreover, according to the above discussion, the transition from communal to private landownership was realized through three main channels: the consolidation of the land reclaimed by peasants, the permission to inherit the bestowed land previously owned by the state, and the further commercialization of land.

Nevertheless, Hulsewe is very suspicious of the thesis that a landlord class emerged out of the dissolution of communal landownership. He contends: 'This is applying, or rather imposing, dogmatic schemes on the material, often leading to conclusions that are not only premature but demonstrably wrong' (Hulsewe, 1985: 234; cf. Lewis, 1990: 6–7). Unfortunately, he does not provide any evidence to support his argument. In fact, his comment seems to be equally dogmatic. A brief analysis of some available materials will indicate that his suspicion is not well grounded.

Firstly, Shang Yang's policy to encourage people to cultivate as much wasteland as possible must have ended up with a situation in which different families had unequal amounts of land. This thesis is supported by one statute from the Shuihudi Qin bamboo strips. As it shows, if the local officials were afraid that animals in the state parks would break out and eat the commoners' crops, they had to make 'an estimate for a levy among those having fields nearby, regardless of their status, the number of people have to be provided according to the number of their fields to build walls or repair them' (Shuihudi, 1990: 47; cf. Hulsewe, 1985: 63).

Secondly, the Qin strips reveal that some people were awarded more land, because of their military merit. How could they cultivate all their land? They must have employed others. A Qin statute seems to support this assumption:

What is 'man-marmot'? 'Man-marmot' refers to those whose children have to go to take care of their master. If they do not go to take care of their master, they should be warranted to be confiscated by government. If they do not take care of their master, but they bring in grain, they are not confiscated (Shuihudi, 1990: 140; cf. Hulsewe, 1985: 177).

It is plausible that the term 'man-marmot' is a contemporary concept to define tenants, like the phrase the 'black-hair people' cited above. For it is clearly stated that they must meet one of the two conditions. They had either to take care of their master or to pay rent in kind to their master. Undoubtedly, the master was the owner of their land and the purpose of the statute was to protect the right of the landlord.

This explanation accords well with the description in contemporary sources. As Han Fei unambiguously states, there were tenants working for landlords (the *Han Fei Zi,* 11\6a). According to the *Shi Ji,* Chen She, the famous leader of the first large-scale peasant rebellion in Chinese history, was also a tenant cultivating for others before being conscripted for statute labour (Sima Qian, 1972: 1949).[70]

Finally, the commercialization of land definitely brought about polarization of classes. Apart from buying and selling land, the rich, especially the merchants, also played the role of moneylenders and the normal interest rate could be as high as 100 per cent. Furthermore, they bought grain in the autumn at half the annual average price, because the supply was then abundant, and sold it at twice the usual price in the spring, when the supply was low. This gave peasants the burden of another 100 per cent interest payment. If the government demanded taxes at the wrong times, the people had to borrow again from the rich, since they had no other choice (the *Guan Zi,* 15\14b–15a). Any disaster, natural or human, could force them to sell their land. It would be bought by the rich and rented back to the previous owners (the *Han Fei Zi,* 19\8a). The precarious situation of small farmers, frequently referred to by contemporary scholars, continued to prevail in the Han dynasty. The rich accumulated their wealth at the expense of the majority. Dong Zhongshu's comment that the rich had large amounts of land, 'while the poor had not even [enough] land into which to stick an awl' (Ban Gu, 24A/15a; Swann, 1950: 181) is most likely a description of his own time, but the process must have started before the end of the Zhan Guo period. Therefore, a landlord class began to constitute an important part of the social scenario, which would have shaped the Chinese economic development for centuries to come. From that time, China entered a new political and economic era.

What were the major characteristics of this new era? How did they influence the economic development of the subsequent dynasties in Chinese history? What is their legacy on the transition from an agrarian society into a modern China? All these questions are extremely complex as well as interesting. It is beyond the scope of this book to offer answers to these questions, because each deserves an independent study in its own right. Nonetheless, it is hoped that the above discussion has provided a concise but comprehensive background knowledge for further research.

7 Conclusion

In the Introduction to this book a brief review of current literature on the AMP and its relationship with Chinese history presented three related questions: 1) Is the AMP conceptually sound? 2) Does it disprove the Marxist theory of history? 3) Has it any empirical validity in explaining Chinese history?

Chapter 1 answered the first question by providing an elucidation and justification of the concept of the AMP within the framework of analytical Marxism. I pointed out that some of Marx's specific remarks about non-Western societies have proved either inadequate or misleading. This is largely due to his lack of precise knowledge on those societies, which was not available during his lifetime.

However, I have contended that it would be wrong to dismiss the AMP simply because some features which Marx attributed to it have nothing to do with the concept (e.g. the alleged need for large-scale irrigation projects). In fact, Marx's other scattered comments, if well constructed, can yield a clear definition of the AMP, namely, that it refers to a stratified society in which communal landownership was predominant. Since I have preserved what seems to be Marx's correct distinction between diverse social and economic formations in the development of world history, my arguments are essentially congruent with Marx's point of view.

In order to appreciate fully the significance of the concept of the AMP, I further outlined Marx's methodological approach to the understanding of history. Marx's starting point of analysis was capitalism, because he intended to expose its inner mechanism. But the specificity of capitalism cannot be completely understood unless it is compared with that of pre-capitalist societies. Therefore, Marx drew a clear distinction between the capitalist mode of production and all pre-capitalist modes of production.

Nevertheless, this is only the first step in discovering the origins of capitalism. In order to perceive the process of capitalist growth, especially the strong barriers to the corrosive influence of capitalism in some pre-capitalist societies, the second step must be taken, that is, to detect the similarities and differences among pre-capitalist societies. It is this distinction which would enable us to grasp the logic of each specific society. Hence the concept of the AMP was employed by Marx to show that 'forms of society reflect material possibilities and constraints' (Cohen, 1988: 133). For the purpose of this book, I compared the AMP with slavery and feudalism. The comparison was by no means systematic, because my

145

major concern was to establish the AMP as a distinctive mode of production. As I have sought to demonstrate, O'Leary's claim that it is impossible to reconstruct a meaningful concept of the AMP cannot be sustained.

Chapter 2 attempted to answer the second question, that is, whether the AMP is compatible with the Marxist theory of history. I examined two charges against the concept of the AMP. First, I refuted the conventional interpretation that societies dominated by the AMP are permanently stagnant. I contended that this is a misconception, because every society is in constant movement. Interaction of different factors formulates a specific combination which will be replaced by another in a given time and space. Economic formations develop at different speeds, but there is no reason to describe those societies in which capitalism did not appear in the first place as permanently stagnant. Most of the pre-capitalist societies did not develop further than they did, because further development was precluded by the emergence of capitalism in the West. We cannot exclude the possibility that a society once dominated by the AMP would be able to breed modern capitalism internally. In short, the AMP had its own dynamics.

But why do economic and social dynamics have different manifestations? A preliminary investigation indicated that this is due to different organizations of production, a variety of material and geographical circumstances, and the influence of traditions in the broadest sense of the word. Each case must be studied specifically if we want to have a correct answer to the question concerned.

Second, evidence was provided to reject the claim that the geographical prefix of the AMP prevents it from being a scientific concept. I have argued that the charge of Eurocentrism against Marx in his writings on non-European societies is at best misleading. In fact, Marx's analysis of colonialism was determined by his dialectical consideration of world history, namely, that the impending urge of capital to expand throughout the world is inherited in its own contradiction, which will dig its own grave. Hence Marx's remarks on non-European societies were an extension of his critique of capitalism, and the concept of the AMP does not carry any negative connotation. In short, the refutation of the AMP by many scholars is one-sided and crudely empiricist.

The remainder of this book sought to answer the third question, namely, whether the concept of the AMP has any empirical validity. In Chapter 3 I focused on the first dynasty of Chinese history – the Shang. First, I argued that although bronze technology had been invented, it was mostly, if not exclusively, used to produce artefacts for conspicuous display by the ruling class.

Second, I examined the available contemporary records to see whether the Shang can be classified as feudalism or slavery. I argued that no solid evidence supports either claim. The first-hand materials are still too scanty to allow us to provide a definite answer on the nature of that period at the present stage.

Finally, I discussed the status of the main labour force – *zhongren* (the multitudes). Both archaeological finds and contemporary literature suggest that they were ordinary members of different lineages or sublineages. Evidence was presented to illustrate that they cannot be defined either as slaves or as serfs.

Chapter 4 was a study of the economy and society in the Western Zhou, that is, the first half of the second dynasty – the Zhou – and its relationship to the AMP. I first explored the development of its productive forces. Available data indicated that there was no qualitative improvement in the major fields of technology in comparison with the Shang. The Zhou industries were largely a continuation of the Shang tradition, though changes in styles did take place.

Second, I examined the relations of production in the Western Zhou and contended that agricultural activities were still greatly controlled by the Zhou kings through their appointees. Labour on a massive scale is confirmed by both archaeological finds and contemporary literary sources.

Third, evidence was provided to refute the claim that the *fengjian* system in the Western Zhou can be defined as feudalism. I contended that feudal Europe and the Western Zhou were different in numerous essential aspects, despite some superficial similarities between the two.

Finally, I discussed the status of those people who are listed in contemporary records as gifts of the Zhou kings such as *chen* and *liren*. I argued that they were unlikely to have been treated by the Zhou rulers either as slaves or as serfs. Based on my distinctions between different modes of production in the first chapter of this book, the Western Zhou was classified as a society dominated by the AMP.

Chapters 5 and 6 were concentrated on the social and economic changes in the Eastern Zhou, that is, the second half of the Zhou dynasty. I contended that this period represented a watershed in Chinese history. The invention of cast iron reduced the cost of farming and other implements. The widespread use of both draught animals and iron ploughs, and many other improvements in agriculturally related techniques made intensive cultivation possible. The increase of both productivity and population encouraged individual farming, which constituted one of the most significant factors in the explanation of the eventual breakdown of lineage-based communities.

On the other hand, the above changes stimulated the ambition of sublineages to expand their territorial control at the cost of others. As a result, constant warfare between those allegedly descending from the same ancestor accelerated the process of dissolution of the time-hallowed *fengjian* system. Local lords in the city-states started to enjoy *de facto* sovereignty in the areas under their control in the Chun Qiu period. By the Zhan Guo times fully-fledged states emerged out of the bloodshed and dominated the scenario for more than two centuries before being wiped out by a man known as Qin Shi Huang Di (the First Emperor of Qin) in 221 BC.

The reasons for Qin's success were investigated in some detail. I have contended that after Shang Yang's reform, the state of Qin adopted a policy which must have been different in some major aspects from those carried out in most of other states. Since strict measures were taken to encourage people to cultivate as much land as possible, they promoted the emergence of private landownership which was eventually recognized by the state. The establishment of the Qin dynasty formally symbolized the end of communal landownership, or the AMP, as the dominant mode of production in China. In short, the empirical validity of the AMP was confirmed, but the concept can be applied only to a certain period of Chinese history, that is, the period from the Shang to the Chun Qiu times.

The above analysis of ancient China in the light of the AMP has two explicit implications. First, it has substantiated the explanatory value of the Marxist theory of history at a time when Marxism is in obituary in popular culture. A Marxist approach to social studies might not be fashionable for the time being, but this does not eliminate the inherited contradictions of capitalism revealed by Marx. Therefore, Marxism retains its vitality in providing a valuable alternative perception of the objective constraints operating on human beings in history. This book has sought to confirm Marx's belief that some actions at a given level of productive forces are at best unlikely or at worst impossible and that the underlying causes of human unfreedom cannot be completely deciphered unless the economic structure in a given society is analyzed. From this perspective, the concept of the AMP offers a useful key for the comparative study of different societies.

Second, the acknowledgement of the existence of the AMP in ancient China can deepen our understanding of the inner mechanism of Chinese society. Questions such as why ancient China developed the way it did and what accounted for China having the longest civilization in the world have prompted answers from scholars with divergent motivations. A systematic explanation of social and other related changes in Chinese history from the standpoint of economic development has been criticised for its so-called inability to offer a causative account with sufficient evidence (Lewis, 1990: 247). This book is a preliminary attempt to demonstrate that such an approach is not only plausible, but well supported by the ever-increasing reliable evidence, both literary and archaeological. As argued above, we have every reason to believe that future archaeological discoveries will supply more details to fill in the gaps of our knowledge.

Of course, it is impossible to squeeze the rich complexity of any period of Chinese history into one book. Therefore, I do not claim to have exhausted all the reasons to account for the complicated process of the formulation of Chinese civilization. Nor does this book aim to explain every phenomenon in the great transition from a society dominated by the AMP to a society in which different modes of production co-existed. As noted in the Introduction, the importance of other factors such as sanctioned violence in ancient China is not denied (cf. Lewis, 1990). Undoubtedly, all aspects of a society deserve serious, independent studies in their own right. I never maintain that every non-material phenomenon needs to be materially explained, but I have sought to show that any form of non-material phenomena is not generated *ex nihilo*. It is from this perspective that special attention has been paid to the technological improvements in order to see in what form exploitation took place in ancient China. Inevitably the main features of economic organization were major focuses of this book and the dynamism of economic development was located, in its final analysis, in material scarcity and people's rationality in improving their situations.

To sum up, this book is an attempt to reach a better comprehension of one of the most crucial periods of Chinese history, in which Chinese civilization was created. It is hoped that the book has offered adequate evidence to delineate some principal characteristics of that civilization which had a significant impact on the later development of Chinese history.

Notes

INTRODUCTION

1. The second part of his contention is that historical materialism is damned without the AMP, since he believes that historical materialism cannot otherwise classify the societies in question (O'Leary, 1989).

2. Elsewhere Marx believed that the concept of private ownership of land 'has been imported by Europeans to Asia only here and there' (Marx, 1972: 616). This is contradictory with some of his writings in the 1850s. For example, in 'Trade with China' Marx came to realise that private property did exist in traditional Chinese society before the British invasion in 1840 (Marx, 1968: 375).

3. All Chinese characters throughout this book are romanized according to the Pinyin system apart from a few names commonly accepted in the West such as Confucius and K. C. Chang. Other forms of spelling in all quotations are also changed accordingly.

4. In general, the AMP as a distinctive mode of production is dismissed by most Chinese scholars. For detailed accounts of the AMP debate among Chinese historians from the 1920s to 1949, see Schwartz, 1954: 143–53; Dirlik, 1978, 1985. The relevant discussions on the concept in China from 1949 to the late 1980s can be found in Ulmen, 1978: 584–7; Lin Ganquan et al., 1982; Hoston, 1985, 1986; Rapp, 1987; Brook, 1989.

5. Analytical Marxism is one of the most important branches of contemporary political philosophy, but it is not confined to philosophy. In the past decade it has greatly influenced the writings of scholars in other disciplines such as political science, economics and sociology. It applies the analytical method, that is, its rigour and conceptual clarity, to central topics in Marx's writings. One of the most crucial contributions is made by G. A. Cohen in his book *Karl Marx's Theory of History* (1978). For further references, see, among others, Roemer, 1986; Ware and Nielsen, 1989; Kymlicka, 1990.

6. In his recent book *History, Labour and Freedom*, Cohen distinguishes two forms of historical materialism: the inclusive and restricted historical materialisms. The former sees the development of productive forces as the only centre of all human activity, 'in the sense that major development in those spheres of activity which lie beyond production and the economy are, in their large lines explained by material and/or economic changes' (Cohen, 1988: 158–9). Meanwhile, the latter is 'primarily a theory about the course of material development itself, rather than about the relationship *between* that development and other developments' (ibid.: 159). Therefore, the latter is much more modest and 'says nothing about economically irrelevant phenomena' (ibid.: 174). Throughout this book the concept of the Marxist theory of history refers to the restricted historical materialism.

7. By ancient China, I refer to the period from the beginning of the Shang dynasty (1766–1122 BC) to the reunification of China under the Qin dynasty in 221 BC.

8. This approach has been doubted by some scholars (Hsu, 1965: 130–1; Chang, 1986: 418), but this book is an attempt to demonstrate that such an approach to ancient China can be well supported by an ever-increasing amount of reliable evidence.

1 THE CONCEPT OF THE ASIATIC MODE OF PRODUCTION

1. He is not the only person to maintain this thesis. Similar argument has already been made, explicitly or implicitly, by many other scholars such as Melotti (1977) and Draper (1977), albeit for different purposes.
2. In *The Late Marx and the Russian Road* Shanin and his associates offered detailed accounts of how Marx sought to give a more concrete analysis of Russian society within his theory of history. The term AMP did not appear in his drafts of a reply to Zasulich, but Marx definitely had the AMP in his mind when he used the concept of 'the archaic formation of society' (Marx, 1983: 103).
3. Among other scholars who have written on the AMP in a more or less similar fashion, see, for example, Thorner, 1966; Avineri, 1968; Hindess and Hirst, 1975; Gouldner, 1980; Gellner, 1988.
4. For further reference to the influence of German philosophy, British political economy and French utopian socialism on Marx and his actual process of formulation of the concept, see, for example, Cohen, 1978; Kolakowski, 1978.
5. For a detailed analysis, see Cohen, 1978: 82–4.
6. It is difficult to claim that Marx did not use mode in the mixed fashion. For example, when introducing the notion of a 'mode of production', Marx pointed out that this mode 'must not be considered simply as being the reproduction of the physical existence of ... individuals. Rather, it is a definite form of activity of these individuals, a definite form of expressing their life, a definite *mode of life* on their part' (Marx and Engels, 1968: 32; all italics in quotations are in the original unless they are noted otherwise throughout this book). Furthermore, in the Preface to *A Contribution to the Critique of Political Economy* where Marx gave arguably his most famous description of his discoveries, he seemed to define the mode of production in this way (Marx, 1970).
7. For further reference, see, for example, Anderson, 1974b; Krader, 1975; Sawer, 1977; O'Leary, 1989.
8. For further reference to Marx's reading list during the 1850s, see O'Leary, 1989: 147–50.
9. In his reply to Marx, Engels stated: 'The absence of property in land is indeed the key to the whole of the East. Herein lies its political and religious history' (Marx, 1968: 427).
10. Both authors refuted Wittfogel (1981) for his distortion of Marx's original idea in this respect and argued that Marx did not intend to reformulate the AMP from a purely political standpoint at all in his later writings. For example, in one of the drafts of a reply to Zasulich Marx wrote: 'The isolation of the rural communes, the lack of connection between the lives of different communes – this localised microcosm does not everywhere appear

as an immanent characteristic of the primitive type. But wherever it is found, it leads to the formation of a central despotism above the communes' (Marx, 1983: 103).

11. For a detailed analysis of this school, see O'Leary, 1989: 162–70.

12. As Cohen has eloquently argued, '[t]he political applicability of historical materialism is limited, since it is a theory about epochal development, and the time horizon of political action necessarily falls short of the epoch' (Cohen, 1988: 133).

13. As Marx and Engels emphasized, there must be at least two conditions for the realization of this transition; first, a Russian revolution which could destroy the present government before the disintegration of the village communities (Marx, 1983: 103); second, this revolution at the same time could become 'the signal for proletarian revolution in the West,' (ibid.: 139) because only a successful socialist revolution in the West would make it possible for Russia to take advantage of the West's advanced technology. Only after that could it start a socialist collective farming and 'reap the fruits with which capitalist production has enriched humanity, without passing through the capitalist regime' (ibid.: 112–13, 121).

   Moreover, it must be stressed that Marx explicitly indicated the purely theoretical nature of his analysis of Russian society (ibid.: 104). And the fact that in his final reply to Zasulich, Marx did not mention most of his theoretical discussions in his previous drafts may imply that Marx was not satisfied with the result of his research. For more reference, see ibid.: 99–139.

14. It is true that efforts should be made to give a concise definition of the concept and that we should be careful in distinguishing the two categories in our analysis, but it seems wrong to deny the logical connection between the conceptual and descriptive accounts of the AMP. Scholars seeking to put them in strict contradiction certainly have misunderstood Marx's intention.

15. Since the first publication of the *Oriental Despotism* in 1957, Wittfogel has been widely criticized. For a Marxist critique, see Nikiforov, 1975, cited in Gellner, 1988: 19; 43. The most recent assault by a Marxologist in the West is made by O'Leary (1989: 235–60).

16. Looking at all the writings of Marx and Engels, O'Leary summarized different interpretations of the AMP into four versions: 1) the form of primitive communism; 2) a form of primitive communism; 3) a transitional order from primitive communism to class-divided society, which nevertheless became a historical cul-de-sac; 4) an independent social order partly coterminous in time and level of development with the other major pre-capitalist social orders (O'Leary, 1989: 135). In fact, few of Marx's writings can be interpreted to endorse the statements of version (1) and version (2).

   Moreover, it is true that Marx once wrote to Engels, 'the Asian or the Indian forms of property constitute the initial one everywhere in Europe' (Marx, 1964: 139; cf. Marx, 1968: 441–2; 1976: 171). Nevertheless, read in its context, it is obvious that Marx did not imply that Europe passed through the AMP but that it developed from the primitive community, of which India offers 'a sample chart of the most diverse forms... more or less dissolved, but still completely recognizable' (Marx, 1973: 882).

17. Gellner reached a similar conclusion that 'the AMP is incompatible with a coherent Marxism' (Gellner, 1988: 47; cf. ibid.: 57).

18. O'Leary followed a similar logic in some of his arguments (O'Leary, 1989: 152–202).

19. In *Anti-Duhring* Engels pointed out the theoretical significance of Marx's methodology, 'to carry out this critique of bourgeois economics completely, it was not enough to be acquainted with the capitalist form of production.... The forms preceding it or still existing alongside it in less developed countries had also to be examined and compared, at least in their main features. By and large, this kind of investigation and comparison has as yet been undertaken only by Marx' (Engels, 1976: 192).

20. Cf. Marx, 1976: 452 where he compared three forms of cooperation. Also in *Capital*, Vol. 3, Marx wrote: 'Usury has a revolutionary effect on pre-capitalist modes of production only insofar as it destroys and dissolves the forms of ownership which provide a firm basis for the articulation of political life and whose constant reproduction in the same form is a necessity for that life. In Asiatic forms, usury can persist for a long while without leading to anything more than economic decay and political corruption. It is only where and when the other conditions for the emergence of the capitalist mode of production are present that usury appears as one of the means of formation of this new mode of production, by ruining the feudal lords on the one hand, and by centralizing the conditions of labour on the other' (Marx, 1981: 732).

21. As I shall argue in the first section of the next chapter, the claim that industrial capitalism did not first come to the world in places such as China is different from the thesis that it is *a priori* impossible for capitalism to grow out of a non-European society.

22. For a convincing elaboration of this book, see Cohen, 1978: 201–15.

23. As Marx eloquently argued in the *Communist Manifesto*, the capitalist mode of production is historically the most revolutionary mode of production in comparison with all the pre-capitalist societies. 'The bourgeoisie cannot exist without constantly revolutionising the instrument of production and thereby the relations of production, and with them the whole relations of society.... Constant revolutionising of production, uninterrupted disturbance of all social conditions, everlasting uncertainty and agitation distinguish the bourgeois epoch from all earlier ones.... It must nestle everywhere, settle everywhere, establish connexions everywhere' (Marx, 1968: 31–2). In the *Grundrisse* Marx further remarked that only a world market created by capitalism could provide 'the possibility of the universal development of the individual' (Marx, 1973: 542). Hence capitalism is an indispensable stage of human development.

24. For detailed discussions of slavery and feudalism, see, among many others, Anderson, 1974a, 1974b; Hilton, 1973, 1976; De Ste Croix, 1981.

25. It would be one-sided to think that the modes of production identified by Marx have exhausted the relevant possibilities. For further reference, see Byres, 1985: 9.

26. Anderson has forcefully argued against the application of feudalism in non–European societies except Japan (Anderson, 1974a, 1974b). But a more recent attempt to refute the temptation to globalize feudalism has been made by H. Mukhia (1981, 1985b), albeit on different grounds. Though I start with their analyses, I shall finish with a different conclusion.

27. In the ensuing pages I shall largely contrast the AMP on the one hand, and slavery and feudalism on the other. This does not mean that I conflate slavery and feudalism into one category. Indeed, there are many differences between the two (cf. Marx, 1964), but this is not the place to extend my analysis into this subject.

28. Although there had been slaves and personal dependence in Chinese history, they were always marginal, and were mainly within household work. Many Chinese scholars have sought evidence to support the claim that China experienced slavery as one of the inevitable stages of its development, but no one is able to prove that it had dominated the whole society, especially the process of production in any period of Chinese history (Balazs, 1967: 147; Melotti, 1977: 178). For further reference on the discussions by Chinese scholars about whether and when China experienced slavery, see Gan Linquan *et al.*, 1982 and the subsequent chapters of this book.

29. It is very important to note that immediately after these comments, Marx quickly added, '*only* from the European point of view' (ibid.: 495–6). It indicates that Marx had in mind the differences between societies.

30. My italics.

31. It is true that Marx did not spell out the conditions of the transition from feudalism to capitalism. However, he did outline many of the essential pre-suppositions for the emergence of capitalism, such as the release of agricultural population, the freedom to hire wage labourers, a high degree of commercialization, accumulation of money wealth and increasing throngs of labourers divested of means of productions. For detailed analyses, see, among others, Polanyi, 1957; Dobb, 1963; Hilton, 1973; 1976; Anderson, 1974a; 1974b; Wallerstein, 1974; Brenner, 1977; 1985; Harman, 1990.

32. In *The German Ideology* Marx further argued that the 'representative system of modern parliamentary democracy is a very specific product of modern bourgeois system, which is as inseparable from the latter as the isolated individual of modern times' (Marx and Engels, 1968: 217–18). To be sure, political emancipation is by no means the final form of human emancipation in general. However, in comparison with the traditional political systems, it is a great step forward and hence a stage to be passed through by all pre-capitalist societies sooner or later. For a more detailed argument, see Marx, 1975.

33. For further reference on the development of criminal law in ancient China, see the first section of Chapter 5.

2   THE ASIATIC MODE OF PRODUCTION AND THE MARXIST THEORY OF HISTORY

1. There are many reasons to explain why Marx over-emphasized the stagnancy of non-European societies. One of them might be the rhetorical requirements of his articles.

2. Similar comments can be found in the writings of many other scholars (Lichtheim, 1967: 69; 75; Avineri, 1968: 5; 9; Tokei, 1979: 23; O'Leary, 1989: 176).

3. As Habib has convincingly argued, some of Marx's writings on Indian history also suggested the existence of economic dynamism in India (cf. Habib, 1985: 46–7).

4. My italics.

5. Why did capitalism develop? It is a question which has been constantly asked by scholars. Up to now, there has never been consensus. Some scholars claim that the development of capitalism is contingent (Gellner, 1988; O'Leary, 1989), while Marxists consider 'history as a protracted process of liberation – from the scarcity imposed on humanity by nature, and from the oppression imposed by some people on others' (Cohen, 1988: vii). If the second thesis is correct, it will not be pure contingency that decides man's rendezvous with capitalism. For an eloquent defence of the second thesis, see Cohen, 1978.

6. O'Leary holds a similar view on the problem, albeit for a different reason (O'Leary, 1989: 177).

7. In his recent book *History, Labour and Freedom* Cohen adopts the so-called 'torch-relay' theory to explain world-wide historical development. The theory says that '[a]dvanced torch-carriers are likely, in time, to yield pride of place to once backward societies, and those societies do not have to repeat all the stages which the societies they begin by emulating went through. The torch shifts to a new carrier partly because the once advanced country or region tends to lock itself into the once progressive economic structure, which has lost its leadership value' (Cohen, 1988: 28). But this shift to a global understanding of Marxism seems to have overlooked the fact that each culture or civilization has its own dynamics of development. We shall never know which culture or civilization would have helped a society embark on a capitalist development before capitalism had come to the world. Therefore, even if Weber's thesis that Protestantism promoted the emergence of capitalism (Weber, 1976) is right, this does not mean that Protestantism is the only religion which is able to help generate capitalism. For example, as some scholars have argued, capitalist economic growth in Japan has its own proto-industrial origins (Howell, 1992: 269–86). (Arguments in support of the explanation that ancient Japan experienced the AMP can be found in Tokei, 1979: 87–91; Hoston, 1986.)

8. Similar comments can also be found in Marx's other writings (cf. Marx, 1968: 84; 418). These passages definitely encourage scholars to conclude that the AMP 'is not capable of giving rise to a higher stage out of itself, and that the revolution to which it is subject is a purely destructive one' (Dunn, 1982: 120).

9. Marx occasionally mentioned that villagers in Eastern societies traded with each other. The merchants travelled between villages. The monarch and his officials participated in the long-distance trade in luxuries (Marx, 1964: 71). Therefore, these conditions cannot be described as those of total autarky. However, Marx did not further develop these ideas.

Moreover, my limited knowledge deprives me of the right to talk about Indian history. Nevertheless, since O'Leary, in his recent attempt to refute the application of the AMP to Indian history, sought to establish his arguments by citing other scholars very selectively, I only intend to point out that firstly Sharma's thesis that India experienced feudalism is by no means the only explanation of Indian history; leaving aside his own admission that despite some evidence in Indian history which may suggest a feudal interpretation, feudalism of the Indian sort in fact differed from European feudalism (Sharma, 1985; criticism of Sharma can be found in, among others, Padhi, 1985: 6; Mukhia, 1985b). Secondly, Sharma, followed by O'Leary, defined feudalism exclusively in terms of its economic imperatives. Marx certainly would not have shared this opinion. On the contrary, Marx defined the feudal mode of production and other pre-capitalist economic formations not only in terms of their economic relations but also in their combination with different extra-economic institutions and ideologies. Marx might concentrate on discussing certain economic aspects at certain points, but he never isolated one aspect from another. Finally, it is important to note that O'Leary did not pay sufficient attention to the arguments of other authorities on Indian history such as Raychaudhuri who have sought to prove the validity of the AMP in India (Raychaudhuri, 1976: 839–47).

10. Obviously, tradition should be understood in the broadest sense of the word.

11. We should bear in mind that Marx's favourite maxim is '[n]ihil humanum a me alienum puto', which can be translated as 'I consider nothing human to be alien to me'.

12. This point has been stressed by authors such as Gellner (1989: vii).

13. No doubt it was truly visible and authentic at its early stage.

14. Eurocentrism is a doctrine which assumes that history is co-extensive only with the European historical tradition. O'Leary unpacked it into three interrelated components: racism, cultural chauvinism and Orientalism (O'Leary, 1989: 24–7). For more references, see, among others, Dawson, 1967; Moore, 1974–5; Said, 1977; Abdel-Malek, 1981.

15. For further reference, see O'Leary, 1989: 25.

16. For detailed arguments, see Hegel, 1905; 1958.

17. For more references, see Marx, 1976: 649; Cohen, 1978: 23, 152; 1988: 126.

18. Limited by his knowledge, he further claimed, tongue in cheek, that '[a]ll the civil wars, invasions, revolutions, conquests, famines, strangely complex, rapid and destructive as the successive action in Hindostan may appear, did not go deeper than its surface' (ibid.: 84). Similar comments about China can be found in Marx, 1968: 418–20.

19. As argued in the first chapter of this book, sometimes Marx himself failed to do so, especially in his analysis of the non-European world. He was too quick in passing his judgement on those societies of which he did not have a thorough knowledge.

20. A few pages later, Marx called the expropriation of the direct producers in England 'the most merciless barbarism, and under the stimulus of the most infamous, the most sordid, the most petty and the most odious of passions' (Marx, 1976: 928).

21. In another place Marx wrote, 'the misery inflicted by the British on Hindostan is of an essentially different and infinitely more intensive kind than all Hindostan had to suffer before' (Marx, 1968: 84).

22. It is from Goethe's Wetostlicher Diwan, 'An Suleika', and can be translated as 'Should this torture then torment us / Since it brings us greater pleasure / Were not through the rule of Timur / Souls devoured without measure?'

23. Marx quoted from Alexei Dmitryevich Saltykov's *Letters sur l'Inde* (Paris, 1848: 61). It can be translated as 'more subtle and adroit than the Italians'.

24. O'Leary claims that '[e]xaminations of Marx and Engels's correspondence have provided ample evidence for those who wish to level' at them charges of so-called Eurocentric racism (O'Leary, 1989: 25). This is a heavily biased judgement. First, he does not provide a single example to prove his claim. Second, If he is right, how can he explain Marx's great contempt of European bourgeoisie in his writings? For example, in one of his notes, Marx described Sir John Budd Phear as an 'ass' (Krader, 1972: 256), and, with ironic condescension, referred to him repeatedly as a Bursch (lad) (ibid.: 262, 271, 281). Fortunately, Sir John Budd Phear was British. Otherwise, for those seeking to find out Marx's Eurocentric racism, this, I suppose, would be one of their ideal examples.

25. Marx's comments on the Irish question represented an excellent example. As Marx wrote, 'quite apart from all phrases about "international" and "humane" *justice for Ireland* – which are taken for granted in the *International Council – it is in the direct and absolute interest of the English working class to get rid of their present connection with Ireland*. And this is my fullest conviction' (Marx and Engels, n.d.: 279–80).

3 THE MYTH OF THE SHANG

1. Some scholars do argue the essential reliability or even validity of the literary record of the later dynasties with regard to the existence of Xia (Chang, 1983: 4; 1986: 315–16; Ho, 1975: 420–1). If Xia ever existed, the nature of the society as revealed by the later textual records was in many ways basically identical with that of the next dynasty, the Shang. No doubt a period of transition must have existed, before the emergence of the Shang, with a certain degree of sophisticated economic and political organizations. However, before the future archaeological finds shed new light on the Xia, it is impossible to have a conclusive analysis of its social and economic features. Hence I exclude it from my analysis.

2. The Shang dynasty is also known as Yin, because the latter was the capital of the dynasty before it was conquered by the Zhou dynasty in 1122 BC. Yin was located near the present Anyang City in Henan Province.

3. For further information, see, among others, Hsu, 1965; Ho, 1975: 1–24; Sima Qian, 1972: 91–110; Chang, 1980: 322–8; Shaughnessy, 1991: xix.

4. For detailed analyses on the emergence of agricultural production in China see, Chang, 1968: 78–121; 1976: 1–21; 1986; Ho, 1975: 43–89.

5. Oracle-bone inscription (*jiaguwen*) refers to the first historical form of Chinese language known to us. It is preserved in the form of oracle records incised on turtle shells and cattle shoulder-blades. *Jiaguwen* was first found in the second half of the last century and since then more than fifteen thousand shards of bones have been found (Hu Houxuan, 1989: 2). The study of Shang oracle-bone inscriptions has become an important research subject with its own nexus of distinctive skills and its own technical literature. Since it provides a direct approach to the Shang society through its own

writings, it is essential to use relevant materials for any discussion on that period of Chinese history. For further information, see, among others, Dong, 1965; Yan, 1978; Keightley, 1978a; Wang Yuxin, 1989.

6. Traditionally, all the Shang oracle-bone inscription charges were regarded by scholars as questions. Since the grammatical form of most of the charges does not differ at all from that of both prognostication and verification, from the 1970s scholars began to doubt the traditional view and proposed that the Shang oracle-bone inscriptions were predictions (Qiu, 1988; 1989: 77–114; Nivison, 1989: 115–25) or attempts to control the future through ritual sacrifice (Allan, 1991: 112–23). This is still a question of debate. Given the premise that a question need not employ a final interrogative particle in Chinese, the great majority of charges can be translated as either statements or as questions. However, it would be a much more serious error to place a question mark after a statement than to place a period after a question. Hence, I shall not translate those inscriptions as questions in this book.

7. This is a controversial matter in both the Shang and Western Zhou studies. There is no agreement as to how the *lei* was pushed and pulled. For further reference, see, among others, Chen Wenhua, 1981: 422–3; Chen Zhenzhong, 1987: 54–78.

8. It is interesting to note that since many storage pits are found in and around the ceremonial places, this may well imply that the Shang was a centralized society. Furthermore, scholars notice that the harvest was also stored in centrally located granaries. Possibly the distribution of grain was also centrally controlled (Cheng, 1960: 197).

9. The Shang bronzes have been classified into seven categories by Cheng Te-K'un. This demonstrates not only the wealth of forms in the bronzesmith's repertoire, but also the almost exclusive emphasis on luxury items (Cheng, 1960: 167–8).

10. Recently another Shang tomb of similar scale has been discovered in Xingan County, Jiangxi Province (Li Xueqin, 1991a).

11. I am very grateful to Dr Allan for enlightening me on this point.

12. He served as an official historian-archivist during the reign of Emperor Wu Ti (140–87 BC) in the Han dynasty. He wrote the first of the official Chinese historical annals, entitled the *Shi Ji* or the Historical Records.

13. For a detailed analysis of the clan or lineage of the monarch, see Chang, 1980: 158–89.

14. *Zhong* can be translated as multitudes. Further explanation of this word will be given in the next section of this chapter.

15. *Di* here refers to God who has the power to decide what should be done. It is also called *Shang Di* (God on High) and primarily is a god of agricultural production (Cheng, 1960: 197, 202, 223). It is important to note that the Chinese conception of God is very different from that of the Western Christian God. For further explanation, see Eno, 1990: 1–26; Allan, 1991: 17, 56, 59–62.

16. The term *hang tu* is also translated as 'stamped earth' (Chang, 1968: 55, 137, 143, 342) and it refers to the technique of making foundations and city walls, which is characteristic of the Shang buildings. It is composed of putting earth into a caisson of wooden planks, and then pounding it

until it is sufficiently compact to withstand the ramming of another layer above it. Successive layers are added in this manner, one above the other, until the desired height is attained. Throughout Chinese history most of the town walls in northern China are constructed by this *hang tu* method. For further information, see An Jinhuai, 1961: 73–80; Shi Zhangru, 1969: 127–68.

17. Keightley believes that it would have taken about ten and a half years to build such a wall (Keightley, 1969: 128–9).

18. The status of *ren* will be discussed in the next section of this chapter.

19. For a systematic description of those archaeological discoveries, see Chang, 1980.

20. Shima Kunio listed 79 examples of similar divinations (Shima Kunio 1967: 124–5).

21. For a systematic discussion of the problem, see Keightley, 1969: 357–79.

22. The *Shang Shu* is one of the earliest historical documents in Chinese history to record the Shang events. Some scholars argue that it was written by Zhou scholars in the cause of their propaganda and hence does not contain valuable descriptions of the Shang (Creel, 1937: 55–95; Chen Mengjia, 1957: 112). But most specialists agree that not everything in the book came out of the imagination of the Zhou authors. Although it is difficult to identify all the forgery, a few sections in it may have preserved, possibly in edited form, some authentic Shang materials (Zhang Xitang, 1958: 198–9; Ho, 1975: 307). Moreover, the chronology of the Shang kings is still not definite. Ho believes that Pangeng was the nineteenth Shang king (Chang, 1980: 69). In 1300 BC Pangeng moved the capital to Anyang. This chapter records his speeches to persuade *zhongren* to go to the new capital with him. It is comprised of not only exhortations, but also threat to invoke ancestral spirits to punish those refusing to go with him (Ho, 1975: 307).

23. Another place where we can find the term *zhongren* is in the 'Chen Gong' of the *Shi Jing* or the Book of Songs (Karlgren, 1950b: 276). Since this verse is believed to originate around the eleventh century BC, it indicates that *zhongren* were also the main labourers at the beginning of Zhou dynasty (Dobson, 1968: xxiii–xxvi).

24. All the Fangs were considered by the Shang as barbarian tribes. The Shang often waged wars against them.

25. Specialists agree that Qin could be the name of a Shang clan whose members were hereditary generals of the Shang royal armies (Keightley, 1969: 31).

26. Presumably it is a place of ancestor-worship.

27. The Qiang refers to probably all the non-Chinese peoples north-west of the Shang state. The Shang not only often fought with them, but also used their captives for the royal sacrifices or royal household slaves such as horse grooms, occasionally as agricultural labourers and auxiliary soldiers (Hu Houxuan, 1944: 5b–7b; Yu Xingwu, 1957: 116; Shirakawa Shizuka, 1958; Li Xueqin, 1959: 80; Keightley, 1969: 372; Chang, 1980: 230).

28. Hu Houxuan claims to have found at least 7426 Qiang individuals that were contemplated for sacrifice in this manner in the oracle-bone inscriptions (Hu Houxuan, 1974: 57).

4 ECONOMY AND SOCIETY IN THE WESTERN ZHOU

1. Some scholars emphasize racial differences between the Shang and the Zhou (Eberhart, 1965: 28), but there is no convincing reason to support such a claim. For further arguments, see, Lattimore, 1962: 547; Chang, 1980, 1986: 362; Allan, 1991: 132.

2. Here I adopt traditional chronology. Scholars propose 18 different dates of the conquest of the Shang by the Zhou (Chang, 1983: 2; cf. Shaughnessy, 1991: 217–87). As indicated above, precise dates are not a prime requisite in a study such as this.

3. Since we do not possess definite knowledge about the timetable of Chinese history before 841 BC, any proposal of the reign period by those kings before King Xuan (827–782 BC) would be tentative in nature. For further reference, see Hsu and Linduff, 1988: 378–90.

4. Chengzhou was built after the conquest of the Shang. The purpose was to prevent a possible rebellion of the subjects of the previous dynasty in its heartland. The area of the present city of Luoyang was chosen as the site of the so-called eastern capital, since it was in a good strategic position to control the east–west route along the Yellow River, and the core of the fertile farming land under the Zhou rule (Hsu and Linduff, 1988: 124). Although they frequently went to Chengzhou to hold ceremonies, the kings of the Western Zhou carried out most of their activities mainly in the old capital, Hao, in the Wei valley of the present Shaanxi Province.

5. The Shang made short inscriptions in their bronzes, but little of historical value. By contrast, almost from the beginning of the dynasty, the Zhou manufactured bronze vessels with inscriptions which documented historical events by that time (Barnard, 1958: 35–6; 1960: 75).

6. To avoid possible controversies, I shall not quote some famous inscriptions, for instance the 'Mao Gong Ding' and 'Ji Zi Bai Pan', which have been questioned by Barnard and Keightley. I am not fully convinced by their claims, but I believe that ample evidence can be found from other inscriptions to support my arguments.

7. It is true that the *Zuo Zhuan* was also interpolated by the Han scholars (206 BC.–AD 25), but I shall only quote those materials taken by contemporary scholars as the most reliable.

8. Critical scholars believe that the *Zhou Li* was certainly not written before the 'Zhan Guo' ('the Warring States', 403–221 BC) period (Wheatley, 1971: 156–7). But a recent archaeological discovery at Yinqueshan in Linyi County of Shandong Province has confirmed that parts of the book might have been written by the Zhan Guo scholars (Yinqueshan, 1985). On the other hand, since it contains some Zhou materials, scholars in China quote the *Zhou Li* freely when they talk about any aspect of the Western Zhou. However, I shall not depend on it, because Western scholars still do not agree on which parts of it originated in remote antiquity.

9. According to some literary records, the Zhou seemed to have appropriated the Shang elite and its skilled labourers to work for the new dynasty. As the 'Shao Gao' chapter of the *Shang Shu* states: 'May the king first employ Yin's managers of affairs, and associate them with our Zhou's managers of affairs.' (Karlgren, 1950a: 15; cf. Hsu and Linduff, 1988: 116–17, 119).

10. Archaeological finds reveal that it is only after the middle reigns of the Western Zhou that bronze vessels were not exclusively owned by the royal court members. The 37 vessels cast by the Qiuwei family are among typical examples. For further reference, see, Qishanxian Wenhuaguan, 1976: 26–33; Zhou Yuan, 1976: 45–50.

11. Many other bronze inscriptions also record the similar claim of the king to be either 'the one man' or the ultimate authority 'over the four quarters'. For further reference, see Tang Lan, 1986: 485–6, 489, 492.

12. A recent discovery of several important bronze inscriptions has stimulated more discussion on the nature of the landownership system in the Western Zhou. Those vessels belonged to the Qiuwei family, and the inscriptions on them reveal that, towards the end of the Western Zhou, it was possible to exchange land among the officials (Qishanxian Wenhuaguan, 1976). Some scholars interpret the ancient Chinese character *she* (deposition) as 'sale', implying that those officials had the full ownership-right on their land (Lin Ganquan, 1976: 47; Zhao Guangxian, 1980: 221–35). But Tang Lan argues that the word *she* implies 'rent' (Tang Lan, 1986: 459–63). Finally, there are scholars maintaining that *she* refers to an exchange. Therefore, those officials only had an incomplete right to dispose of the land which was entrusted by the Zhou king. The overall control of landownership rights by the king was also indicated by the fact that exchanges of land had to be reported to the royal court with the approval of the official who had been originally given the land by the king. This hypothesis is most likely correct, because in most cases agreements would include a statement indicating explicitly that they were not only registered in the royal archives, but also verified by the royal ministers (Huang Shengzhang, 1981; Du Zhengsheng, 1985: 20; Hsu and Linduff, 1988: 276–9). On the other hand, the transfer of land did indicate that local officials had the discretionary power to dispose of the land they used. This was merely one of the first steps towards the eventual emergence of the concept of private property in China during the second half of the Eastern Zhou. For further reference, see next two chapters.

    Finally, it is worth stressing that the poem quoted above is considered by most scholars to have been written towards the end of the Western Zhou. If so, it may well imply that throughout the Western Zhou, it was a deep-rooted belief that all the land belonged to the king.

13. This is confirmed by some peculiar traditions of the Zhou. For example, first, primogeniture replaced the Shang practice of fraternal succession. Second, the animism of the Shang disappeared with the emergence of the Zhou. Third, bronzes during the Shang dynasty were mainly used for ritual purposes, while the Zhou secularized them almost from the very beginning of the dynasty. Apart from ritual ceremonies, they produced bronzes with long inscriptions commemorating military campaigns or glorious family histories, and so on, (Hsu and Linduff, 1988: 190).

14. It is known as *zong fa* in Chinese. The phrase consists of two characters. The first, *zong*, is a combination of two graphs: a 'rooftop' and an 'offering table'. The second character, *fa*, refers to 'a system of rules or regulations'. As one phrase, *zong fa* means that a group of people performs certain rituals to serve ancestors, but, in fact, it is a way of maintaining order through ancestral worship. According to traditional understanding, the *zong fa* was

segmented into branches, each of which was regarded as a subordinate to the line from which it was derived. The principal line was that of the king *da zong*. The major line was only a relative term in comparison with the segment, and vice versa. Hence the whole society was the segmentation of lineages, and everybody within the Zhou control was classified as belonging to one of the lineages (Chang, 1980).

15. How this system functioned is still not clearly understood by specialists. Both archaeological discoveries and classical literature indicate that each lineage was itself highly stratified, along blood lines. It consisted of several sublineages, and the members of each sublineage were related to one another according to a genealogically demonstrable relationship. Individual lineages, and even individual members within each lineage or sublineage, belonged to different strata (Chang, 1976: 72–92; Chun, 1990).

16. Some later writings give various numbers. For example, the *Zuo Zhuan* says that King Wu conferred land upon 15 of his brothers and another 40 people with the same surname (CQZZZ, 1981: 1494–5), while Xun Zi (298–238 BC) says that there were 71 of them altogether, of which 53 belonged to members of the royal family (the *Xun Zi*, 1979: 87). But, according to the *Yi Zhou Shu* or the Lost History of the Zhou, possibly compiled in the third or fourth century BC, the Zhou army conquered 99 cities, and imposed its authority on 652 others . However, when Ma Duanlin (fl. 1273 A.D.) wrote the *Wenxian Tongkao* or the Comprehensive Examination of Documents and Composition, the number of grantings became 1773 (Ma Duanlin, 1936: 2059b). In no way can we confirm or disprove these figures. For an attempt to map these places, see Wheatley, 1971: 65.

17. The king would address the people with his own surname as 'paternal uncles' and those with other surnames as 'maternal uncles' (CQZZZ, 1981: 1018; Guo Moruo, 1976: 262).

18. Traditionally, scholars believed that there was a royal domain in which the king ruled directly, while the other areas were governed independently by his relatives. However, Creel has convincingly argued that there was no such a distinction in the Western Zhou. Instead of being a loose confederation of lords, the Zhou empire was under the efficient control of the kings (Creel, 1970: 363–6).

19. Legge correctly translates *fengjian* as 'appointment (established) over the States' (Legge, 1871: 645), while Karlgren does not translate it directly (Karlgren, 1950b: 266).

20. A similar approach can be found in Bodde: 1956: 90–1; Keightley: 1969; Eberhard: 1977: 24; Hsu and Linduff, 1988: 177–85; Lewis, 1990: 28–35.

21. Cf. the first section of the next chapter.

22. For further reference, see the fourth section of Chapter 1.

23. For further reference, see the fourth section of Chapter 1.

24. As Needham correctly puts it, the Chinese town was 'not a spontaneous accumulation of production, nor of capital or facilities of production, nor was it only or essentially a market-centre; it was above all a political nucleus, a node in the administration network, the seat of the bureaucrat' (Needham, 1971: 71).

25. They had to pay tributes of various kinds as well as leading their army to launch military campaigns according to the orders of the king, etc.

26. Sometimes other phrases such as *ximing*, *ciming* and *celi* were also used. According to specialists, they were interchangeable with *ceming* in the ancient Chinese language (Qi Sihe, 1981: 51–2).

27. Occasionally it was held in the residential hall of the recipients and in the later period of the Western Zhou the king sometimes asked one of his trusted people to perform such a ceremony (Qi Sihe, 1981: 54; Hsu and Linduff, 1988: 250).

28. Traditionally, the Zhou aristocracy was considered to have five ranks (the *Zhou Li*: 18/21b–22b), but recent scholarship does not support the above division (Chen Pan, 1969: 686–7; Creel, 1970: 326–33). Thus, it is misleading to translate Chinese terms such as *Gong, Hou, Bo, Zi, Nan* into English as Duke, Marquis, Earl, Baron and Knight. Naturally, there is no such hierarchy of positions in which the duke ranked above the marquis and the marquis above the earl, etc. (Guo Moruo, 1954b: 39b–42a). Nevertheless, for the sake of convenience, I use some of the above-mentioned Western aristocratic titles in this book. It is worth stressing that the translations are customary and that they cannot be taken literally.

    Moreover, in order to support their claim that Zhou feudalism was eventually institutionalized, some scholars argue that the burial pattern of the aristocracy was neatly regulated during the mid-Western Zhou (Hsu and Linduff, 1988: 172–3). However, as Shaughnessy has convincingly demonstrated, the archaeological findings do not provide distinctive evidence of this (Shaughnessy, 1990: 204–5).

29. It is translated as 'steward' by Legge, 1871: 323–33; Creel, 1970: 119–20; Hsu and Linduff, 1988: 231.

30. The Chinese character *guo* has been translated as 'state' by most scholars. However, early Zhou graphs for *guo* depict a wall with gate towers. Hence the etymology of the word suggests that originally it only signified a fortified stronghold. This implies that *guo* was a town where an appointed official stayed. Later on it also referred to the vicinity of the city, and acquired the meaning of state only after the fall of the Western Zhou (Jiao Xun, 1888: 1/13–4; CQZZZ, 1981: 47; Hsu and Linduff, 1988: 268–9). As I shall further explain in the subsequent pages, the development of different meanings of the word *guo* was a parallel to the expansion of Zhou territory as part of the *fengjian* system. Nevertheless, it does not suggest the existence of independent states. Indeed, all the *guo* in the Western Zhou had to follow strict regulations set up by the king. Thus, it may create possible misunderstandings for non-specialists, if *guo* is interpreted as 'state' in English. Here I follow Wheatley to translate it as 'city-state', but it should not be confused with the concept of the Greek *polis*. The former 'refers simply to the geographic range of the political unit and does not imply democratic or popular rule' (Lewis, 1990: 267; cf. Ito Michiharu, 1975: 172–224; Kaizuka Shigeki, 1978a: 255–382; 1978b: 119–32; Du Zhengsheng, 1979; Tong Shuye, 1980).

31. Like *guo* ('city-state'), the word *bang* also has different meanings in Chinese. In the Western Zhou times it only referred to a city or a town. It was much later on that it acquired the meaning of an independent state (Hou Wailu, 1955: 151–60). Thus it is apparently inappropriate to translate this word into English as 'state' at this point (Karlgren, 1950b: 19, 196, 227, 242).

32. I here follow Hsu's translation (Hsu and Linduff, 1988: 115; cf. Shaughnessy, 1991: 3–4).
33. It is probably the name of an area.
34. This is chiefly decided by the 'slash and burn' method of cultivation. Since the hostile environment and low level of technology would soon exhaust the soil, peasants had to move to the new land after cultivating a plot for several years at a time (Yang Kuan, 1965; Zhang Zhenglang, 1973: 93). On the other hand, the increased territory required both the expansion and concentration of military power. Hence the administrative control in the Western Zhou was heavily mixed with military characteristics.
35. For further reference about the movements of other city-states, see Chen Pan, 1969; Hsu and Linduff, 1988: 158–63.
36. He was the grandson of the famous Duke of Zhou, one of the younger brothers of King Wu.
37. Tang Lan believes that the city-state of Shen is in the present Runan County, Henan Province (ibid.: 322). But, as Yang Bojun has convincingly argued, it is located at Laocheng of the present Shenqiu County, Henan Province (Yang Bojun, 1981: 527; 1360–1).
38. According to Mencius, such inspection took place twice a year (Meng Zi zhushu, 2A\6a; cf. Mencius, 1984: 30–2; but there is no independent information to confirm it.
39. More examples can be found in ibid.: 158, 166: Guo Moruo, 1976: 267–8.
40. The word *yuan* is a measure word in the Western Zhou, and Tang Lan believes that one hundred *yuan* approximate 1250 kg (Tang Lan, 1986: 309–12).
41. It is the name of a place.
42. For further reference, see, Tang Lan, 1986: 377, 389, 471.
43. For detailed information, see, the 'Shi Yin Gui', 'Cai Gui' (Tang Lan, 1986: 485–6, 473–4) and the 'Shi Ao Gui' (Guo Moruo, 1958: 149a, b).
44. This aspect of *ceming* has been emphasized by scholars such as Granet (1930: 112–13) and Maspero (1978). As Wheatley correctly points out, the Zhou *fengjian* has 'partaken of the character of an *exequatur* rather than of the *commendatio* of medieval Europe' (Wheatley, 1971: 121).
45. Both Creel and Keightley define the appointees as 'proto-bureaucrats' (Creel, 1964: 169; Keightley, 1969: 154).
46. According to Tang Lan, when king Zhao was not at the court, Queen Wang Jiang was empowered to carry out the king's duty (ibid.).
47. There are also cases in which the degree of responsibility given to a person changed. For example, two bronze inscriptions indicate that a musician was promoted from assistant in charge of small bells to assistant in charge of both small and large bells, as well as drums. Yet, in both inscriptions the phrase 'give you the post of your ancestors' is included. As Hsu correctly points out, it is unlikely that each official should follow exactly the same career path of his ancestor (Hsu and Linduff, 1988: 250).
48. Certain scholars seek to contend that subinfeudation existed in the Western Zhou (Chen Mengjia, 1956c: 105; Hsu and Linduff, 1988: 178–80), but there is no conclusive evidence to support their claim (Creel, 1970: 372–5).
49. Zheng was still located in the area between the present Fufeng County and Fengyang County in the western part of Shaanxi Province by that time. It

was later on that the Zheng lineage was ordered to move to the area of present Hua County in the eastern part of Shaanxi Province. Finally, it moved to the area of present Xinzheng County, Henan Province (Tang Lan, 1986: 369–70).

50. Other examples of promotions can be found in Guo Moruo, 1958: 102b, 139b.

51. The Chinese equivalent of the English word 'country' or 'state' is *guojia*, which literarily is a combination of two characters: *guo* ('state') and *jia* ('family'). For the ancient Chinese, state (*guo*) is nothing but a larger family (*jia*). This idea originated in the Western Zhou, and was systemized by Confucius and his followers in the later dynasties.

52. Keightley believes that, like other poems in the *Shi Jing*, this ode merely represents the ritual liturgy of the Zhou temple and court. Hence all agriculturally related poems cannot be taken as a real description of the Zhou agricultural conditions in general (Keightley, 1969: 285–6). His claim is contestable, since most authorities in this area agree that the *Shi Jing* is unsurpassed for its authenticity and textual excellence (Karlgren, 1964; Waley, 1960; Gao Heng, 1980a). No description in those poems explicitly indicates that they are purely liturgical in nature. As Guo Moruo convincingly argues, if we regard the poems related to agriculture as exaggeration by the poets, why were the later poets unable to exaggerate to such extent (Guo Moruo, 1957: 118)?

53. The character *si* has been translated by some scholars as *si tian* (private land) (Karlgren, 1950b: 244; Waley, 1960: 161; Sun Zuoyun, 1966: 178). Here I follow Guo Moruo who considers *si* as 'plough'. For further reference, see Guo Moruo, 1957: 97; cf. Li Yunyuan, 1991: 95.

54. There are different interpretations of 'the thirty *li*'. Traditionally, 'thirty *li*' was thought to be the space occupied by 10 000 families (Legge, 1871: 584), but this calculation depended on the *Zhou Li* which is a much later work. The phrase reappeared in another poem 'Xiao Yia, Liu Yue', when it refers to the area in which the peasants lived (Karlgren, 1950b: 120). Presumably it refers to a large area, but not necessarily to 10 000 families (Amano Motonosuke, 1959: 95; 1962; Li Yanong, 1962: 70–5; Hsu and Linduff, 1988: 347).

55. Here the character *ou* refers to *ougeng* (pair cultivation). As indicated in the last chapter, this method of cultivation was popular in Shang times. All the contemporary literary sources clearly suggest that the Zhou continued the Shang tradition in field-work. For instance, the poem 'Zai Shan' documents similar sentences: 'They clear away the grass and the bushes. / Loud is the sound of their ploughing. / In thousands of pairs are the weeders, / they work in both the wet land and the field dykes' (based on Karlgren, 1950b: 250). We do not have a definite knowledge about the exact content of this method of farming. Sun Changshu suggests two possible ways. The first method might be that people face each other to loosen earth clods or to pick up root systems of plants by jacking them up, using digging-sticks for leverage. They might also do the work by standing shoulder to shoulder to open up irrigation troughs, or pile up ridges for planting (Sun Changshu, 1964: 51; Yang Kuan, 1964: 41; Chen Zhenzhong, 1987: 54–78; Hsu and Linduff, 1988: 351).

56. According to Chen Mengjia, the original meaning of *ji* is 'to till' (Chen Mengjia, 1956a: 533; cf. Kimura Masao, 1954: 124–5).

57. For more references, see, Jia, 615; 1369; Qian, 5. 20. 2; Hou, 28. 16; Heji, 9511; Yi, 966; Guo Moruo, 1976: 184.

58. Here I follow Chen Mengjia (1957: 112) in translating *li* as 'to give' instead of 'to regulate' (Karlgren, 1950b: 244) or 'appreciate' (Guo Moruo, 1957: 99). For further reference, see Keightley, 1969: 286–7.

59. Whether this part of the *Guo Yu* should be relied upon is still controversial. Some scholars insist that the *Guo Yu* has not transmitted the Western Zhou materials (Yang Bojun, 1981: 44), but most authorities believe that it depicts a basically correct outline at the end of the Western Zhou and the 'Chun Qiu' period (Wheatley, 1971: 151-5; Hsu and Linduff, 1988).

60. Perhaps it was an appeal to the *Shang Di* for a favourable harvest at the same time.

61. This term has different explanations. Legge translates it as 'minister of instruction' (Legge, 1872: 388), while Karlgren takes it as 'director of the multitudes' (Karlgren, 1950a: 139). Waley translates it as 'master of land' (Waley, 1960: 248), but here I follow Hsu to render it as 'minister of land' (Hsu and Linduff, 1988: 234). For further reference, see Keightley 1969: 259-60; Maspero, 1978: 45.

62. The *Guo Yu* also stresses the importance of the *si tu* in the *ji tian* ceremony towards the end of the Western Zhou (the *Guo Yu*, 1959: 8).

63. This method was practised by rulers of almost all subsequent dynasties throughout Chinese history.

64. Accordingly, other poems are also interpreted in this fashion. For example, the 'Zai Shan' is said to describe a peasant going to the public field with his family, while the 'Liang Si' is believed to refer to a peasant's work in the field of his landlord (Fu Zhufu, 1980: 58–67). This explanation is not tenable, because there was no individual landlord who had the legal right to own a piece of land in the Western Zhou.

65. Some verses indicate that even the farming tools were owned collectively. For instance, the 'Da Tian' reads: 'The great fields give a large crop; / we have seen to the seed-grain, we have seen to the tools;/ when all is ready, we go to work; / with our sharp plough-shares / we start working on the southern acres; / we sow the many kinds of grain, / they grow straight and large; / so that the wish of the distant descendant is satisfied' (based on Karlgren, 1950b: 166). It is very likely that 'the distant descendant' in the poem refers to the head of the lineage or sublineage.

66. There are different explanations as to the precise meaning of these three terms. *Zi* may refer to those recently-reclaimed new fields which have to wait for a year for actual planting. *Xin* refers probably to the land in its second-year preparedness, ready for planting, while *yu* presumably refers to well-treated land in its third-year preparedness, ideal for actual planting (Yang Kuan, 1965: 10–14; 45–8; Ho, 1975: 51–2). For a different interpretation, see, Legge, 1871: 582; Hsu and Linduff, 1988: 354.

67. The non-changing land refers to those fields that could be planted continually without lying fallow. Ho believes that this method of cultivation was possible on some land during the Western Zhou (Ho Ping-ti, 1975: 51–3).

Nevertheless, I do not find his argument convincing. For example, he clearly overestimates the fertility of the loess soil in ancient China (Ho, 1984: 723–33). Without improvement in farming tools and extensive use of fertilizers, it is hard to believe that there could exist 'non-changing land' of any kind. No evidence indicates that the above technologies were already available in the Western Zhou.

Moreover, Ho fails to offer solid evidence to prove that climatic and vegetational environment in ancient North China was similar to that of the present-day (Chang, 1986: 78–9).

68. It is obvious that once-changing land refers to the fields that only need one year fallow.

69. It refers to fallow land.

70. One of the latest systematic defence of this argument is provided by Chen Hanping (1986).

71. By the time the *Han Shu* or the Record of Han was written by Ban Gu (AD 32–92), there appeared new versions of the well-field system (Ban Gu, 24A/2b–4a).

72. For more information, see Chapter 6.

73. Kang Shu and Tang Shu are said to be two younger brothers of King Wu (Hsu and Linduff, 1988: 186).

74. The Chinese spelling of this Zhou is different from the 'Zhou' which is the name of this dynasty, although both have the same pronunciation.

75. Li Yanong believes that the Zhou adult male population was approximately sixty to seventy thousand persons when it started its campaign against the Shang. This, certainly, is a rough estimation. However, almost all specialists agree that the Zhou had much less population than the Shang (Li Yanong, 1962: 166–9; Hsu and Linduff, 1988: 69–70).

76. The theory is traditionally attributed to the Duke of Zhou (Ho, 1975: 328–38). Since there is a lack of independent information to confirm it, we do not know whether the traditional view is correct or not. Yet, from some preserved Shang sayings in the Western Zhou texts, the *Shang Shu,* it seems plausible to presume that the theory originated in Shang times. A breakthrough was possible for the Zhou only after they were stimulated by Shang wisdom (Legge, 1865: 408–9; Creel, 1970: 93–9; Hsu and Linduff, 1988: 109–10; Ano, 1990: 23–30).

77. Its religious origin has been discussed by Ho, 1975: 333–6; Hsu and Linduff, 1988: 99–100.

78. Some scholars give a rationalist and humanist explanation of this theory, because they argue that the theory stresses human effort. As Hsu remarks: 'This was humanism in its incipient form, a type of thinking that determined the subsequent orientation of Chinese thinking, both politically and philosophically' (Hsu and Linduff, 1988: 111; cf. Ho, 1975: 333–8). Nevertheless, this liberal interpretation is not shared by other scholars (Shaughnessy, 1990: 204–4).

79. As Chang convincingly contends, the Shang and Zhou shared a common culture, and they differed only in details (Chang, 1980: 347–50).

80. This is an extension of the Shang concept that the centre of their domain was the nucleus of the universe, the physical centre of the world (Hsu and Linduff, 1988: 96-9).

81.   The 'Da Feng Gui' (Guo Moruo, 1958: 1) inscription suggests that King Wu even conducted the Shang ceremony of *I Si*, which collectively paid homage to all the Shang ancestors. Through this ceremony king Wu, presumably, intended to authorize himself as the legitimate successor of the Shang dynasty (Li Xueqin, 1959: 9; Hsu and Linduff, 1988: 100). In the *Shang Shu* the king claimed to employ the virtue to bring harmony to all the people in China (cf. Legge, 1865: 418).

82.   It took place not long after the establishment of the Zhou as a dynasty, and was soon put down under the alleged leadership of the Duke of Zhou (CQZZZ, 1981: 1213; Hsu and Linduff, 1988: 186).

83.   According to historical records, some Shang people were ordered to move to the west to build the new Eastern capital Chengzhou, and some eventually settled down in the Wei valley (Ding Shan, 1956: 87–9; Hsu and Linduff, 1988: 117–18). These movements from one place to another resembled the settlements of different Zhou lineages throughout China by the decree of the Zhou kings. This only proves the existence of forced labour rather than slavery in the Western Zhou.

84.   A detailed description of the functions of the *chen* can be found in Keightley, 1969: 366–9.

85.   There are many bronze inscriptions, recording bestowal of *chen* upon other appointees. For example, the 'Er Zun' documents a conferral of ten households of *chen* upon Er (Chen Mengjia, 1956a: 81–2), while the 'Chu Gui' says that the king gave Chu ten households of Yi-barbarian *chen* from a tribe called Yi (Guo Moruo, 1958: 119b).

86.   The exact meaning of 'Pian' is not clear. Scholars suggest that it probably refers to a living area within a city (Chen Mengjia, 1956a: 323; Keightley, 1969: 166–7).

87.   Guo Moruo believes that they could be slaughtered by their masters, but he does not provide a single example (Guo Moruo, 1954a: 100).

88.   The only possible evidence is the 'Hu Ding'. It documents an exchange of horses, silk, and men, which indicates that five men were equivalent in value to one horse and one piece of silk. It has been used repeatedly by Guo Moruo and others to support their claim that slaves could be bought and sold by their masters (Guo Moruo, 1954a: 104; Yang Kuan, 1965: 75). However, this evidence is questionable. First, Keightley has cast serious doubts about its authenticity (Keightley, 1969: 197–9). Secondly, another authority in Chinese epigraphy, Yang Shuda, has offered a different explanation of this inscription. According to him, the word *mai* (sell) should be read as *shu* (redeem) (Yang Shuda, 1954: 58). Finally, even if it is a true inscription, it is the only record of slave transaction among thousands of Western Zhou bronzes.

89.   Keightley defines them as forced labourers (Keightley, 1969: 215), but this does not by itself mean that they were not slaves.

90.   Most scholars believe that the place 'Yi' refers to an area near the present Dantu County, Jiangsu Province (Tang Lan, 1986: 152–3). But others contend that 'Yi' refers to the area just south of the present Luoyang City, Henan Province (Huang Zhangsheng, 1983: 295–305; Shaughnessy, 1990: 204–5).

91.   For a detailed discussion of these interpretations, see Keightley, 1969: 222–7.

92. There can be no doubt that war captives were used for ritual sacrifices. Nevertheless, the numbers were definitely small, and they occupied a position external to the main structure of the Zhou society (Pulleyblank, 1958: 185-228; Wheatley, 1971: 203).

93. This theory was later used by the new rulers to justify their overthrow of the previous dynasties in China. Each claimed to have received the Mandate from Heaven to bring peace and prosperity to the people.

5   THE GREAT TRANSITION IN THE MAKING: THE EASTERN ZHOU

1. There are different opinions as to when the Zhan Guo started, but in this study I follow Yang Kuan to take 476 BC as the beginning of the period (Yang Kuan, 1980: 3–5).

2. The authors of this book are not known. But the materials seem to have been selected from the records of the Zhan Guo diplomats, strategists, politicians and so on. They were originally preserved in the Han (206 BC–AD 220) imperial library. Though it underwent alteration later on, it is believed to have reflected the general framework of the Zhan Guo period (Hsu Cho-yun, 1965: 191–2).

3. It is not clear who wrote this work and at what time, and to what extent the Han scholar Liu Xin (53 BC–AD 23) excised his recension (Hsu, 1965: 185–6; Wheatley, 1971: 154–5). After a careful study of the text, Karlgren believes that it is a contemporary work of the *Zuo Zhuan* (Karlgren, 1926: 58–9, 64–5). But I shall follow most scholars in using those materials which are believed to be compatible with the data found in the *Zuo Zhuan* and other reliable sources.

4. I shall not cite the *Gongyang Zhuan* or The Tradition According to Gongyang and the *Guliang Zhuan* or The Tradition According to Guliang to support my arguments in the discussion of the Chun Qiu period, since scholars agree that they were written in a much later time than the *Zuo Zhuan* (Yang Bojun, 1981: 43).

5. For example, the difficult situation of the city-state of Zheng is described in CQZZZ, 1981: 950–89.

6. Here I use the word 'state', because the previous city-states became fully-fledged territorial states, and their rulers enjoyed the political sovereignty over their individual territory by the Zhan Guo period.

7. Below them there was a class known as *shi*. They were descendants of rulers or ministers, but in due course they were reduced to no more than officials of one minister or another (Hsu, 1965: 7–8, 34–7, 88–9; Wheatley, 1971: 124).

8. By now the Eastern Zhou had greatly exceeded the Western Zhou in extent.

9. It is around the present Xingyang County of Henan Province.

10. It is probably around the eastern part of the present Wenxi County, Shanxi Province (ibid.: 1073).

11. For further reference, see Chapter 4.

12. For the genealogy in the city-state of Lu, see Hsu, 1965: 78–9. The genealogies of other city-states in the Chun Qiu period can be found in Blakeley, 1983.

13. For further reference on the struggles for survival among different clans in other city-states see: CQZZZ, 1981: 1474 for the city-state of Chu; ibid.: 1729–32 for the city-state of Song; ibid.: 1203, 1234–6, 1480 for the city-state of Qi.

14. He was once the Chancellor of the city-state of Qi and was credited as the author of the *Guan Zi* or *The Book of Master Guan*. It contains lengthy discussions with the Duke of Huan (r. 685–43) over proposed measures for reform. But scholars tend to agree that the book was most likely written by scholars in the Ji Xia school. The school was set up by King Xuan of Qi around 302 BC in Linzi, the present Zibo City of Shandong Province and was the centre of Chinese intellectual activity for more than half a century. The above thesis has been confirmed by a recent discovery of bamboo strips at Yinqueshan in Linyi of Shandong Province in 1972. Therefore, the book reflects the social conditions and state policies of the Zhan Guo period rather than the reality of Guan Zhong times. For further references, see *Guan Zi*, Xiao Gongquan, 1979: 5; Qiu Xigui, 1981: 245; Yinqueshan, 1985; Rickett, 1985: 15; 1989: 201.

15. He controlled the government in the city-state of Zheng from 543 BC to 522 BC (CQZZZ, 1981: 1180, 1421).

16. Creel has argued that written codes had been used extensively even in the Western Zhou (Creel, 1970: 161–8; 1980: 22–55). The *Zuo Zhuan* does mention the introductions of different legal codes in the Shang and Western Zhou, but none of its descriptions is clearly stated (CQZZZ, 1981: 1275; Bodde, 1986: 27).

17. It is interesting to note that the concept of natural law which accompanied the formation of the Roman empire did not appear in Chinese history (Cicero, 1928: 211; Needham, 1956: 518–69; Finnis, 1980).

18. As recent studies show, the Legalists were not the only people to have made contributions to the centralization of state power during the Zhan Guo period. The concept of Legalism is used here in a broad sense to refer to those advocating changes from traditional society to political organization of a new kind. For further reference, see Li Xueqin, 1985: 484; Hulsewe, 1986: 234–5.

19. Some of his economic policies will be discussed in the first section of the next chapter.

20. The *Shang Jun Shu* or *The Book of Lord Shang* was most likely not written by Shang Yang himself. However, scholars agree that it reflects the basic ideas of Lord Shang (Bodde, 1986: 34). As a recent discovery of Qin law strips at Shuihudi of Hubei Province has confirmed, after Shang Yang's reform, the state of Qin developed a detailed legal system. It contains specific regulations aimed at the smooth functioning of government and maintenance of its stability. It reveals how Legalist ideas were realized there. Hence, it represents not only a great step in the secularization of traditional society, but also a climax of the political development in the Eastern Zhou period. For further reference on the Qin law, see Hulsewe, 1985; Shuihudi, 1990.

21. Creel has argued that Shen Buhai (d. 337 BC), who was once the Chancellor of the state of Han, also made a great contribution in the process of bureaucratization of the government in ancient China (Creel, 1974).

 Moreover, it should be stressed that the Chinese spelling of the word Han here is different from another Han which is the name of the dynasty immediately following the Qin dynasty in 206 BC.

22. Some of his economic policies will be discussed in the first section of the next chapter.

23. The origin and specific development of this system have been discussed in Bodde, 1938: 135–9, 238–43; Yan Gengwang, 1961; Creel, 1964: 155–83; Wheatley, 1971: 179–82; Yang Kuan, 1980: 209–13, 230–2; Li Jiahao, 1987: 49–58.

24. A detailed analysis can be found in Hsu, 1965: 34–52.

25. This does not mean that kinship disappeared completely. Some of its features have persisted throughout Chinese history (cf. Baker, 1979; Faure, 1986).

26. Traditionally, Shang Yang was credited with having advocated the idea that law should be applied to all the people indiscriminately, regardless of their social positions (*Shang Jun Shu*, 4\5a–b; cf. Duyvendak, 1928: 273). But as the recent discovery of the bamboo strips at Shuihudi in Hubei Province shows, this policy was not strictly carried out. This feature of Chinese law has been inherited throughout its history.

27. It was modified by the rulers of the subsequent dynasties and became one of the most distinctive features of Chinese civilization. For instance, based on such a system, the Han dynasty introduced a civil service examination not later than 160 BC to select senior officials. As Creel correctly points out, China had established, many centuries before any other nation, a highly bureaucratic administration of society (Creel, 1970: 22–7, 53). Since then, the state has always been the expression of the rulers' will in China.

28. This is not the place to discuss in detail the great achievements in different fields of science in ancient China, unless they have immediate relevance to serve my arguments. For further information, see Yang Kuan, 1980; Li Xueqin, 1985.

29. Some scholars in China argue that there seemed to be a period in the first half of the Eastern Zhou in which bronze agricultural tools were rather widely used, at least in the lower Changjiang valley area (Yu Xingwu, 1957; Guo Moruo, 1976: 247–8; Li Xueqin, 1980a; 1985: 478–9; 1991a: 4–5). Bronze tools might have stimulated, to certain extent, the development of agricultural production, but evidence is still too scanty to allow a meaningful and reliable estimation. Thus we have to wait for more archaeological discoveries to enrich our understanding of the significance of bronze tools in ancient China.

30. The impact of this technological revolution on the changes of economic structure, especially that of landownership will be examined in the next chapter.

31. Prior to this finding, an iron dagger with bronze handle had been dated to the early Chun Qiu period at Jingjiazhuang site in Lingtai County of Gansu Province in 1979. Unfortunately, heavy erosion prevented metallographic

analysis from yielding any result (Liu Dezhen and Zhu Jiantang, 1981: 298–301; Li Xueqin, 1985: 318–9).

Furthermore, the fact that the iron sword is connected with a bronze handle and a jade face-guard shows that metallurgical iron must have been very precious by then. Therefore, it is perfectly plausible to assume that people had not known the technology for a long time when the sword was made (Yu Weichao, 1991).

32. Two other possible pieces of evidence which can be dated to the same period come from the verses 'Si Tie' and 'Gong Liu' in the *Shi Jing*. But the texts are ambiguous and subject to different explanations (cf. Karlgren, 1950b: 80, 206).

33. It is said to be a term of measurement.

34. Another two archaeological discoveries in Changsha of Hunan Province in 1976 and 1977 seem to further support my argument. According to the relevant report, the two sites should be dated to around the late Chun Qiu period. Among other objects two *ding* tripods were found, one in each site. Scientific analysis reveals that both tripods were made of cast iron (Wen Wu, 1978: 44–8; Li Xueqin, 1985: 321–2).

35. Most of these iron artefacts are listed in Lei Congyun, 1980: 92–102. But Li Xueqin tends to be more cautious and dates some of them to the early Zhan Guo period (Li Xueqin, 1985: 320).

36. Cf. the previous section of this chapter.

37. Another piece of evidence is preserved in the *Zuo Zhuan*. It indicates that the army of the city-state of Jin and that of Zheng fought at 'Tie' (*iron*) in 493 BC. Presumably the place is famous for its iron production, though the text does not give any definite explanation (CQZZZ, 1981: 1611).

38. For further reference, see ibid.: 23\1a; 24\7a; Needham, 1958: 4–9; Li Xueqin, 1985: 328; Zhang Hongyan, 1988: 268.

39. They were Qin, Qi, Yan, Han, Zhao, Wei and Chu. The most definite study of the political struggles among these states can be found in Yang Kuan, 1980; cf. Lewis, 1990.

40. The discoveries of more iron foundries dating to the Zhan Guo period in other states indicate that massive productions of iron implements were not confined to the state of Qin (Li Jinghua and Wang Wenqiang, 1991: 189–92).

41. Other archaeological remains also suggest that recasting of tools was not confined to the state of Qin (Bray, 1984: 162).

42. Twenty years later, another famous Chancellor Zi Chan in the same city-state carried out a new reform, but we are not well informed about whether it was related to irrigation or not (CQZZZ, 1981: 1181).

43. There is more documentation of irrigation projects in the Chun Qiu period, but the texts are either ambiguous or unreliable (Chi, 1963: 65–6; Sima Qian, 1972: 1407–15; Ho 1975: 47; Yang Kuan, 1980: 36–44).

44. It is the ancient name for the present Sichuan Province.

45. For further information on other great irrigation projects around the same period, see Chi, 1963: 96–7; Hsu, 1965: 131–3; Sima Qian, 1972: 1407–15.

46. Through comprehensive studies, many scholars have convincingly proved that it is a mismarriage to combine the concept of oriental despotism with the development of irrigation projects. As argued by Ho, 'insofar as ancient

China is concerned, the theory of the "hydraulic" genesis of culture or of despotism is completely groundless' (Ho, 1975: 48).

47. The Zhou rulers promoted the image that Hou Ji was their ancestor, but there is no reliable data to confirm the story. As to the other two people, our knowledge is also based on legends (Qi Sihe, 1981: 85; Chen Shuitian, 1988).

48. The book *Lun Yu* is a collection of Confucius's speeches, mostly with his disciples. It has been translated as *The Analects* in English. Scholars believe that it was compiled by his students a generation or so after his death.

49. They must have been made of stone or wood. Bray even argues that this invention was perhaps a further modification of a traction-spade of some kind (Bray, 1984: 162–6). However, it is extremely difficult to identify them with certainty, although traces of them have been found in different archaeological sites (Mu Yongkang and Wei Zhengjin, 1978: 67–73). The first reason is that the shapes of those archaeologically available tools are difficult to distinguish. Secondly, wooden tools perish easily in most conditions. If some early ploughs were indeed made of wood, they are no longer accessible to us. However, as my discussion in the subsequent pages seeks to demonstrate, ploughs of different kinds were all indigenously developed in China.

50. It is worth stressing that there must have been gradual improvements both in variety and quality of those tools, though scholars are not yet able to offer a detailed account of this evolution.

51. It is around the present Tengzhou City of Shandong Province.

52. Waley was one of the first Western scholars to reinstate this hypothesis (Waley, 1948: 803–4).

53. The strips can be dated to 217 BC, but the area in which they were found was conquered by Qin in approximately 279 BC.

54. Guo Moruo believes that people in the Western Zhou already realized the importance of rotten grass as fertilizer (Guo Moruo, 1976: 248). It is plausible that from a much earlier time the ancient proto-Chinese peasants left the wild grass in the field after cutting it. The dead grass would be transformed into green fertilizer later on. But the available materials have not yet provided a definite answer as to when and to what extent its importance was realized by the peasants. Therefore, even if the ancient proto-Chinese had some knowledge about the effects of the green fertilizer, their main purpose was presumably to get rid of the grass, rather than anything else, before the mid-Zhan Guo period.

55. It is an eclectic collection of different essays compiled under the patronage of the Qin Chancellor Lu Buwei (290–235 BC). Traditionally, it is believed to have been written around 240 BC (Needham, 1959: 195). Despite some modifications in the later years, it preserves a reasonably faithful record of the Zhan Guo period.

56. Yang Kuan, basing his argument on an ambiguous statement in the *Zuo Zhuan,* reckons that people in the Chun Qiu period were capable of two harvests in a year (CQZZZ, 1981: 27). But Tong Shuyie has convincingly refuted the thesis. For further reference, see Tong Shuyie, 1980: 372–3.

57. It was discovered at Yinqueshan in Linyi of Shandong Province in 1972. Scholars believe that they were probably written by scholars in the state of Qi during the mid-Zhan Guo period (Qiu Xigui, 1981: 246).

58. According to Ho, one picul is equal to about twenty litres (Ho, 1975: 85; cf. Hulsewe, 1985: 19).

59. As argued above, Ho seems wrong to presume that there was no substantial change in productivity from Neolithic times to around 400 BC (Ho, 1975: 82–3).

60. They were presumably places under the control of a minister, that is, *qing* or *daifu*.

61. The Chinese spelling of this 'Wei' is different from that of the state of Wei during the Zhan Guo period discussed in the first section of this chapter.

62. It is in the present Hua County of Henan Province.

63. Scholars tend to agree that there were about three people on each chariot, which was followed by approximately ten infantrymen (Guo Moruo, 1976: 270; Lan, 1979; CQZZZ, 1981: 13). Moreover, it is still not clear how the infantrymen could catch up with the fast-moving chariots, since there were around four horses in front of each chariot. But it is beyond doubt that chariot-fighting was the main form of war, and it was not replaced by infantry-fighting until the Zhan Guo period in China (ibid.).

64. It is around the present Tong County and Qi County in Henan Province.

65. It was originally located to the east of present Xuchang City of Henan Province.

66. According to Tong Shuyie, the city-state of Jin moved its capital at least five times around the same period (Tong Shuyie, 1980: 225–7), while Chu moved its capital as many as six times (ibid.: 230–6). For the movement of other city-states, see CQZZZ, 1981: 347 for the city-state of Qi; ibid.: 1254 for the city-state of Lai; ibid.: 1604 for the city-state of Cai. Moreover, the constant movement of some city-states did not mean that there were no places in which people already settled down permanently. The *Zuo Zhuan* offered much evidence to indicate that some fertile land had already attracted people not to move again during the Chun Qiu period. For further reference, see the first section of the next chapter.

67. This estimate is very preliminary. Since there were three people on each chariot followed by ten infantrymen, the total number of soldiers should be 325 000. I add another 175 000 to the figure to include those in supply of equipment and of other related services. This means that there were seven more people with each chariot on average. The figure given here is most probably larger than the real one. However, since we lack first-hand reliable data, this somewhat arbitrary number is provided to guarantee that the upper limit of my estimation is correct.

68. To be sure, this estimate does not include those people living around or even within different city-states, but not yet integrated into Chinese civilization. They are excluded from my calculation, because we do not have sufficient information about them.

69. Similar descriptions can also be found in the Yinqueshan bamboo strips (Yinqueshan, 1985: 127).

70. Archaeological discovery of the ancient city of Linzi does not seem to confirm the historical description (Shandong sheng wenwu guanli chu, 1961: 289–97; Wheatley, 1971: 145, 149; Bodde, 1986: 98–9). Based on the same passage, Wheatley believes that there were 210 000 inhabitants in Linzi (Wheatley, 1971: 190).

71. He lived around the end of the Zhan Guo period. The authenticity of his book *Wei Liao Zi*, or The Works of Master Wei Liao, has always been doubted by some scholars. But the recent discovery of the Yinqueshan strips has proved that a similar copy of the book had already existed around the beginning of the Han dynasty. Thus it may well reflect the reality of the third century BC (Yinqueshan, 1985: 73–80).

6 THE DYNAMISM OF ANCIENT CHINA

1. Cf. the second section of Chapter 5.
2. Cf. the discussion in the ensuing pages.
3. As indicated in the Chapter 4, this term refers to labour service of a kind. Since all the land belonged to the Zhou king, he had the right to appropriate part of the harvest, although the exact amount of the tribute is not known.
4. It is in the present southeast of Shandong Province.
5. Similar accounts can be found in ibid.: 766; the *Guo Yu*, 1959: 5–6, 8, 74–5; the *Li Ji*, 14/12a.
6. For further information on other interpretations, see Wu Tingyu, 1987: 47.
7. For further reference on the topic, see Chapter 4.
8. Obviously the word *yuan* here is understood as rotation, since in ancient Chinese this character was homophonous with another, *huan,* which means 'switch', or 'rotate' (Duan Yucai, 2\37a–b).
9. The *shoutian* (land-bestowal) system was adopted in most states from the mid-Zhan Guo period on. It implies that individual peasants received fixed amounts of land from the state. For further reference, see the next section of this chapter.
10. For further reference, see the next section of this chapter.
11. Although some scholars believe that those exchanges took place between individual peasants (Guo Moruo, 1976: 325; Du Zhengsheng, 1983: 41), it seems implausible to me, since the existence of independent peasants during that time is still in question (Zhao Guangxian, 1980: 190).
12. For a detailed description, see Li Xueqin, 1983.
13. It is in the southern part of the present Xuchang City of Henan Province.
14. Of course, it is not difficult to find many more examples of forced annexations of lands, very often in the form of wars, in the *Zuo Zhuan.*
15. In many cases the nobles had to return the land (*zhi yi*) conferred upon them by the rulers of their city-states (ibid.: 1156, 1166, 1167, 1688).
16. Though we cannot exclude the possibility that occasional exchanges of land did happen in reality, we are not able to trace back those transactions with certainty.
17. This has been testified by the struggles between different sublineages described in the first section of the last chapter.
18. The Chinese spelling of this word is different from another Zheng which is the name of a city-state in the Chun Qiu period.
19. This is one of the three most controversial concepts pertaining to the evolution of taxation in ancient China. The other two concepts are *zhu* and *che.*

They were first mentioned together by Mencius (*Meng Zi zhushu,* 5A\4a–b; cf. Mencius, 1984: 96). However, Mencius was himself not able to make clear what their differences were and how they evolved. Therefore, all the later discussions on the topic are doomed to be speculations based on different interpretations of some plausible evidence. It seems unlikely that we can find an acceptable compromise to resolve the contradictions among different evidence in the near future. Nevertheless, since they are not immediately relevant to the present discussion, I should refrain from further comment. For further reference, see, among others, Amano Motonosuke, 1959: 141–4; Hsu, 1965: 108; Yang Lien-sheng, 1969: 92–76; Jin Jingfang, 1983; Hou Jiaju, 1986: 16–21.

20. It can also be understood as either an obligation or a taxation.
21. Legge is mistaken to believe that the tax was levied on the land of the whole city-state (Legge, 1872: 825).
22. Hou Jiaju suggests that before 594 BC Lu's taxation was about 10 per cent of the total harvest. After the reform, it was increased to 20 per cent. In 483 BC it was increased to 40 per cent (Hou Jiaju, 1986: 18). Although there is no independent information to verify these figures, an overall tax increase seems beyond doubt. One of the reasons will be discussed in the next paragraph of this section (cf. Sato Taketoshi, 1957: 1–24).
23. The exact size of one *mu* by that time is not clear. But some scholars suggest that it might have equated a size of 1 x 100 paces. According to one estimation, one foot was approximately 23.1 cm. long and a pace consisted of six feet. Hence one *mu* was about 200 square metres or 0.02 hectare (Gao Min, 1979: 168–70; Hulsewe, 1986: 215).
24. He was in charge of the government affairs of Zheng from 543 to 522 BC.
25. This is the earliest document of mutual surveillance system in Chinese history. It was later adopted and developed by Shang Yang in the state of Qin during the Zhan Guo period. Yang Bojun is apparently wrong to presume that the word *wu* (five) is a kind of taxation (Yang Bojun, 1981: 1181). For further reference, see the next section.

   Moreover, it is worth stressing that this system was inherited and modified by the subsequent imperial dynasties to control their population. This later version is known as the *baojia* system (cf. Yang Lien-sheng, 1957).
26. As indicated above, Zheng is not the first city-state to do so. Apart from the city-state of Lu, the *Zuo Zhuan* also clearly indicates that five years before Zi Chan became Chancellor of Zheng, similar policies had already been adopted in the southern city-state of Chu. In 548 BC Wei Yan, the Minister of the Army, was ordered to conduct a survey of all resources. He measured the forest and distinguished the good land from the bad in order to determine the amount of tribute (CQZZZ 1981: 1106–7).
27. The exact content of this *qiu fu* (*qiu* taxation) is not agreed upon by scholars. For further reference, see Gao Heng, 1980b: 150–2; Yang Bojun, 1981: 783–4; Hou Jiaqiu, 1986: 18–21; Lewis, 1990: 58–9.
28. For another extolment by Confucius on Zi Chan before his death, see ibid.: 1360.
29. The political philosophies of the so-called 'one hundred schools' have been extensively discussed by scholars (Feng Youlan, 1952; Xiao Gongquan, 1979; Schwartz, 1985).

30. He was in charge of the governmental affairs in the state of Wei when Duke Wen of Wei (403–387 BC) was in power.

31. The great reforms taking place in the state of Qin will be discussed in some detail below.

32. This area was under the control of the state of Qi during the Zhan Guo period.

33. We are not informed about the precise criteria required to divide land into different categories.

34. The exact amount of land distributed to each family is not clear. According to different sources, it seems that each family would receive either 100 *mu* of fertile land, or 200 *mu* of medium-grade or 300 *mu* of poor. There are some discrepancies between different descriptions. Since the natural conditions were different from one place to another, it was difficult to implement the policy with the same standard everywhere (*Zhou Li zhushu*, 10/9a; 15/9a; the *Guan Zi*; the *Xun Zi*, 1979: 172; Yinqueshan, 1985: 145–6).

35. For further reference, see the *Xun Zi*, 1979: 172, 179.

36. One *qing* is equivalent to the size of 100 *mu*. According to some recent archaeological discoveries, the size of one *mu* changed from 1 x 100 paces to that of 1 x 240 paces, which is about 0.47 hectare. But we still do not know how it developed in different places. On the other hand, scholars seem to agree that the new *mu*, that is, an area of 0.46 hectare, was introduced in the state of Qin after Shang Yang's reform (Gao Min, 1979: 168–70; Hulsewe, 1985: 19).

37. One bushel (*shi*) is about 20 litres.

38. There is little doubt that the discovered Qin bamboo strips represent merely a small portion of its total legal codes.

39. Why, then, did they not bother to state unambiguously that the bestowed land belonged to the receivers permanently? Perhaps it was such a common event that people simply took it for granted. We cannot expect the ancient people to think in the way we prefer. Of course, this is pure conjecture. We have to await future archaeological discovery to offer a definite answer.

40. Qin is traditionally considered as a backward state before the mid-Zhan Guo period. Two reasons are stressed by scholars. First, although it was once the centre of the Western Zhou polity, the invasion of the non-Chinese around the 771 BC greatly hindered its development. Second, much of its population consisted of the so-called 'barbarians' who had come under the influence of Chinese culture not long previously (Sima Qian, 1972: 2234; the *Xun Zi*, 1979: 234). In recent years some scholars argue that Qin was less backward than it has been depicted in the classical texts (Hulsewe, 1986: 213). But no compelling evidence suggests that Qin was better developed than those eastern states (cf. Ota Yukio, 1980: 13–24, 46; Lin Jianming, 1980).

41. For a detailed discussion, see Duyvendak, 1928.

42. The exact rate of taxation in Qin and other states during the Zhan Guo period is not clear. It must have been different from one state to another, and within each state it would have changed along with the changes of economic policies (Wen Wu, 1976: 94; Huang Jinyan, 1981: 61–82; Hulsewe, 1986: 219).

43. Married sons were considered as heads of different families (Duyvendak, 1928: 15).

44. Evidence indicates that military bravery was encouraged towards the end of the Chun Qiu period in some city-states (CQZZZ, 1981: 1614). Moreover, according to contemporary sources, this tradition was preserved in some states during the Zhan Guo period (the *Xun Zi*, 1979: 234). However, Qin seemed to be the only state which set up a comprehensive system to award soldiers for their military merit. As will be discussed below, this policy not only had a revolutionary effect on the transition from communal to private landownership, but also constituted one of the most crucial reasons for Qin's eventual success in conquering all other states in 221 BC.

45. Kroll classifies the status of the five families as slaves, but the word *li* in the text does not warrant such an interpretation. In fact, it implies 'having power over' in a very general sense here (cf. the *Xun Zi*, 1979: 236; Kroll, 1990: 70).

46. Of course, we cannot exclude the possibility that fallow systems of some kind were practised by the peasants in the state of Qin as a result of having more land to cultivate after Shang Yang's reform. But it is worth stressing that this system is not necessarily related to the *shoutian* system under the present discussion (cf. Li Jiemin, 1981: 47–60; Hulsewe, 1986: 216).

47. *Qianmo* refers to roads and paths running either north–south or east–west (Cheng Yaotian, 541/43a–44a). Yang Kuan contends that the different explanations depended on the course of the rivers in different geographical conditions (Yang Kuan, 1982: 84; Shuihudi, 1990: 108). *Feng* are the earth-mounds dividing different fields. Another archaeological discovery of Qin wooden tablets from Qingchuan County of Sichuan Province in 1979 has confirmed that such a mound was four feet or just over one metre high, with sides of the same length (Sichuansheng bowuguan *et al.*, 1982: 11; cf. Hulsewe, 1985: 212). Most scholars believe that *qianmo* is *feng* (Tang Zangong, 1981: 57; cf. Hulsewe, 1985: 164), but a recent study by Huang Shengzhang has convincingly proved that the above understanding is wrong. According to Huang, *feng* and *qianmo* represent two different things. The former refers to any border-mound within the state, while the latter represents the ownership-right one has over a piece of land (cf. Huang Shengzhang, 1991: 87). Finally, *jiang* refers to borders between different fields.

48. Some scholars believe that the *qianmo* system is a symbol of the so-called well-field system which existed before Shang Yang's reform (Xu Xichen, 1983: 276; Bodde, 1986: 36). But this is not a well-grounded thesis, because, first, nowhere did Sima Qian make such an equation. Second, as indicated above, the existence of a well-field system in Qin is still in question.

49. Following another tradition, some scholars interpret the sentence in a totally different way. According to them, it means that Shang Yang adopted the *shoutian* system which was prevalent in the state of Qi by that time (Wu Shuping, 1976: 150). As argued above, this thesis cannot be borne out by contemporary evidence (cf. Hiranaka Reiji, 1967: 21–41; Moriya Mitsuo, 1968: 86–110; Koga Noboru, 1980: 92–108, Li Jiemin, 1981: 46–60).

50. The two wooden tablets contain a Qin statute on agriculture and were written on 29 September 309 BC.

51. According to the Yinqueshan strips, if the size of one *mu* is small, the taxation will be very heavy on the peasants. If the peasants have not enough to eat, there will be no increase of population and hence it is impossible for the state to grow strong. For further reference, see Wen Wu, 1976: 94–5.

52. Shang Yang was killed after being accused of plotting a *coup d'état* in 338 BC.

53. Following Hiranaka, Hulsewe argues that the concept of private property in Qin is different from the modern one. He believes that the right of a Qin peasant over his land was closer to the right of occupation rather than private property (Hiranaka, 1967: 3–22; Hulsewe, 1986: 217). In fact, similar ideas are also expressed by some Chinese scholars. It is certainly true that the modern concept of private property first came into existence along with the emergence of a bourgeois class in the West. There are variables in the concept in the modern sense which did not exist in ancient Greek and Roman times, but this does not mean that there was no private property protected by the states in the ancient West. The same is true with the concept of private property in Chinese history. For further reference, see Powelson, 1990: 165–79.

54. The term 'commoners' refers to peasants in the Zhan Guo period.

55. To be sure, it is not from generosity that the government allowed those peasants to return to cultivate their land. What the government really cared about was to gain more taxes from each harvest.

56. These people have been classified as slaves by most scholars (Lin Jianming, 1980: 91–9; Shuihudi, 1990: 149; cf. Hulsewe, 1985: 15–17, 27–8). As indicated above, slaves, especially family chattels, existed throughout Chinese history, but no serious scholar believes that slave labour has ever constituted a major part of the productive forces.

57. Some sources seem to suggest that slaves were given to the commoners to honour their military merits (Shang Jun Shu, 5\2b–3a; cf. Duyvendak, 1928: 299–300; Shuihudi, 1990: 153; cf. Hulsewe, 1985: 193).

58. One statute even suggests that some families had more than one slave (Shuihudi, 1990: 118; Hulsewe, 1985: 148–9), and no evidence implies that any land was given to slaves.

59. Another statute indicates that commoners were also permitted to borrow bond-women belonging to the government to work for them (Shuihudi, 1990: 32; cf. Hulsewe, 1985: 30).

60. A person who was less than six feet is classified as small by the Qin Law. Six feet was equivalent to 1.96 metres of modern times (Shuihudi, 1990: 33; cf. Hulsewe, 1985: 31).

61. It means that he had pocketed the taxes.

62. Note that this statute is said to be a revised version of a previous one (Sichuansheng bowuguan *et al.,* 1982: 11). It is plausible to assume that it has been improved in comparison with the previous version, which was probably formulated by Shang Yang some fifty years before.

63. As repeatedly indicated above, all the trades were strictly regulated by government officials. This prevented merchants from setting up free associations of any kind. Hence an opposition force which might have had a potential bargaining power did not emerge (cf. Hulsewe, 1985: 229–31).

64. This tradition was inherited and became one of the most important social and economic phenomena in the subsequent dynasties.
65. For further reference on Lu Buwei and other famous merchants during that period, see Sima Qian, 1972: 2505–14, 3253–84.
66. It is a contemporary term to refer to commoners.
67. It cannot be denied that there still was a large amount of land which belonged to the Qin state as a result of its expanding power (Qiu Xigui, 1981: 150–1). Furthermore, the available Qin codes indicate that different labour forces such as bond-servants, were employed by the state to carry out farming activities in the state-controlled land (Lin Jianming, 1980: 91–7; Qiu Xigui, 1981: 252–7; Shuihudi, 1990: 42–5; cf. Hulsewe, 1985: 30–3). But more and more land seemed to have been converted into private hands through the state policies discussed above (Qiu Xigui, 1981: 287–8).
68. 'Landlord' refers to those who employ others to work on their land, while 'small peasants' work on their own small piece of land.
69. For further references on the co-existence of modes of production, see, among others, Wolpe, 1980; 1985; Davidson, 1989.
70. All men between the ages of 15 and 60 except higher-ranking officials had to perform heavy statute labour in Qin (Hulsewe, 1984: 195–204; Shuihudi, 1990: 87, 132; cf. Hulsewe, 1985: 177).

Bibliography

Abdel-Malek, A, *Civilizations and Social Theory: Social Dialectics,* Vol. I, Macmillan, London, 1981.

Adams, R. M., *The Evolution of Urban Society: Early Mesopotamia and Prehispanic Mexico*, Aldine , Chicago, 1966.

Allan, S., *The Shape of the Turtles: Myth, Art, and Cosmos in Early China*, State University of New York Press, Albany, 1991.

Althusser, L., *For Marx*, tr. Brewster, B., Allen Lane, London, 1969.

Amano Motonosuke, 'Chugoku kodai nogyo no tenkai', *Tohogakuho*, 1959 (30): 67–166.

——, *Chugoku nogoshi kenkyu*, Ochanomizu Shobo, Tokyo, 1962.

Ames, R. T., *The Art of Rulership: A Study in Ancient Chinese Political Thought*, University of Hawaii Press, Honolulu, 1983.

An Jinhuai, 'Shilun Zhengzhou Shangdai chengzhi – Aodu', *Wenwu*, 1961 (4–5): 73–80.

An Zhimin, 'Zhongguo gudai de shidao', *Kaogu xuebao*, 1955 (10): 27–52.

Anderson, P., *Passages From Antiquity to Feudalism*, New Left Books, London, 1974a.

——, *Lineages of the Absolute State*, New Left Books, London, 1974b.

Ano, R., *The Confucian Creation of Heaven: Philosophy and Defense of Ritual Mastery*, State University of New York Press, Albany, 1990.

Anyang Gongzuodui, 1977: See Zhongguo shehui kexue yuan kaogu yanjiu suo Anyang gongzuo dui, 1977.

——, 1979: See Zhongguo shehui kexue yuan kaogu yanjiu suo Anyang gongzuo dui, 1979.

Avineri, S. (ed.), *Karl Marx on Colonialism and Modernization*, Doubleday, Anchor, Garden City, New York, 1968.

Bailey, A. M. and Llobera, J. P. (eds), *The Asiatic Mode of Production: Science and Politics*, Routledge and Kegan Paul, London, 1981.

Baker, H. D. R., *Chinese Family and Kinship*, Columbia University Press, New York, 1979.

Balazs, E., *Chinese Civilization and Bureaucracy*, ed. A. F. Wright, Yale University Press, New Haven, Conn., 1967.

Ban Gu, *Han Shu*, Sibubeiyao edition.

Banerjee, D., 'Marx and Transformality of 'Asiatic' Societies', *Essays in Honour of Professor S. C. Sarkar*, People's Publishing House, New Delhi, 1976.

——, 'In Search of a Theory of Pre-capitalist Modes of Production', *Marxian Theory and the Third World*, ed. D. Banerjee, Sage Publications, New Delhi, 1985: 13–40.

Barnard, N., 'A Recently Excavated Inscribed Bronze of Western Chou Date', *Monumenta Serica*, 1958 (17): 12–46.

——, 'A Recently Excavated Inscribed Bronze of the Reign of King Mu of Chou', *Monumenta Serica*, 1960 (19): 67–113.

——, *Bronze Casting and Bronze Alloys in Ancient China*, Nagoya: Australian National University and Monumenta Serica, monograph 14, 1961.

——, 'Chou China: A Review of the Third Volume of Cheng Te-K'un's Archaeology in China,' *Monumenta Serica*, 1965 (24): 307–442.

Beijing daxue lishixi kaogu jiaoyanshi, *ShangZhou kaogu*, Wenwu, Beijing, 1979. Abb. as Beida Lishixi.

Beijingshi wenwu guanlichu, 'Beijingshi Pingguxian faxian Shangdai tongqi', *Wenwu,* 1977 (11): 1–8.

Bielenstein, H., *The Bureaucracy of Han Times*, Cambridge University Press, Cambridge, 1980.

Bing: see Zhang Bingquan, 1957–1967.

Blakeley, B. B., *Annotated Genealogies of Spring and Autumn Period Clans*, Vol. 1, Chinese Materials Center, San Francisco, 1983.

Bloch, M., *Feudal Society,* Vol. I, Routledge and Kegan Paul, London, 1962a.

——, *Feudal Society*, Vol. II, Routledge and Kegan Paul, London, 1962b.

Bodde, D., *China's First Unifier: A Study of the Ch'in Dynasty as Seen in the Life of Li Ssu*, E. J. Brill, Leiden. Sinica Leidensia Vol. III, 1938.

——, 'Feudalism in China', *Feudalism in History*, ed. R. Coulborn, Princeton University Press, Princeton, 1956.

——, 'The State and Empire of Ch'in', *The Cambridge History of China, Vol. I: The Ch'in and Han Empires, 221 BC–220 AD,* eds D. C. Twitchett and M. Loewe, Cambridge University Press, Cambridge, 1986.

——, 'The Idea of Social Classes in Han and Pre-Han China', *Thought and Law in Qin and Han China*, eds W. L. Idema and E. Zurcher, E. J. Brill, Leiden, 1990: 26–41.

Bray, F., *Science and Civilization in China, Vol. 6, pt 2, Agriculture*, Cambridge University Press, Cambridge, 1984.

Brenner, R., 'The Origins of Capitalism', *New Left Review*, July–August, 1977 (105): 25–82.

——, 'The Social Basis of Economic Development', *Analytical Marxism*, ed. J. Roemer, Cambridge University Press, Cambridge, 1986: 23–53.

Brook, T. (ed.), *The Asiatic Mode of Production in China*, M. E. Sharpe, London, 1989.

Byres, T. J., 'Modes of Production and Non-European Pre-Colonial Societies: The Nature and Significance of the Debate', *The Journal of Peasant Studies*, 1985 (12.2–3): 1–18.

Carrere d'Encausse, H. and Schram, S. (eds), *Marxism and Asia, 1853–1964*, Penguin, Harmondsworth, 1969.

Chang, K. C., *The Archaeology of Ancient China*, 2nd edn, Yale University Press, New Haven and London, 1968.

——, 'ShangZhou qingtongqi qixing zhuangshi huawen yu mingwen zonghe yanjiu chubu baogao', *Bulletin of the Institute of Ethnology and Phinology*, Academia Sinica, Taipei, 1970 (30): 239–315.

——, *Early Chinese Civilization: Anthropological Perspectives*, Harvard University Press, Cambridge, Mass., 1976.

——, *Shang Civilization*, Yale University Press, New Haven, 1980.

——, *Art, Myth and Ritual: The Path to Political Authority in Ancient China*, Harvard University Press, Cambridge, Mass., 1983.

——, *The Archaeology of Ancient China*, 4th edn, Yale University Press, New Haven, 1986.

Changsha tielu dongzhan jianshe gongcheng wenwu fajuedui, 'Changsha xin faxian Chunqiu wanqi de tongjian he tieqi', *Wenwu*, 1978 (10): 44–8. Abb. as Wen Wu.

Chao Kang, *Man and Land in Chinese History: An Economic Analysis*, Stanford University Press, Stanford, 1986.

Chaudhuri, K. N., *Trade and Civilization in the Indian Ocean: An Economic History from the Rise of Islam to 1750*, Cambridge University Press, Cambridge, 1985.

——, 'The Indian Ocean Societies', *History Today*, July, 1992 (42).

Chen Banghuai, *Jiaguwen lingshi*, Renmin, Tianjing, 1959.

Chen Hanping, *XiZhou ceming zhidu yanjiu*, Xuelin, Shanghai, 1986.

Chen Liangzuo, 'Woguo lidai nongtian shiyong zhi lufei, *Dalu zazhi*,1973 (46.5): 22–47.

——, 'Woguo gudai de qingtong nongju – Jianlun nongju de yanbian', *Hanxue zazhi*, 1984a (2.1): 136–66.

——, 'Woguo gudai de qingtong nongju – Jianlun nongju de yanbian', *Hanxue zazhi*, 1984b (2.2): 363–402.

Chen Mengjia, 'XiZhou tongqi duandai (1)', *Kaogu xuebao*, 1955a (9): 137–75.

——, 'XiZhou tongqi duandai (2)', *Kaogu xuebao*, 1955b (10): 69–142.

——, *Yinxu puci zongshu*, Kexue, Beijing, 1956a.

——, 'XiZhou tongqi duandai (3)', *Kaogu xuebao*, 1956b (1): 56–114.

——, 'XiZhou tongqi duandai (4)', *Kaogu xuebao*, 1956c (2): 85–94.

——, 'XiZhou tongqi duandai (6)', *Kaogu xuebao*, 1956d (4): 85–122.

——, *Shangshu tonglun*, Shangwu, Shanghai, 1957.

Chen Pan, *Chunqiu dashibiao lieguo juexing ji cunmiebiao zhuanyi*, Academia Sinica, Taipei, 1969.

Chen Shuitian, *Zhongguo gudai shenhua*, Guji, Shanghai, 1988.

Chen Wenhua, 'Shi lun woguo nongju shishang de jige wenti', *Kaogu xuebao*, 1981 (4).

Chen Zhongyi and Zhao, Wang,' Zhongguo Lishishang de chengshi renkou', *Shihuo Monthly*, July, 1983 (13.3–4): 9–31.

Chen Zhenzhong, 'Ougeng shuyi', *Jingji yanjiusuo jikan*, Zhongguo shehui kexueyuan, Beijing, 1987 (9): 54–78.

Cheng Te-k'un, 'The Carving of Jade in the Shang Period', *Transactions of the Oriental Ceramic Society*, 1957 (29): 13–30.

——, *Archaeology in China Volume 2: Shang China*, Cambridge, 1960.

——, *Archaeology in China Volume 3: Chou China*, Cambridge and Toronto, 1963.

Cheng Yaotian, Gouxue jiangli xiaoji, *Huang Qing jingjie*, Xuehai shuyuan, Guangzhou, 1829 (541): 51–3.

Chi Ch'ao-ting, *Key Economic Areas in Chinese History*, 2nd edn, Paragon Book Reprint Corp., New York, 1963.

Chun, A. J., 'Conceptions of Kinship and Kingship in Classical Chou China', *T'oung Pao*, 1991 (76): 16–48.

Cicero, M. T., *The Republic III*, tr. C. W. Keyes, Harvard University Press, Cambridge, Mass., 1928.

Cohen, G. A., *Karl Marx's Theory of History: A Defence*, Oxford University Press, Oxford, 1978.

——, *History, Labour and Freedom*, Clarendon Press, Oxford, 1988.

Cohen, J., 'Review of Cohen, Karl Marx's Theory of History', *Journal of Philosophy*, 1982 (79.5).

Confucius, *The Analects (Lun Yu)*, tr. D. C. Lau, Chinese University Press, Hong Kong, 1983.

——, *Chun Qiu Zuo Zhuan zhu*, Annotated by Yang Bojun, Zhonghua, Beijing, 1981. Abb. as CQZZZ.

——, *Chun Qiu Gongyang Zhuan zhushu*, Annotated by Xu Yan (Tang Dynasty), *Shisan jing zhushu*, Yiwen, Taipei, 1976 (7). Abb. as Gongyang Zhuan.

——, *Chun Qiu Guliang zuan zhushu*, Annotated by Yang Shixun (Tang Dynasty). *Shisanjing zhushu*, Yiwen, Taipei, 1976 (7). Abb. as Guliang Zhuan.

Creel, H. C., *The Birth of China: A Study of the Formative Period of Chinese Civilization*, Reynal & Hitchcock, New York, 1937.

——, 'The Beginnings of Bureaucracy in China: The Origin of the Hsien', *Journal of Asian Studies*, 1964 (23): 155–83.

——, *The Origins of Statecraft in China, Vol. I: The Western Chou Empire*, University of Chicago Press, Chicago and London, 1970.

——, *Shen Pu-hai: A Secular Philosopher of the Fourth Century BC*, University of Chicago Press, Chicago and London, 1974.

——, 'Legal Institutions and Procedures during the Chou Dynasty', *Essays on China's Legal Tradition*, eds J. A. Cohen, R. R. Edwards and Fu-mei Chang Chen, Princeton University Press, Princeton, 1980.

Croce, B., *History as the Story of Liberty*, tr. S. Spriggi, New York, 1957.

Cui: see Guo Moruo, 1945.

Currie, K., 'The AMP: Problems of Conceptualising State and Economy', *Dialectical Anthropology*, 1984 (8): 251–68.

——, 'Marx, Lubasz, and the Asiatic Mode of Production: A Comment', *Economy and Society*, 1985 (14.3): 399–403.

Davidson, A., 'Mode of Production: Impasse or Passe?', *Journal of Contemporary Asia*, 1989 (19.3): 243–78.

Dawson, R., *The Chinese Chameleon: An Analysis of European Conceptions of Chinese Civilization*, Oxford University Press, London, 1967.

De Sainte Croix, G. E. M., *The Class Struggle in the Ancient Greek World*, Duckworth, London, 1981.

Ding Shan, *Jiaguwen suojian shizu jiqi zhidu*, Kexue, Beijing, 1956.

Dirlik, A., *Revolution and History: Origins of Marxist Historiography in China, 1919–1937*, University of California Press, Berkeley, 1978.

——, 'The Universalisation of a Concept: "feudalism" to "Feudalism" in Chinese Marxist Historiography', *The Journal of Peasant Studies*, 1985 (12.2–3): 197–227.

Dobb, M., *Studies in the Development of Capitalism*, Routledge and Kegan Paul, London, 1963.

Dobson, W. A. C. H., *The Language of the Book of Songs*, Toronto, 1968.

Dong Zuobin, *Xiaotun dierben: Yinxuwenzi: jiabian*, Shanghai, 1948. Abb. as Jia.

——, *Xiaotun dierben: Yinxuwenzi: yibian*, Shanghai, pt. 1, Nanjing, 1948, pt 2, Nanjing, 1949, pt 3, Taipei, 1954. Abb. as Yi.

——, *Yinlipu*, 2 vols, Academia Sinica, Taipei, 1964. Reprint of 1945 edition.

——, *Jiaguxue liushinian*, Yiwen, Taipei, 1965.

Draper, H., *Karl Marx's Theory of Revolution*, Monthly Review Press, New York and London, 1977.

Du Zhengsheng, *Zhoudai chengbang*, Lianjing, Taipei, 1979.
——, 'Bianhu Qimin de chuxian jiqi lishi yiyi', *Bulletin of Institute of History and Philology,* Taipei, 1983(54.3): 77–111.
——, 'Zhoudai fengjian jieti hou de junzheng xin zhixu', *Bulletin of Institute of History and Philology*, Taipei, 1984 (55.1): 73–113.
——, 'Cong fengjianzhi dao junxianzhi de tudi quanshu wenti', *Shihuo Monthly*, Feb., 1985 (14.9–10): 12–44.
——, 'Guanyu Zhoudai guojia xingtai de lice – "fengjian chengbang" shuo chuyi', *Bulletin of Institute of History and Philology*, 1986 (57.3): 465–500.
Duan Yucai, *Shuowen jiezi zhu*, Compiled by Xu Shen (d.ca. 120 A D,), Annotated by Duan Yucai (AD1735–1815), Yiwen, Taipei, 1974.
Dunn, S., *The Fall and Rise of the Asiatic Mode of Production*, Routledge and Kegan Paul, London, 1982.
Duyvendak, J. J. L, *The Book of Lord Shang, a Classic of Chinese School of Law*, Arthur Probsthain, London, 1928.
Eberhard, W., *Conquerors and Rulers*, Brill, Leiden, 1965.
——, *A History of China*, rev. 4th edn, London, 1977.
Elvin, M., *The Patterns of the Chinese Past*, Stanford University Press, Stanford, 1973.
Engels, F., *Anti-Duhring*, Foreign Language Press, Beijing, 1976.
——, *Anti-Duhring*, Marx and Engels, *Collected Works*, Lawrence and Wishart, London, 1987 (25).
Eno, R., 'Was There a High God Ti in Shang Religion?', *Early China*, 1990 (15): 1–26.
Fairbank, W., 'Piece-mold Craftsmanship and Shang Bronze Design', *Archives of the Chinese Art Society of America,* 1962 (14).
Fan Wenlan (ed.), *Zhongguo tongshi jianbian*, Shanghai, 1947.
Fang Falian (Chalfant, F. H.), *Jinzhang Suocang jiagu puci* (The Hopkins Collection of Inscribed Oracle Bones), The Chalfant Publication Fund, New York, 1939. Abb. as Jin.
Faure D., *The Structure of Chinese Rural Society: Lineage and Village in the Eastern New Territories, Hong Kong*, Oxford University Press, Oxford, 1986.
Feng Youlan, *A History of Chinese Philosophy*, tr. D. Bodde, Princeton, 2nd edn, 1952.
Feuerwerker, A., 'Chinese Economic History in Comparative Perspective', *Heritage of China: Contemporary Perspectives on Chinese Civilization*, ed. P. S. Ropp, University of California Press, Berkeley, 1990: 224–41.
Finley, M. I., 'Slavery', *International Encyclopedia of the Social Sciences*, New York, 1968 (14).
Finnis, J., *Natural Law and Natural Right*, Clarendon Press, Oxford, 1980.
Fu Sinian, *Fu Mengzhen xiansheng ji,* Vol. 4, National Taiwan University, Taipei, 1952.
Fu Zhufu, *Zhongguo jingji shi luncong*, Sanlian, Beijing, 1980.
Gao Heng, *Shi Jing jinzhu*, Guji, Shanghai, 1980a.
——, *Wenshi shulin*, Zhonghua, Beijing, 1980b.
Gao Min, *Yunmeng Qinjian chutan*, Henan Renmin, 1979.
Gardella, R., 'Squaring Accounts: Commercial Bookkeeping Method and Capitalist Rationalist in Late Qing and Republican China', *Journal of Asian Studies*, May 1992 (51.2): 317–39.

Gellner, E., *State and Society in Soviet Thought*, Blackwell, Oxford, 1988.
——, 'Foreword' to O'Leary, B., *The Asiatic Mode of Production*, Blackwell, Oxford, 1989.
Gernet, J., *A History of Chinese Civilization*, tr. J. R. Foster, Cambridge University Press, Cambridge, 1982.
Gettens, R. J., R. S. Clarke and W. T. Chase, *Two Early Chinese Bronze Weapons with Meteoritic Iron Blades*, Washington, DC, Freer Gallery of Art, 1971.
Godelier, M., 'The Concept of the 'Asiatic Mode of Production' and Marxist Models of Social Evolution', *Relations of Production, Marxist Approaches to Economic Anthropology*, ed. D. Seddon, Cass, London, 1978: 209–57.
Godes, M. I., 'The Reconfirmation of Unilinealism', *The Asiatic Mode of Production: Science and Politics*, eds A. M. Bailey and J. R. Llobera, Routledge and Kegan Paul, London, 1981.
Gouldner, A., *The Two Marxisms: Contradictions and Anomalies in the Development of Theory*, Macmillan, London, 1980.
Granet, M., *Chinese Civilization*, tr. K. E. Innes and M. R. Brailsford, Routledge and Kegan Paul, London, 1930.
Gu Derong, 'Zhongguo gudai renxun renshengzhe de shenfen tanxi', *Zhongguoshi yanjiu*, 1982 (2): 112–23.
Gu Donggao, 'Chun Qiu dashi bao', *HuangQing jingjie xubian*, Nanqing shuyuan, Jiangyin, 1888 (67–133). Guan Zi, Sibubeiyao edn.
Guo Baojun, 'B qu fajue ji zhiyi', *Anyang fajue baogao*, 1933 (4): 579–596.
——, 'Yijiu wulingnian chun Yinxu fajue baogao', *Kaogu xuebao*, December, 1951 (5): 1–61.
——and Lin Shoujin, 'Yijiu wuer nian qiuji Luoyang dongjiao fajue baogao', *Kaogu xuebao*, 1955 (9): 91–116.
Guo Moruo, *Nulizhi shidai*, Renmin, Beijing, 1954a.
——, *Jinwen congkao*, Kexue, Beijing, 1954b.
——, *Yinqi cuibian*, Beijing, 1945. Abb. as Cui.
——, 'Ze Gui ming kaoshi', *Kaogu xuebao*, 1956 (1): 7–9.
——, *Qingtong shidai*, Kexue, Beijing, 1957.
——, 'Liang Zhou jinwenci daxi kaoshi', Kexue, Beijing, 1958.
——, *Zhongguo gudai shehui yanjiu*, Shanghai, 1930; rev. edn., Kexue, Beijing, 1960.
——, 'Ban Gui de Zaifaxian', *Wenwu*, 1972 (9): 2–13.
——(ed.), *Zhongguo shigao*, Vol. 1, Renmin, Beijing, 1976.
——(ed.), *Zhongguo shigao*, Vol. 2, Renmin, Beijing, 1979.
——(chief ed.) *Jiaguwen heji*, 13 vols, ed.-in-chief Hu Houxuan, Zhonghua, Beijing, 1978–82. Abb. as Heji.
Guo Yu, Shangwu, Beijing, 1959.
Guo, Ruoyu *Yinqi shiduo*, Laixunge, Beijing, 1951. Abb. as Shiduo.
Habib, I., 'Classifying Pre-colonial India', *Journal of Peasant Studies*, 1985 (12.2–3): 44–53.
Hall, J. W., 'Feudalism in Japan: A Reassessment', *Comparative Studies in Society and History*, 1962 (5.1): 15–51.
Han Fei, *Han Fei Zi*, Sibu congkan edn.
Harman, C., 'From Feudalism to Capitalism', *International Socialism*, 1990 (2).
Hayashi Minao, 'Chugoku senshin jidai no hato', *Shirin*, 1966 (49): 234–62.
——, 'In shu jidai no zusho kigo', *Tohogakuho (Kyoto)*, 1968 (39): 1–117.

He Hao, 'Chunqiushi Chu mieguo xintan', *Jianghan luntan*, 1982 (4): 55–63.
He Qinggu, 'Lun Zhanguo shangye de fazhan', *Zhongguoshi yanjiu*, 1981 (2): 15–22.
He Qunchang, *Han Tang jian fengjian tudi suoyouzhi xingshi yanjiu*, Renmin, Shanghai, 1964.
Hegel, G. W. F., *The Philosophy of History*, tr. J. Sibree, Bell, London, 1905.
——, *The Philosophy of Right*, tr. T. M. Knox, Oxford, 1958.
Heji : See Guo Moruo, 1978–82.
Henansheng Bowuguan, 'Zhengzhou Shangcheng yizhi nei faxian Shangdai hangtu taiji he nuli gutou', *Wenwu*, 1974 (9): 1–2.
Hibbert, A. B. 'The Origins of the Medieval Town Patriciate', *Past and Present*, Feb. 1953: 15–27.
Hilton, R. H., *Bond Men Made Free*, Temple Smith, London, 1973.
——(ed.), *The Transition from Feudalism to Capitalism*, New Left, London, 1976.
Hindess, B. and Hirst, P., *Pre-capitalist Mode of Production*, Macmillan, London, 1975.
——, *Modes of Production and Social Formations: an Autocritique*, Routledge and Kegan Paul, London, 1977.
Hiranaka Reiji, *Chukoku kodai no densei to zeiho*, Toyoshi kenkyukai, Kyoto, 1967.
Ho Ping-ti, *The Cradle of the East*, Chinese University of Hong Kong Press, Hong Kong, 1975.
——, 'The Paleoenvironment of North China: A Review Article', *The Journal of Asian Studies*, 1984 (43.4): 723–33.
Hobsbawm, E. (ed.), *Pre-capitalist Economic Formation*, Lawrence and Wishart, London, 1964.
Hoston, G., *State and Revolution in China and Japan: Marxist Perspectives on the Nation-state Revolution in Asia*, Ph.D. Thesis, Harvard, 1985.
——, *Marxism and the Crisis of Development in Prewar Japan*, Princeton University Press, Princeton, 1986.
Hou: see Luo Zhenyu, 1916.
Hou Jiaju 'Jingtian congkao', *Dalu zazhi*, September, 1983 (67.3): 11–30.
——, 'Chunqiu Luguo fushui kao', *Zhonghua wenhua fuxing yuekan*, 1986 (19.4): 16–21.
Hou Wailu, *Zhongguo gudai shehuishi lun*, Renmin, Beijing, 1955.
Howell, D., 'Proto-industrial Origins of Japanese Capitalism', *The Journal of Asian Studies*, May 1992 (51.2): 269–86.
Hsu Cho-yun, *Ancient China in Transition: An Analysis of Social Mobility, 722–222 B.C.*, Stanford University Press, Stanford 1965.
——, and K. M. Linduff, *Western Chou Civilization*, Yale University Press, New Haven, 1988.
Hu Houxuan, *Jiaguxue Shangshi luncong*, Vol. I, Qilu University, Changdu, 1944.
——, *Jiaguxue Shangshi luncong*, Vol. II, Qilu University, Changdu, 1945.
——, *Zhanhou Jingjin xinhuo jiaguji*, Qunlian, Shanghai, 1949. Abb. as Jingjin.
——, *Zhanhou nanbei suojian jiagu lu*, Laixunge, Beijing, 1951. Abb. as Nanbei.
——, *Jiagu xucun*, 3 vols, Qunlian, Shanghai, 1955. Abb. as Xucun.
——, 'Shi "yu yi ren"', *Lishi yanjiu*, 1957 (1): 75–78.
——, 'Zhongguo nuli shehui de renxun he renji', pt. 2, *Wenwu*, 1974 (8): 56–67.
——, '"Jiaguwen nongye ziliao xuanji kaobian" xu', *Yindu xuekan*, 1989 (2): 2–3.

Hu Qianying, 'Fenghao kaogu gongzuo sanshinian de huigu (1951–81)', *Wenwu*, 1982 (10).

Huang Jinyan 'Qindai zufu yaoyi zhidu chutan', *Qinhan shilun,* Shaanxi Renmin, 1981: 61–82.

Huang Jingluo 'Yan Xiadu chengzhi daocha baogao', *Kaogu*, 1962 (1): 10–19, 51.

Huang Jun, *Yezhong pianyu sanji*, Beijing, 1942. Abb. as Ye.

Huang, R., *China: A Macro-History*, M. E. Sharpe, New York, 1988.

Huang Shengzhang, 'Weiheding zhong zhu yu zhutian jiqi qianshe de XiZhou tianzhi wenti', *Wenwu*, 1981 (9): 79–82.

——, 'Qingchuan xin chutu Qinmudu jiqi xiangguan de wenti', *Wenwu*, 1982 (9): 71–5.

——, 'Tongqi mingwen Yi Yu Ze de diwang jiqi yu Wuguo de guanxi', *Kaogu xuebao*, 1983 (3): 295–305.

——, 'Qin Fengzongyi washu jiqi xiangguan wenti kaobian', *Kaogu yu wenwu,* 1991 (9): 81–90.

Huang Zhanyue, 'Guanyu Zhongguo kaishi yietie he shirong tieqi de wenti', *Wenwu*, 1976 (8): 62–70.

——, 'Yunmeng Qinlu jianlun', *Kaogu xuebao*, 1980 (1): 1–28.

Hulsewe, A. F. P., 'Some remarks on Statute Labour during the Ch'in and Han period', *Orentalia Veneziana* I, ed. M. Sabattini, Olschki, Florence, 1984: 195–204.

——, *Remnants of Ch'in Law*, E. J. Brill, Leiden, 1985.

——, 'The Influence of the "Legalist" Government of Qin on the Economy as Reflected in the Texts Discovered in Yunmeng County,' *The Scope of State Power in China*, ed. S. R. Schram, School of Oriental and African Studies, University of London and The Chinese University Press, Hong Kong, 1986.

Ito Michiharu, 'Shukyo men kara mita Indai no ni-san no mondai', Toyoshi kenkyu, 1960 (20): 36–58.

——, *Chugoku kodai ocho no keisei*, Sobunsha, Tokyo, 1975.

Jaksic, M., 'Exploitation in the Mode of Capitalism and in the Asiatic Mode of Production', *Journal of Contemporary Asia*, 1990 (20.2): 224–38.

Ji zhong Zhoushu (Yi Zhoushu), Sibucongkan edition.

Jia: see Dong Zuobin, 1948.

Jiang Tao, 'Guoguo mudi fajue jishi', *Wenwu tiandi*, 1992 (1): 9–13.

Jiao Xun, 'Qunjing gongshitu', *HuangQing jingjie xubian*, Nanqing shuyun, jiangyin, 1888.

Jin: see Fang Falian.

Jin Jingfang, *Zhongguo nuli shehui de jige wenti*, Beijing, 1962.

——, *Zhongguo nuli shehuishi*, Renmin, Shanghai, 1983.

Jin Zutong, *Yinqi yizhu*, Shanghai, 1939. Abb. as Zhu.

Jingdu: see Kaizuka, Shigeki, 1960.

Jingjin: see Hu Houxuan, 1949.

Kaizuka Shigeki, *Kyoto daigaku jinbun kagaku kenkyujo shozo kokotsu moji*, Institute of Humanistic Sciences, Kyoto University, Kyoto, 1960. Abb. as Jingdu.

——, 'Kinbun ni arawareta reki no mibun ni tsuite', *Tohogakuho*, 1962 (23): 1–5.

——, *Chugoku no kodai kokka, Kaizuka Shigeki chosaku shu,* Vol. 1, Chuo Koron, Tokyo, 1978a.

——, 'Chugoku kodai toshi kokka no seikaku', *Kaizuka Shigeki chosaku shu,* Vol. 2, Chuo Koron, Tokyo, 1978b.

Kane U. L., 'Aspects of Western Chou Appointment Inscriptions: the Charge, the Gifts and the Response', *Early China,* 1981–2(2): 14–28.

Karlgren, B., *The Authenticity and Nature of the Tsuo Chuan,* Goteborg Hogskolos Arsskrift, 22, n.3, 1926.

——, *The Book of Documents,* Bulletin of the Museum of Far Eastern Antiquities (Stockholm), 1950a (22): 1–81.

——, *The Book of Odes,* Stockholm, Museum of Far Eastern Antiquities, 1950b.

——, *Glosses on the Book of Odes,* Stockholm, 1964.

Keightley D. N., *Public Work in Ancient China: a Study of Forced Labor in the Shang and Western Chou,* Ph.D. Thesis, Columbia University, 1969.

——, *Sources of Shang History: The Oracle-Bone Inscriptions of Bronze Age China,* University of California Press, Berkeley and Los Angeles, 1978a.

——, 'The Religious Commitment: Shang Theology and Genesis of Chinese Political Culture', *History of Religions,* 1978b (17): 211–25.

——, 'Early Civilization in China: Reflections on How It Became Chinese', *Heritage of China,* ed. P. S. Ropp, University of California Press, Oxford, 1990.

Kimura Masao, 'Sekiden to shoho', *Toyo shigaku ronshu,* Vol. 3, Tokyo kyoiku daigaku, 1954.

Koga Noboru, *Kan Choajoto senpaku kenkyoteiri seido,* Yusankaku, Tokyo, 1980.

Kokin, M. and Papaian, G., *Tszin-Tian, Agrarnyi Stori Drenogo Kitaia* (Tszin-Tian, the Agrarian Order of Ancient China), Leningrad, 1930.

Kolakowski, L., *Main Currents of Marxism,* 3 vols, Oxford University Press, Oxford, 1978.

Kosminsky, E. A., *Studies in Agrarian History of England in the Thirteenth Century,* Oxford, 1956.

Krader, L. (ed.), *The Ethnological Notebooks of Karl Marx,* van Gorcum, Assen, 1972.

——, *The Asiatic Mode of Production, Source, Development and Critique in the Writings of Karl Marx,* van Gorcum, Assen, 1975.

Kroll, J. K., 'Notes on Ch'in and Han Law, in Thought and Law', *Ch'in and Han China,* eds W. L. Idema and E. Zurcher, E. J. Brill, Leiden, 1990: 63–78.

Kusuyama Shusaku, 'Sho Yo enten ni tsuite', Tohogaku, 1973 (46): 70–87.

Kymlicka, W., *The Contemporary Political Philosophy,* Clarendon Press, Oxford, 1990.

Lan Yongwei, *Chunqiu shiqi de bubing,* Zhonghua, Beijing, 1979.

Lattimore, O., *Studies in Frontier History,* Oxford University Press, Oxford, 1962.

Legge, J., *The Chinese Classics, Vol. III: The Shoo King or the Book of Historical Documents,* Hong Kong and London, 1865.

——, *The Chinese Classics, Vol. IV: The She King or The Book of Poetry,* Hong Kong and London, 1871.

——, *The Chinese Classics, Vol. V: The Ch'un Ts'ew with the Tao Chuen,* Hong Kong and London, 1872.

Lei Congyun, 'Sanshi nianlai Chunqiu Zhanguo tieqi faxian shulue', *Zhongguo lish bowuguan guankan,* 1980 (2): 92–102.

Lewis, M. E., *Sanctioned Violence in Early China,* State University of New York Press, Albany, 1990.

Li Ji, 'Ji xiaotun chutu zhi qingtongqi(zhongpian)', *Zhongguo kaogu xuebao*, 1949 (4): 1–70.
——, 'Yinxu youren shiqi tushuo', *Bulletin of Institute of History and Philology*, Academia Sinica, 1951 (23): 523–615.
——, 'Xiaotun taoqi ziliao zhi huaxue fenxi', *Taida Fuguxiaozhang Sinian xiansheng jinian wenji*, National Taiwan University, Taipei, 1952: 123–38.
——, *The Beginnings of Chinese Civilization*, University of Washington Press, Seattle, 1957.
——, 'Yinxu chutu de gongyie chengji-sanli', *Bulletin of the College of Arts*, National Taiwan University, 1976 (25): 1–64.
Li Ji zhushu, Sibubeiyao edition.
Li Jiahao, 'Xian Qin wenzi zhong de "xian"' *Wenshi*, March, 1987 (28): 49–58.
Li Jiannong, *Xian Qin liang Han jingji shigao* Sanlian, Beijing, 1957.
Li Jiemin, '"Kai qianmo" bianzheng', *Wenshi*, March, 1981 (11): 47–60.
Li Jinghua and Wang, Wenqiang, 'Henan Hebishi Guxian Zhanguo he Handai yetie yizhi chutu de tienongju he nongjufan', *Nongye kaogu*, 1991 (3): 189–192.
Li Xixing, 'Cong Qishan xian fengchucun fajue yizhi kan XiZhou de jiazu gongshe', *Kaogu yu wenwu*, 1984 (5): 70–5.
Li Xueqin, *Yindai dili jianlun* Kexue, Beijing, 1959.
——, 'Cong xinchutu qingtongqi kan changjiang xiayou wenhua de fazhan', *Wenwu*, 1980a (8): 35–40, 84.
——, 'Qinguo wenwu de xin renshi', *Wenwu*, 1980b (8): 25–31.
——, 'Lun Duo You Ding de shidai ji yiyi', *Renwen zazhi*, 1981 (6): 87–92.
——, 'XiZhou jinwenzhong de tudi zhuanrang', *Guangming ribao*, 1983.
——, *Eastern Zhou and Qin Civilizations* tr. K. C. Chang, Yale University Press, New Haven, 1985.
——, 'Xingan dayangzhou damu de qiji', *Wenwu tiandi*, 1991a (1): 4–5.
——, 'Sanmenxia Guoguo gumu xinfaxian yu Guoguoshi', *Zhongguo wenwu bao*, 3rd Feb. 1991b.
Li Yanong, *Zhongguo de nulizhi yu fengjianzhi*, Renmin, Shanghai, 1954.
——, *Yindai shehui shenghuo*, Renmin, Shanghai, 1955.
——, *XiZhou yu DongZhou*, Renmin, Shanghai, 1956.
——, *Xinranzhai shilunji*, Renmin, Beijing, 1962.
——, *Li Yanong shilunji*, Renmin, Shanghai, 1964.
Li Yunyuan, 'XiZhou nongshishi "Yi Xi" bianjie', *Nongye kaogu*, 1991 (1): 93–5, 103.
Li Zhiting, 'XiZhou fengguo de zhengqiu xingzhi', *Hangzhou daxue xuebao*, 1981 (3): 48–53.
Lichtheim, G., *The Concept of Ideology and Other Essays*, Random House, New York, 1967.
Lin Ganquan, 'Dui Xizhou tudi guanxi de jidian xinrenshi', *Wenwu*, 1976 (5): 45–9.
——(ed.), *Zhongguo fengjian tundi zhidushi*, Zhongguo shehui kexueyuan, Beijing, 1990.
Lin, Ganquan, Tian, Renlong and Li, Zude , *Zhongguo gudaishi fenqi taolun wushinian*, Renmin, Shanghai, 1982
Lin, Jianming, 'Li chen qie bian', *Zhongguo shi yanjiu*, 1980 (2): 91–9.
——, *Qinshi gao*, Renmi, Shanghai, 1981.
Liu, E., *Tieyun canggui*, Beijing (?), 1903. Abb. as Tie.

Liu Dezhen, and Zhu Jiantang, 'Gansu lingtai xian jingjiazhuang Chunqiu mu', *Kaogu*,1981 (4): 298–301.
Liu Yu, 'XiZhou jinwen zhong de jizuli', *Kaogu xuebao*, 1989 (4): 495–522.
Loewe, M., 'The Orders of Aristocratic Rank of Han China', *T'oung Pao*, 1960 (48).
Lu Wenyu, 'Xi Zhou caiyi zhidu shulue', *Lishi yanjiu*, 1991 (3): 20–31.
Lu Zhenyu *Yin Zhou shidai de Zhongguo shehui*, Sanlian, Beijing, 1962.
Lubasz, H., 'Marx's Concept of the Asiatic Mode of Production: A Genetic Analysis', *Economy and Society*, 1984 (13.4): 456–83.
Luoyangshi wenwu gongzuodui, '1975–1979 Luoyang beiyao XiZhou zhutong yizhi fajue', *Kaogu*, 1983 (5): 430–41.
Luo Zhenyu, *Yinxu shuqi Qianbian*, N.p., 1913. Abb. as Qian.
——, *Yinxu shuqi kaoshi*, N.p., 1915.
——, *Yinxu shuqi qinghua*, N.p., 1914. Abb. as Qinghua.
——, *Yinxu shuqi houbian*, N.p., 1916. Abb. as Hou.
——, *Yinxu Shuqi xubian*, N.p., 1933. Abb. as Xu.
Luo Zhenyue, 'Qinguo shoutianzhi de jidian bianxi', *Qiusuo*, 1985 (1).
Ma Duanlin, *Wenxian tongkao*, Shangwu, Shanghai, 1936.
Mad'iar, L. I., *The Economics of Agriculture in China* (Zhongguo nongcun jingji), tr. Cung Hua, Shanghai, 1928.
Mandel, E., *The Formation of the Economic Thought of Karl Marx*, New Left Books, London, 1971.
Marx, K., *Economic and Philosophical Manuscripts of 1944*, Moscow, 1961.
——, *Pre-capitalist Economic Formation*, ed. E. Hobsbawm, Lawrence and Wishart, London, 1964.
——, *Capital: A Critique of Political Economy*, 3 vols, International Publishers, New York, 1967a, 1967b, 1967c.
——, *Karl Marx on Colonialism and Modernization*, ed. S. Avineri, Doubleday, Anchor, Garden City, New York, 1968.
——. *A Contribution to the Critique of Political Economy*, tr. S. W. Ryazanskaya, and intro. M. Dobb, Progressive Publishers, Moscow, 1970.
——, *Theories of Surplus Value*, Vol. I, Moscow, 1969; Vol. III, Moscow, 1972.
——, *Grundrisse*, tr. with a foreword by M. Nicolaus, Penguin/New Left Review, London, 1973.
——, *On the Jewish Question, Marx and Engels: Selected Works*, Vol. 3, London, 1975.
——, *Capital*, Vol. 1, Penguin/New Left Review, London, 1976.
——, *Capital*, Vol.2, Penguin/New Left Review, London, 1978.
——, *Capital*, Vol. 3, Penguin/New Left Review, London, 1981.
——, *The Late Marx and the Russian Road, Marx and the 'Peripheries of Capitalism,'* ed. T. Shanin, Macmillan, London, 1983.
Marx, K. and Engels, F., *Manifesto of the Communist Party*, Foreign Language Publishing House, Moscow, 1959.
——, *The German Ideology*, Lawrence and Wishart, London, 1965.
——, *The German Ideology* (complete text), tr. C. Dutt *et al.*, Moscow, 1968.
——, *Selected Correspondence*, Foreign Language Publishing House, Moscow, n.d.
Maspero, H., *China in Antiquity*, tr. F. A. Kieraman, Jr., The University of Massachusetts Press, 1978.
Masubuchi Tatsuo, *Chugoku kodai no shakai to kokka*, Kobundo, Toykyo, 1960.
Melotti, U., *Marx and the Third Word*, Macmillan, London, 1977.

Mencius, *Mencius* Vol. 1, tr.. D. C. Lau, Chinese University press, Hong Kong, 1984.

Meng Zi, *Meng Zi zhushu*, Sibubeiyao, edin.

Michael, F., *The Taiping Rebellion: History and Documents*, Vol. 2, University of Washington Press, Seattle, 1971.

Moore, C., 'The Prolet-Aryan outlook of Marxism: Were Marx and Engels White Racists?' *Berkeley Journal of Sociology*, 1974–5 (19): 125–56.

Moriya Mitsuo, *Chugoku kodai no kazoku to kokka*, Toyoshi Kenkyukai, Kyoto, 1968.

Mu Yongkang and Wei, Zhengjin, 'Majiabang wenhua he langZhu wenhua', *Wenwu*, 1978 (4): 67–73.

Mukhia, H., 'Was There Feudalism in India?', *The Journal of Peasant Studies*, 1981 (8.3): 273–310.

——, 'Marx on Pre-colonial India', *Marxian Theory and the Third World*, ed. D. Banerjee, Sage Publications, New Delhi, 1985a: 173–84.

——, 'Peasant Production and Medieval India', *The Journal of Peasant Studies*, 1985b (12.1–2–3): 228–51.

Mumford, L., *The City in History*, Harcourt Brace and World, New York, 1961.

Nanbei: see Hu Houxuan, 1951.

Needham, J., *Science and Civilization in China, Vol. 2: History of Scientific Thought*, Cambridge University Press, Cambridge, 1956.

——, *The Development of Iron and Steel Technology in China*, Newcomen Society, London, 1958.

——, *Science and Civilization in China, Vol. 3: Mathematics and the Sciences of the Heavens and the Earth*, Cambridge University Press, 1959.

——, *Clerks and Craftsmen in China and the West*, Cambridge, 1970.

——, *Science and Civilization in China, Vol. 4/3: Physics and Physical Technology: Civil Engineering and Nautics*, Cambridge University Press, Cambridge, 1971.

Ning Ke, 'Shilun Zhongguo fengjian shehui de renkou wenti', *Zhongguo shi yanjiu*, 1980 (1): 3–19.

Nishijima Sadao, *Chugoku kodai teikoku no keisei to kozo – niju to shakusei no kenkyu*, Tokyo Daigaku, Tokyo, 1961.

Nivison D., 'The "Question" Question', *Early China*, 1989 (14): 115–25.

O'Leary, B., *The Asiatic Mode of Production*, Blackwell, Oxford, 1989.

Ota Yukio, 'Sho Yo henpo no saikento hosei', *Rekishigaku kenkyu*, August 1980 (483): 13–24, 46.

Padhi, S., 'Property in Land, Land Market and Tenancy Relations in the Colonial Period: a Review of Theoretical Categories and Study of a Zamindari District', *Essays on the Commercialization of Indian Agriculture*, eds, K. N. Raj, *et al.*, Oxford University Press, Delhi, 1985: 1–50.

Plekhanov, G., *Selected Philosophical Works*, Vol. 1, Lawrence and Wishart, London, 1981.

Pirenne, H., *Medieval Cities*, Princeton University Press, New Jersey, 1925.

——, *Economic and Social History of Medieval Europe*, New York, 1937.

——, *Early Democracies in Low Countries*, W. W. Norton, New York, 1971.

Polanyi, K., *The Great Transformation*, Beacon Press Books, 1957. Reprint of 1944.

Powelson, J. P. 'Property in Chinese Development: Some Historical Comparisons', *Economic Reforms in China: Problems and Prospects,* eds. J. A. Dorn and Wang Xi, University of Chicago Press, Chicago, 1990: 165–79.

Puci: see Rong geng and Qu Runmin, 1933.

Pulleyblank, E. G. 'The Origins and Nature of Chattel Slavery in China', *Journal of the Economic and Social History of the Orient*, 1958 (1.1. pt 2): 185–221.

Qi Sihe , *Zhongguoshi tanyan*, Zhonghua, Beijing, 1981.

Qi Wentao, 'Gaishu jinnian lai Shandong chutu de ShangZhou qingtongqi', *Wenwu*, 1972 (5): 3–16.

Qian: see Luo Zhenyu, 1913.

Qinghua: see Luo Zhenyu, 1914.

Qiu Xigui 'Zhanguo wenzizhong de "shi"', *Kaogu xuebao*, 1980 (3): 285–96.

——, 'Sefu chutan', *Yunmeng qinjian yanjiu*, Zhonghua, Beijing, 1981: 226–301.

——, 'Guanyu Yinxu puci de mingci shifou shi wenju de kaocha', *Zhongguo yuwen*, 1988 (1): 1–22.

——, 'An Examination of Whether the Charges in Shang Oracle-Bone Inscription are Questions', tr. E. L.Shaughnessy, *Early China*, 1989 (14): 77–172.

Qishanxian Wenhuaguan, 'Shaanxisheng Qishanxian dongjiacun XiZhou tongqi shixue fajue jianbao', *Wenwu*, 1976 (5): 26–44.

Rapp, J. A., *Despotism and Leninist Party State Autonomy: The Chinese AMP Debate in Comparative Perspective*, Ph.D. Dissertation, University of Wisconsin-Madison, 1986.

——, 'The Fate of the Marxist Democrats in Leninist Party State', *Theory and Society*, September 1987 (16.5).

Rawski, E. S., 'Research Themes in Ming–Qing Socioeconomic History – the State of the Field', *The Journal of the Asian Studies*, 1991 (50.1): 84–111.

Raychaudhuri, T., 'The AMP and India's Foreign Trade in the 17th Century', *Essays in Honour of Professor S. C. Sarker*, People's Publishing House, New Delhi, 1976.

Raychaudhuri, T. and Habib, I., *Cambridge Economic History of India, Vol. 1, c. 1200–1750 A.D.*, Cambridge University Press, Cambridge, 1982.

Rickett, W. A. *Guanzi: Political, Economic and Philosophical Essays from Early China*, Vol. 1, translation of Chpts. 1–34, Princeton University Press, Princeton, 1985.

——, 'Guanzi Xuekan', *Early China*, 1989 (14): 201–11.

Roemer, J., *Analytical Marxism*, Cambridge University Press, Cambridge, 1986.

——, *Free to Lose*, Radius, London, 1988.

Rong Geng and Qu, Runmin, *Yinqi puci,* Harvard-Yenching Institute, Beiping, 1933. Abb. as Puci.

Rozman, G. R. (ed.) *The East Asia Region: Confucian Heritage and its Modern Adaptation*, Princeton University Press, Princeton, 1991.

Said, E., *Orientalism*, Routledge and Kegan Paul, London, 1977.

Sato Taketoshi, 'Shunju jidai Rokoku no fusei sei kaikaku ni kansuru ichi kosatsu', *Chugoku kodai no shakai to bunka*, Tokyo Daigaku , Tokyo, 1957.

——, 'Senshin jidai no zaisei', *Kodaishi koza,* Vol. 5, 1962: 383–403.

Sawer, M., *Marxism and the Question of the Asiatic Mode of Production*, Martinus Nijhoff, The Hague, 1977.

Schwartz, B. A, 'Marxist Controversy in China', *Far Eastern Quarterly*, Feb. 1954: (13.2).

——, *The World of Thought in Ancient China*, Harvard University Press, Cambridge, Mass., 1985.

Shandong sheng wenwu guanli chu, 'Shandong Linzi Qi gucheng shijue jianbao', *Kaogu*, 1961 (1): 289–97.

Shang Chengzuo, *Yinqi yicun*, Jinling daxue, Nanjing, 1933. Abb. as Yicun.

——, *Shang Jun Shu*, Sibubeiyao edition.

——, *Shang Shu zhushu*, Sibubeiyao edition.

Shanin, T. (ed.), *The Late Marx and the Russian Road, Marx and the 'Peripheries of Capitalism'*, Macmillan, London, 1983.

Shanxisheng wenwu guanli weiyuan hui, 'Shanxisheng wenguan hui Houma gongzuozhan gongzuo de zong shouhuo', *Kaogu*, 1959 (5): 222–8.

Sharma, R. S., 'How Feudal was Indian Feudalism?' *The Journal of Peasant Studies*, 1985 (12.2–3): 19–43.

——(ed.), *Survey of Research on Social and Economic History of India*, ICSSR, Ajanta Publications, Delhi, 1986.

Shaughnessy, E. L., 'The Date of the "Duo You Ding" and its Significance', *Early China*, 1983–5: 55–69.

——, 'Western Chou Civilization: A Review Article,' *Early China*, 1990 (15): 197–205.

——, *Sources of Western Zhou History: Inscribed Bronze Vessels*, University of California Press, Berkeley, 1991.

Shaw, W. H., *Marx's Theory of History*, Hutchinson, London, 1978.

Shen Changyun, 'Cong Yinqueshan zhushu "shoufa" "shouling" deng shisan pan lunji Zhanguo shiqi de shoutianzhi', *Zhongguo shehui jingji yanjiu*, 1991 (2): 1–7, 14.

Shen Wenzhuo, 'Fu yu ji', *Kaogu*, 1977 (5): 335–8.

Shi Jing (Maoshi zhengyi), Sibubeiyao, edn.

Shi Jing: see Karlgren, 1950b.

'Shi Qingchuan Qindu de tianmu zhidu', *Wenwu*, 1982 (7): 83–5.

Shi Weichang, 'Yelun Qin zi Shangyang bianfa houde tudi zhidu', *Zhongguo shehui jingjishi yanjiu*, 1986 (4): 16–25.

Shi Zhangru, 'Diqici Yinxu fajue: E qu gongzuo baogao', *Anyang fajue baogao*, 1933 (4): 709–28.

——, 'Yindai de hangtu banzhu yu yiban jianzhu', *Bulletin of Institute of History and Philology*, Academia Sinica, 1969 (41): 127–68.

Shiduo: see Guo Ruoyu, 1951.

Shima Kunio, *Inkyo bokuji kenkyu*, Kyuko Shoin, Tokyo, 1958.

——, *Inkyo bokuji sorui*, Kyuko Shoin , Tokyo, 1967.

Shirakawa Shizuka, 'In no kiso shakai', *Ritsumeikan soritsu gojishunen kinen ronbun shu Bungaku hen*, Ritsumeikan, Kyoto, 1951: 260–96.

——, 'In no ozoku to seiji no keitai', *Kodaigaku*, 1954 (3): 19–44.

——, Indai yuzuku ko, sono ni, Jaku', *Kokotsu Kinbungaku Ronso*, 1957 (6): 1–62.

——, 'Kyozoku ko', *Kokotsu Kinbungaku Ronso*, 1958 (9).

——, *Kokotsu kinbungaku ronshu* , Hoyu Shoten, 1973.

Shuihudi Qinmu zhujian zhengli xiaozu, *Shuihudi Qinmu zhujian*, Wenwu, 1990. Abb. as Shuihudi.

Sichuansheng bowuguan and Qingchuanxian wenhuaguan, 'Qingchuanxian chutu Qin gengxiu tianlu mudu', *Wenu*, 1982 (1): 1–15.

Sima Qian, *Shi Ji*, Zhonghua, Beijing, 1972.

Southall. A., *Alur Society*, W. Heffer & Sons, Cambridge, 1956.

Sun Changshu, 'Leisi de qiyuan jiqi fazhan', Renmin, Shanghai, 1964.

Sun Zuoyun, Shijing yu Zhoudai shehui yanjiu, Zhonghua, Beijing, 1966.

Swann, N. L. (tr.) *Food and Money in Ancient China: The Earliest Economic History of China to A.D. 25*, Princeton University Press, Princeton, 1950.

Tang Zangong, 'Yunmeng Qinjian suosheji tudi suoyouzhi xingshi wenti chutan', Yunmeng Qinjian Yanjiu, Zhonghua, Beijing, 1981: 53–66.

Tang Lan, 'He Zun mingwen jieshi', *Wenwu*, 1976a (1): 60–3.

——, 'Yong qingtongqi mingwen lai yanjiu Xi Zhoushi', *Wenwu*, 1976b (3): 31–9.

——, 'Shaanxisheng Qishanxian dongjiacun xinchutu XiZhou zhongyao tongqi mingci de shiwen he zhushi', *Wenwu*, 1976c (6): 55–9.

——, 'Luelun XiZhou weishi jiazu jiao cang tongqiqun de zhongyao yiyi', *Wenwu*, 1978 (2): 19–24.

——, *Xi Zhou qingtongqi mingwen fendai shizheng*, Zhonghua, Beijing, 1986.

Thorner, D., 'Marx, India and the Asiatic Mode of Production', *Contributions to Indian Sociology*, December 1966 (11): 33–66.

Tie: see Liu E. 1903.

Tokei, F., *Essays on the Asiatic Mode of Production*, Akademiai, Budapest, 1979.

——(ed.), *Primitive Society and Asiatic Mode of Production*, Mta Orientalisztikai Munkakozosseg, Budapest, 1989.

Tong Shuyie, *Chunqiu Zuozhuan yanjiu*, Renmin, Shanghai, 1980.

——, *Chunqiu shi*, Shandong daxue chubanshe, 1987.

Ulmen, G. L. *The Science of Society: Toward an Understanding of the Life and Work of Karl August Wittfogel*, Moulton Publishers, The Hague, 1978.

Waley, A., 'Note on Iron and the Plough in Early China', *Bulletin of the London School of Oriental Studies*, 1948 (12. 3–4): 803–4.

——(tr.), *The Book of Songs*, Grove Press, New York, 1960.

Walker, R. L., *The Multi-State System of Ancient China*, The Shoe String Press, Hamsden, Conn. 1950.

Wallerstein, I., *The Modern World System*, Academic Press, New York, 1974.

Wang Guowei, *Guantang jilin,* Zhonghua, Taipei, 1959. Reprint.

Wang Min, 'Guoguo mudi xin faxian', *China Pictorial*, 1991 (5): 34–9.

Wang Qingyun, *Shiqu yuji*, N. p. 1935. Reprint.

Wang Yuhu, 'XianQin nongjiayan sipian bieshi', Nongye, Beijing, 1981.

Wang Yumin, 'XianQin renkou chuyi', *Shanghai shifan daxue xuebao*, 1990 (2): 33–42.

Wang Yuxin, *Jiagu xue tonglun*, Zhongguo shehui kexue chubanshe, 1989.

Wang Zengxin, 'Liaoning Fushunshi Lianhuabao yizhi fajue jianbao' *Kaogu*, 1964 (6): 286–93.

Ware, R. and Nielsen, K. (eds) *Analyzing Marxism: New Essays on Analytical Marxism, Canadian Journal of Philosophy*, Supplementary Vol., 1989 (15).

Weber, M., *The Religion of China*, New York, Macmillan, 1951.

——, *Economy and Society*, 3 vols, Bedminster Press, New York, 1968.

——, *The Protestant Ethic and the Spirit of Capitalism*, London, Allen and Unwin, 1976.

Wei Liao Zi, *Wei Liao Zi zhuyi*, annotated by Hua Luzong, Zhonghua, Beijing, 1979.

Wei Si, 'Shilun beibi de zhineng yu YinShang shiqi de shangpin jingji', *Zhongguo shehui jingjishi yanjiu*, 1985 (1): 9–12.

Wen Wu, 1976: see Yinqueshan Hanmu zhujian zhengli xiaozu.

Wen Wu, 1978: see Changsha tielu dongzhan jianshe goncheng wenwu fajuedui.

Wheatley, P., *The Pivot of the Four Quarters: a Preliminary Enquiry into the Origins and Character of the Ancient Chinese City*, Edinburgh University Press, Ediburgh, 1971.

Wilbur, C. M., *Slavery in China During the Former Han Dynasty, 206 C–A.D 25*, Field Museum of Natural History, Chicago, 1943.

Wittfogel, K. A., *Oriental Despotism*, Vintage Books, New York, reprint of 1957 edition, 1981.

Wolpe, H. (ed.), *The Articulation of Modes of Production*, Routledge and Kegan Paul, London, 1980.

——, 'The Articulation of Modes and Forms of Production', *Marxian Theory and the Third World*, ed. D. Banerjee, Sage Publications, New Delhi, 1985: 89–104.

Wu Qichang, 'Qin yiian Zhongguo tianzhishi', *Shehui kexue jikan* (Wu Han University), 1935 (5): 534–83, 833–72. Partially translated into English by E-tu Zen Sun and J. De Francis in *Chinese Social History*, Octagon Books, New York, 1966: 55–102.

Wu Shuping, 'Cong Yinqueshan Hanmu zhujian "wu wen" kan Sunwu de fajia sixiang', *Sun Zi bingfa*, eds *Yinqueshan Hanmu zhujian zhengli xiaozu*, Wenwu, 1976: 141–161.

——, 'Yunmeng Qinjian suo fanying de Qindai shehui jieji zhuangkuang', *Yunmeng Qinjian yanjiu*, Zhonghua, Beijing, 1981: 79–130.

Wu Tingyu, *Zhongguo lidai tudi zhidu shigang*, *Jili daxue chubanshe*, 1987.

Xiao Gongqian, *A History of Chinese Political Thought*, tr. F. W. Mote, Vol. 1, University of Princeton Press, Princeton, 1979.

Xiao Tong, 'XiZhou mo rengong zhitie de faxian duiyu yanjiu Guanzhong de zhongda yiyi', *Guanzi xuekan*, 1991 (4): 34–8.

Xiaotun, see Zhonngguo shehui kexueyuan kaogu yanjiusuo, 1980.

Xiong Tieji and Wang, Duanming 'Qindai de fengjian tudi suoyouzhi', *Yunmeng Qinjian yanjiu*, Zhonhua, 1981: 67–78.

Xu: see Luo Zhenyu, 1933.

Xu Fuguan, *Zhou Qin Han zhengzhi shehui jiegou zhi yanjiu*, Xuesheng , Taipei, 1974.

Xu Xichen, 'Jin "zuoyuantian" jie binglun yuantian ji jingtian' *Zhongguo gudaishi luncong* Vol. 8, eds *Zhongguo xianQinshi xuehui mishuzhu*, Fujian Renmin chubanshe, 1983: 261–76.

Xu Xitai, 'Zhouyuan kaogu gongzuo de zhuyao shouhuo', *Kaogu yu wewu*, 1988 (5–6): 106.

Xu Zhongshu, 'Leisi kao', *Bulletin of Institute of History and Philology*, Academia Sinica, 1930 (2.1): 11–59.

——, 'XiZhou Qiangpan mingwen qianshi', *Kaogu xuebao*, 1978 (2): 139–48.

Xucun: see Hu Houxuan, 1955.

Xun Zi, *Xun Zi xinzhu*, Annotated by Beijing Daxue 'Xun Zi' zhushizu, Zhonghua, Beijing, 1979.

Yan Yiping, *Jiagu Xue*, Yiwen, Taipei, 1978.

Yan Gengwang, *QinHan difang xingzheng zhidu*, 2 vols, Academia Sinica, Taipei, 1961.

Yang Bojun, (ed.), Chun Qiu Zou Zhuan zhu, Zhonghua, Beijing, 1981.

Yang Kuan, *Gushi xintan*, Zhonghua, Beijing, 1964.

Bibliography 197

——, *Zhan Guo shi*, 2nd edn rev., Renmin, Shanghai, 1980.
Yang Lien-sheng, *Money and Credit in China*, Harvard University Press, Cambridge, Mass., 1952.
——, 'The Concept of "Pao" as a Basis for Social Relationships in China', *Chinese Thought and Institutions*, ed. J. K. Fairbank, University of Chicago, Chicago, 1957.
——, *Studies in Chinese Institutional History*, Harvard University Press, Cambridge, Mass., 1961.
Yang Shuda, *Jiweiju jinwenshuo*, Kexue, Beijing, 1954.
Yang Zuolong, 'Qin Shangyang bianfa hou tianzhi wenti shangque', *Zhongguoshi yanjiu*, 1989 (1) 1–13. *Jizhong Zhoushu* (Yi Zhou shu), Sibucongkan edition.
Ye: see Huang Jun, 1942.
Yi: see Dong Zuobin, 1948–54.
Yicun: see, Shang Chengzuo, 1933.
Yinqueshan Hanmu zhujian zhengli xiaozu (eds), *Sun Zi bingfa*, Wenwu, 1976. Abb. as Wen Wu, 1976.
Yinqueshan Hanmu zhujian zhengli xiaozu (eds), Yinqueshan Hanmu zhujian, Wenwu, Beijing, 1985. Abb. as Yinqueshan.
Yu Haoliang and Li, Junming, 'Qinjian suo fanying de junshi zhidu', *Yunmeng Qinjian yanjiu*, Zhonghua, 1981.
Yu Weichao, 'Shangcunling guoguo mudi xinfaxian suo jieshi de jige wenti', *Zhongguo kaogu xuebao*, 3 Feb. 1991.
Yu Xingwu, 'Cong jiaguwen kan Shangdai shehui xingzhi', *Dongbei Renmin daxue renwen kexue xuebao*, 1957 (2–3): 97–136.
——, 'Luelun XiZhou jinwen zhong "liu dui" he "ba dui" jiqi tuntianzhi', *Kaogu*, 1964 (3): 152–5.
——, 'Cong jiaguwen kan Shangdai nongtian kenzhi', *Kaogu*, 1972 (4): 40–1, 45.
Yu Yi, 'DongZhou kaogu shang de yi ge wenti', *Wenwu*, 1959 (8): 64–5.
Zeng Chaoyu and Yin, Huanzhang, 'Shilun hushu wenhua', *Kaogu xuebao*, 1959 (4).
Zhang Bingquan, *Xiaotun dier ben: Yinxu wenzi, bingbian*, Taipei, Pt 1. section 1 (1957); section 2 (1959); Pt. 2. section 1 (1962); section 2 (1965); Pt 3. section 1 (1967). Abb. as Bing.
Zhang Hangyan, *Chunqiu Zhanguo chengshi jingji fazhan shilun*, Liaoning daxue chubanshe, Shenyang, 1988.
Zhang Jinguang, 'Shilun Qin zi Shang Yang bianfa hou de tudi zhidu', *Zhongguo shi yanjiu* , 1983 (2): 26–42.
——, 'Lun Zhongguo gudai de qianmo fengjiang zhidu', *Nongye kaogu*, 1991 (1): 228–37.
Zhang Shouzhong, '1959 nian Houma "niucun gucheng" nan DongZhou yizhi fajue jianbao', *Wenwu*, 1960 (8–9): 11–14.
Zhang Xitang, *Shang Shu yinlun*, Xian, 1958.
Zhang Yachu and Liu, Yu, *XiZhou jinwen guanzhi yanjiu*, Zhonghua, Beijing, 1986.
Zhang Yinlin, 'Zhoudai de fengjian shehui', *Qinghua xuebao*, 1935 (10.4): 803–36, tr. by E-tu Zen Sun and J.de Francis, in *Chinese Social History*, Octagon Books, New York, 1966: 21–36.
Zhang Zhenglang, 'Puci poutian jiqi xiangguan zhu wenti', *Kaogu xuebao* 1973 (1): 93–118.

Zhang Zhengming, 'Chudu bian', *Jianghan luntan*, 1982 (4): 64–8.

Zhang Zhenxin, 'Handai de niugeng', *Wenwu*, 1977 (8): 57–63.

Zhanguo Ce, Compiled by Liu Xiang, Guji, Shanghai, 1978.

Zhao Guangxian, *Zhoudai shehui bianxi*, Renmin, Beijing, 1980.

Zhao Lisheng, *Zhongguo tudi zhidu shi*, Qilu chubanshe, Jinan, 1984.

Zhongguo shehui kexue yuan kaogu yanjiu suo, *Fengxi fajue baogao*, Wenwu, Beijing, 1962. Abb. as Kaogu yanjiusuo.

——, *Xiaotun nandi jiagu*, Zhonghua, Beijing, 1980. Abb. as Xiaotun.

Zhongguo shehui kexue yuan kaogu yanjiu suo Anyang gongzuo dui 'Anyang Yinxu wuhaomu de fajue', *Kaogu xuebao*, 1977 (2): 57–98. Abb. as Anyang gongzuodui.

——, 'Yijiu liujiu zhi yijiu qiqi nian Yinxu muzang fajue baogao', *Kaogu xuebao*, 1979 (1): 27–146. Abb. as Anyang gongzuodui.

Zhou Li zhushu, Sibubeiyao edition.

Zhou Yuan, 'Jubo Qiuwei liangjia de xiaozhang yu Zhouli de benghuai', *Wenwu*, 1976 (6): 45–50.

Zhouyuan kaogudui, 'Fufeng yuntang XiZhou guqi zhizhuo zuofang yizhi fajue jianbao', *Wenwu*, 1980 (4): 27–35.

Zhu: see Jin Zutong, 1939.

Zhu Fenghan, 'Yinxu puci zhong de "zhong" de shenfen wenti', *Nankai xuebao* 1981 (2): 57–74.

Zou Heng, *Xia Shang Zhou kaoguxue lunwenji* Wenwu Beijing, 1980.

Index

199